URI GELLER: MY STORY

This is the autobiography of the famous and controversial Israeli psychic known throughout the world as the man who—apparently by force of will—bends keys and spoons, mends broken radios and stopped watches, and who has demonstrated in controlled experiments at the University of London, the Stanford Research Institute and elsewhere, staggering extra-sensory powers. It is Uri's first book and it tells, in his own words, how he came to realize his incredible powers and how they affected him. 'It amazes me,' he says, 'every time these things happen. I want to jump up and point them out to people.' He describes an event in a 'magical mystery garden' when he was three or four, and he recalls his first telepathic and clairvoyant experiences: reading his mother's mind, and on several occasions sensing potential disasters. This book goes beyond anything written elsewhere about this extraordinary man, and it ends with the strangest event of all—one never before revealed—at once the epitome and the culmination of all that has gone before.

URI GELLER: MY STORY

An Autobiography

THE
COMPANION BOOK CLUB
LONDON AND SYDNEY

This edition, published in 1976 by
The Hamlyn Publishing Group Ltd,
is issued by arrangement with
Robson Books Limited

Made and printed in Great Britain
for the Companion Book Club
by Odhams (Watford) Ltd
600872084
11.76/308

This book is dedicated to
those who have worked, contributed, and loved
for the past two-and-a-half years,
and especially to my mother and father
who devoted all their efforts and energies
to bringing me up into something so
unbelievable and so unknown

ACKNOWLEDGEMENTS

Many people have helped me as I was writing my book and otherwise. I thank you: Robert and Kirsten Abel, Charles Anderson, Mark and Dianne Anderson, Bob Banker, Robert and Stephanie Barrat, Dr Edward Bastin, Dr David Bohm, Jim Bolen, Bryce Bond, Dr Dean Brown, Sara Bursak, Eldon Byrd, Jean Byrd, Elizabeth Cater, Zmira Chen, Solveig Clark and her family, Bart Cox, James and Brenda Crenshaw, Iris Davidesco, David Dimbleby, Arnold Dolin, Sir Val Duncan, Peter and Anita Edler, Moshe Farkash, Dr Wilbur Franklin, Lu Fenton, John G. Fuller, Margaret Geller, Tibor and Eva Geller, Ingrid Goldberg, Vicki Golden, Felice Gordon, Merv Griffin, Dr John Hasted, Ron and Nancy Hawke, Peter Hielscher, Jim and Desiree Mazel Hurtak, Brian Inglis, Byron and Maria Janis, Stefan Janis, Joker, Joselito and Joseline Jacinto, Nancy Kahan, Yasha Katz, Betty Kenworthy, Kasey Kirby, Ephraim Kishon, Rae Knight, Ed Koster, Benjamin and Anita Levi, Goddard and Brigitta Lieberson, Larry and Gloria Lighter, Michael Magzis, Ron and Carmen Markham, Jean Mayo, Kevin McCormick, Capt. Edgar Mitchell and Anita, Richard Moore, Gianna Morello, Del Newman, Maxine Nightingale, Dr Glenn Olds and Eva, Brendan O'Regan, Charles Panati, Gidon and Lea Peleg, Dr Ralph Pelligra, Hagai and Ruth Pinsker, Dr Andrija Puharich, Dr Harold and Adrienne Puthoff, David and Sue Richardson, Piri Rosner, Amnon and Roni Rubinstein, Lo Sachs, Dr Louis and Edna Shenkman, Dr Michael and Ralla Shenkman, Don Scheuch, Werner Schmid and Brothers, Ioav Shacham, Shipi Shtrang, Arie, Hava and Hanna Shtrang,

Soshi and Iaakov Shtrang, Bob and Judy Skutch, Ray and Mary Kathryn Stanford, Robert Stigwood, George Swanson, John and Anna Swanson, Mother Swanson, Russell and Joan Targ, Prof. John Taylor, Telos and Venus, John and Sue Tishman, Melanie Toyofuku, Werner Triepke, Tzuki, Charles Van Doren, Trina and Frida Vatter and their family, Lyall Watson, Dr Paul and Maudine Wheeler, Bill Whitehead, Bob Williamson, Dolly and Kelly Williamson, Priscilla Williamson, C. V. and Joanne Wood, Jun Ichi Yaoi, Jimmy Young, Ila Zibell.

To all detractors and sceptics, I give love.

URI GELLER
February, 1975

1. It Happens Every Day

CHAPTER ONE

WHEN I WENT into the tiny BBC radio studio to be interviewed on the Jimmy Young Show that November morning in 1973, I wasn't prepared for what was going to happen. I was ready for something, but nothing as big and as mind-blowing as what followed. I liked Jimmy Young. He was a beautiful person, I knew right away, very warm and friendly. I usually can tell immediately whether I'm going to like a person. Jimmy made me feel right at home, which was good because I was a little nervous, as I usually am when I go before an audience.

The Jimmy Young Show has a large radio audience. It reaches all over England, up into Scotland, and to Ireland, and I'm sure he's very popular with his listeners. The audience reaction that followed proved that.

Jimmy began with the usual questions. He asked when I had first found out that I was able to bend keys, nails or other metal objects just by touching them lightly and when I had learned I could start up a watch or clock that hadn't run for years. I said I had noticed these things way back in my first years in school, much to the surprise of my classmates, teachers, parents—and myself. In fact, I am still surprised, and have a sense of wonder when these things happen.

Then he asked me if I would demonstrate for him. Of course I had agreed to try before I went on the show. Jimmy took a thick Yale key from his pocket and put it down in front of me. I did what I usually do, laying my hand over the key and wishing it to bend. Jimmy was watching carefully, and by this time the engineers in the control room were peeping through their window. Everybody was expectant and excited. I continued to be a little nervous myself, because sometimes these demonstrations do not work, which is very embarrassing for me. I am confident that they will work most of the time, but there is still that chance that they won't.

Just as I started to put my hand over the key, I remembered the events of a radio broadcast in Texas a few months before, which even I had trouble believing. I had taped a show there, and it went on the air several days after I had left. On that show, I had done the usual demonstration of bending keys and nails, while the commentator described what was happening. What happens is very simple but also very startling. The key begins to bend slowly as I either rub it lightly with my fingers or hold my hand over it. Then it continues bending after I take my hand away. Sometimes it bends only slightly and stops. Other times, it continues up to a 45-degree angle, or even to a right angle. Sometimes it will seem to melt, without heat, and half the key will drop off. I'm never sure myself what a key will do.

After the taped interview had been played on the air in Texas, I had received a signed affidavit from three employees of the Texas Attorney General's Office. An attorney there had suggested to three women employees that they listen to the broadcast and, just for fun, that they put some metal objects on the table in the records room there, and concentrate on them. To the surprise of everyone, as their affidavit reported, a spoon handle bent to about 45 degrees, a door key completely broke in half, and a large paper clip vanished. I know how unbelievable this sounds, but their affidavit is real, and there apparently was no motive for them to make the story up. They would hardly gain anything from it. What puzzled me most was that this was a delayed broadcast, and I had already left Texas when it went on the air.

As I sat in the BBC studio in London four months later and concentrated on the key Jimmy Young had given me to bend, this story came back to me. It must have been that memory that prompted me to suggest that people listening in their homes might concentrate on their keys—or spoons or forks— and see what happened. The words just seemed to slip out. And then I added: 'If there are any broken watches in your house, please concentrate on them and try to make them work. Just take them in your hand and concentrate on them.'

Just about this time I took my hand away from Jimmy Young's key. It was starting to bend, and it continued to do so. As we watched, he was so startled that he almost shouted: 'It's bending right in front of me. I can't believe it!' The key *was* bending, as I had seen happen so many times before. His words, intense and excited, were being broadcast live all through England, Scotland, and Ireland. We continued talking, and I continued demonstrating.

The studio producer rushed in with a bunch of notes. I didn't know at first what they were all about, so I kept talking. I explained how I was always as baffled as anyone else when I bent a key or spoon.

The producer continued running in and out of the studio with one note after another. Then I realized what was happening. The entire BBC switchboard had lit up like a Christmas tree. There were phone calls from England, from Ireland, from Scotland, from all over the British Isles. All England seemed to be bending. The phone calls were reporting that knives, forks, spoons, keys, and nails were bending in homes everywhere, near and far from London. A lady from Harrow reported that she was stirring soup when suddenly the ladle started bending. The gold bracelet of a girl in Surrey buckled and bent. A police constable said that several knives and spoons had curled up. A jeweller reported that half the pieces on a tray of cutlery bent. A watchmaker said that his tweezers had done the same. There were reports of watches and clocks starting up that hadn't run for years.

There was complete confusion at the BBC. After the Texas experience, I had half-expected this to happen. I thought that, if people really wanted things to happen in their homes and really concentrated, I could trigger it, because what I do could serve to release the same strange energy in other people. But I was still astounded that so many calls had come in from so many places. The BBC switchboard was absolutely jammed.

When I returned to the Hyde Park Hotel after the radio show, reporters from all the wire services and newspapers were waiting for me. The news of what had happened all over England had gone out fast. There were journalists from Reuters, the Associated Press, the UPI, many British newspapers—even from Japan. They showered me with questions and asked me to demonstrate how I bend keys and spoons and rings, which I did for them. Everyone seemed to be wondering what was going to happen when I repeated the performance the next night on 'David Dimbleby's Talk-In,' one of the BBC's most popular television shows.

I was wondering myself. If so many things had occurred as a result of a radio show—where no one could see what was happening—what would the results be from the more powerful influence of television? I'd heard that the audience would be very big because of hold-overs from the Miss Universe awards, scheduled just before my appearance.

I woke up the next morning to find big front-page headlines in all the London papers. Some of them aimed at humour: 'URI PUTS BRITAIN IN A TWIST,' or 'URI CATCHES BRITAIN BENDING.' I had never had such attention before. I guess there isn't anyone who doesn't enjoy seeing his name in the front-page headlines, and I am no exception. In addition, the news had gone out all over the world, they told me, through the wire services.

I was also a little perplexed, as I usually am, because I am convinced that there is something very serious beyond the strange things that happen to metal and other objects. For the past few years, I had been doing everything I could to find out just what it all meant. But in England that fall I didn't have much time to think about philosophy. I was preparing for a lecture-demonstration tour through many countries of Europe and elsewhere, and the pace of it left little time for reflection.

As usual, I was a little nervous when I returned to the BBC the next day, again afraid that nothing would happen when I tried to repeat the demonstration for the television cameras. There were going to be two other guests on the show. One of them was Professor John Taylor, a well-known mathematician from the Department of Mathematics at King's College of the University of London. I had heard that he was fair-minded. The other guest was to be Dr Lyall Watson, a well-known biologist and author of *Supernature*.

David Dimbleby is a very pleasant man. He and others had brought things for me to experiment with—forks, spoons, keys, and several broken watches. Just before the show started, the host and the other guests went into another room to prepare a drawing, which would be sealed in an envelope for me to guess and duplicate during the programme.

If it hadn't been for the amazing occurrences during the radio show the day before, perhaps I wouldn't have been so nervous. But I didn't want the television show, in front of such a big audience, to be a letdown. Also, I knew that a scientist like John Taylor was bound to be sceptical, even if he saw things happen in front of his eyes.

When the show went on the air, everything seemed to be working right. I concentrated on the sealed envelope, closed my eyes, and waited for whatever picture might appear in the sort of screen that I always see in my forehead. It wasn't long before I saw a shape very clearly—that of a sailboat. The envelope was opened, and, sure enough, it was a drawing of a sailboat. They were astonished. But that was only the beginning.

Various things were spread out on a table: forks, spoons, broken watches, and keys. I suggested that the audience concentrate while I was concentrating. Dimbleby held a spoon in his hand, and I stroked it lightly with two fingers. It bent almost double in a very short time. As the spoon was bending in Dimbleby's hand, a fork on the table bent without anyone touching it. I stroked another fork, and it bent until the handle broke off and dropped on the table. Then I began concentrating on the broken watches on the table. They began starting up almost immediately. Lyall Watson's watch, which had been running perfectly, suddenly stopped. The hands inside one of the other watches suddenly curled up against the glass.

Professor Taylor, who had begun the programme with a sceptical attitude, seemed to be shocked by what was happening. So did the others. The demonstration couldn't have been more successful. And any doubts I'd had about the effect of the television show throughout Britain were cleared up immediately. The BBC switchboard was again jammed, so jammed that it was almost put out of commission. The same thing had again happened in homes everywhere. Even on the Channel Island of Guernsey, three families had seen their spoons bend and broken clocks start up. Fourteen callers reported receiving the drawing of the sailboat telepathically.

The headlines were even bigger as a result of the television programme, and again the press filled my hotel room. They came for interviews, but they also came with challenges. I was used to the challenges, because all my life many people have accused me of using magic tricks or illusions. I can understand why they do. If I were to read in the newspaper about someone who did these things, I would have doubts, too. I would want to see it first-hand, and I would want to make sure myself that there were no tricks being played.

I was glad about what happened on the BBC shows, because thousands of other people, all across Britain, were involved. At least I couldn't be accused of trickery, as I often was. There was no possible way I could arrange for objects to bend and watches to start in thousands of homes all over the country. The newspapers sent people out to check the viewers and listeners directly; they confirmed dozens of the cases reported to the BBC switchboard. There was no doubt whatever that these things had happened. My main question was: Did many people have these powers, and had they been triggered by listening to the radio show and watching the television programme?

I still am not sure about this. For the two years before the BBC broadcasts, I had been going through scientific tests in the United States at the Stanford Research Institute at Menlo Park, California. The first results had confirmed that something strange and new was happening, both with the metal objects involved and with telepathy experiments. The researchers there had indicated that, if the tests continued to check out as they had, they would have a serious effect on modern science. This of course was exciting. One scientist even mentioned that, if what was happening were fully confirmed, science would have to take a whole new look at the theories of Galileo, Newton, and Einstein.

One of the British newspaper articles that pleased me mos was by Clifford Davis, TV editor of the *Daily Mirror* and also a magician, a member of the Inner Magic Circle, England's leading association of magicians. He wrote in the *Mirror:* 'Any worth-while magician could perform similar feats, but it would be trickery. Uri must be genuine.' His story continued: 'Anyone performing feats like this under such conditions cannot be a fake. Uri has stood up to thirteen laboratory tests in the United States. It shows that in rare cases the power of the mind can move or even bend inanimate objects.'

Since many magicians had been trying to prove I was

nothing more than an illusionist, it was good to have one of them come out like this in print, even though I have learned to ignore those who say what I do is false. *I* know what I do is real, and that is what counts.

The events in England were real, not the results of magic, and they were important. For the first time other people, hearing and watching someone who has these powers and energies, found them manifested in their own homes. They were important also because they could help create more interest in scientific studies about unknown energies. I feel that these powers come from far outside me, that I am like a tube that channels them. And beyond that is what the powers mean to the whole mystery of the universe. I know that something unusual is going on here, and I'd like other people, as many as possible, to know about it, to explore it together. I know it was and is important to work with scientists. But whatever I have to show or to say becomes more important if it has reached millions of people.

I told this to Bryan Silcock, science editor of the *Sunday Times*, as he rode with me in a taxi to Heathrow airport after the two BBC shows. Silcock is a respected science reporter, and the *Sunday Times* is one of the best papers in London. I knew that what he wrote about our interview would carry weight with many intelligent readers, including scientists. I was glad that he was taking the time to talk to me. During the ride he held out one of his own keys, and I stroked it lightly with my fingers. It began to curl up almost immediately. Silcock, at first sceptical, was very impressed. At the airpor, at KLM ticket agent who had seen the television show the night before asked me to start up her broken watch. I held it between my palms for a few seconds, and it moved directly to the correct hour. I also bent a thick letter opener. Silcock was amazed. He wrote his column in the *Sunday Times* under the headline: 'URI BENDS A KNIFE—AND MY CYNICAL MIND.' The column said: 'Uri Geller finally boarded his flight for Paris leaving this initially highly sceptical science correspondent with his mind totally blown. I missed his television programme. Even if I had seen it, I would probably have remained a doubter. But it is utterly impossible to remain sceptical after seeing Uri Geller in action. . . . He says that he is prepared to go on doing so until the bulk of scientific opinion is convinced. He is prepared to take part in any genuine scientific experiment.'

Silcock also quoted a comment by John Taylor about what had happened on the TV programme. 'We know what he can do,' Professor Taylor said, 'I would like to try to find out how. Some kind of explanation along conventional scientific lines might be possible. I would very much like to get in touch with people who had odd experiences during the TV programme, as they might have similar, but less developed, powers.'

Professor Taylor would later do so, with amazing results. But at that moment there was little time for savouring his remarks and Silcock's. I was on my way to Paris for an interview with *Paris Match* as part of the tour, which was to cover England again, then the United States for a short time, followed by Germany, Switzerland, Norway, Sweden, Denmark, Holland, and Japan.

Just before I left London, representatives from one of the Sunday papers had asked me to work with them on a stunt they thought would be interesting and amusing. I was going to be in Paris, but I told them I'd concentrate very hard at 12.30 p.m. London time, and we'd see what would happen. The paper, *Sunday People*, had a circulation of 15 million, so I felt fairly confident that something would happen.

I suggested to the paper that its readers surround themselves with various metal things and, at 12.30 p.m., hold spoons and forks in their hands and concentrate with me on the objects, even though I would be across the Channel in France. I also suggested that they stroke the objects lightly with thumbs or fingers. If they had any broken watches, they were to do the same with them. I told the editors that often nothing happens at all, but it would be interesting to see if anything did.

I was at Orly Airport in Paris on Sunday, November 25, preparing to return to London. I concentrated hard, beginning at 12.15, in an attempt to send thoughts and energies across the Channel. If the effort worked, it would show again that the energies could be transferred. And it certainly could not be dismissed as an ordinary illusionist's trick. I was keenly interested in the outcome.

At exactly 12.30, I shouted: 'Bend!' I don't know if the people at the airport thought I was crazy or what. But I do know that within a few days the editors of the paper were mind-blown. *Sunday People* received more than a thousand letters. Hundreds of broken clocks and watches that had been written off as useless had started up, and forks and spoons had bent all over England again. The watch of a woman in Dorset that hadn't run for forty years started up. A watch in Birmingham started, but the hands went backwards. In one home, the screws popped out of a cupboard hinge, and in another the bars of a birdcage bent.

The newspaper made a final tabulation of the results from their readers:

Clocks and watches restarted	1,031
Forks and spoons bent or broken	293
Other objects bent or broken	51
	1,375

Dr Edward Bastin, a mathematician at the Cambridge University Language Research Unit told the newspaper: 'A question that now needs to be asked is whether the owners influenced the objects by themselves, or whether Uri did so through them.' This, as I've already stated, was a question I wanted to have answered myself.

Another paper, the *Sunday Mirror,* thought it might discredit me. It sent one of the keys I had bent to a metallurgist who specialized in metal fatigue. Chris Amon, the metal expert, told the newspaper: 'There are no tricks, no fake key, nothing suspicious at all.' He said it would take 63 pounds of pressure to bend that particular key, which, by the way, I hadn't even touched. I had just concentrated on it, and it had curled up without my touching it.

The events in Britain towards the end of 1973 marked the first time that the effect reached thousands of people and came directly into their lives. Those who thought I was some kind of illusionist or magician would find it impossible to explain those events. They were happening far away from me, and to other people. The evidence was there for all to see: the BBC phone calls, the newspaper interview follow-ups, the long series of newspaper articles, the direct demonstrations to the reporters, and the hundreds of thousands of television viewers who not only saw these energies at work, but who participated in them.

But, in spite of everything, there still were magicians who claimed that I was simply a clever illusionist. They were fanatical and jealous. They claimed that they could duplicate what I did by tricks. But none of them wanted to try under the controlled scientific conditions that I had been working under for many months at Stanford Research Institute, or with other reputable research groups who had already tested me or were planning to in the future. I would agree to any magician's sitting on a panel that examined me, as long as he went through the same controlled scientific tests I did, and there were scientists present.

The critics who were against me often tried to explain how I did my demonstrations. Some of them said I used acid on the metal objects I bent. Others even said that I must use a laser beam of some sort. If they had stopped to think how ridiculous their charges were, they would not have made them. If I used anything like acid, my fingers would have burned and dropped off years ago. If there were such a thing as a portable laser generator, and I had used one, I probably would have burned myself up altogether by this time. As I understand, a laser machine has to be able to generate thousands of volts of electricity in the most complex sort of electronic equipment. I would probably be exhausted from trying to carry it around—if I could at all.

None of the critics in England tried to explain how the two broadcasts and the experiment across the Channel from France reached so many people in their homes. There was no possible way that this phenomenon could have been caused by show business magic. They were silent about that. They have also stayed silent about the starting up of clocks and watches that haven't run for years. Mostly, they are content with showing how some keys or nails can be made to appear bent by sleight of hand, or how some apparently miraculous mental telepathy feats can be faked.

Magicians *can* do some of the things I do and make them look real. They are often very skilful at it. When they perform on a stage under their own prescribed conditions, they never fail. But when they try to do them under laboratory conditions, they fail miserably. I readily admit that I sometimes fail, and it's rather embarrassing when I do. Since I'm convinced that what I do comes from an energy force far outside of me, I'm never sure when I will fail. If I were a professional magician, which I'm not, I am certain I would practise to the point where I, like they, would never fail either. As it is, I know I would make a pretty miserable excuse for a professional magician.

The reception of the press in England at the end of 1973 was really impressive. Bryan Silcock wrote a second article in the *Sunday Times* that was encouraging to me. He said: 'If people really can bend metal by mind power, it will mean a revolution in science and our whole way of thinking about the world, more profound than anything since Newton turned the universe into a piece of clockwork three centuries ago.'

An article in the *Times* said the fact that an illusionist could, under certain conditions, appear to duplicate some of the things I was doing did not explain how objects could be affected in homes hundreds of miles away from the BBC studios.

But none of what happened in England in the late fall of 1973 was as startling as the news I later received in a letter from a well-known scientific consultant in England. What he told me was incredible. There is still no explanation, and I wonder if there ever will be.

CHAPTER TWO

LET ME ASSURE the reader, I understand that it is hard for him to believe or comprehend the things I do unless he experiences them himself. Because they have been happening to me ever since I was a small child, I sometimes forget that I can't just talk about them and expect people to believe me. These events are so mingled with my personality and my beliefs that it's not difficult for *me* to accept them any more. If I could go to every person's living room to talk and demonstrate these energies in front of him, it would be the easiest thing in the world to convince people. But I'm only one person. I'm trying to pass my knowledge on through a book or a record, or through radio or television, or through the scientific publications, and I'm not sure it comes across as well as I hope it will.

It's almost as if a person came to me and said: 'Listen, I saw a dog yesterday playing a harmonica.' I would say: 'Come on now, I don't believe that.' But if I saw the dog in front of me with a harmonica, playing a tune, then I would have to believe it. I would of course be very sceptical and check first. 'Wait a minute. Is that a real dog? Is there a hidden harmonica, and is somebody else playing the tune? Is there a hi-fi set rigged somewhere inside the dog? What kind of harmonica is that, and what kind of dentistry did the dog have to enable it to play?' But if I checked all these things and had experts check them, and if I personally inspected the dog's mouth, felt the vibrations on the harmonica as it played directly in the mouth, and took the harmonica apart and made sure that there was no solid-state amplifier or tape inside it, then I would have to admit that it was real. Even then, I'd be a little wary.

But if I just read about it in a newspaper or a magazine or a book, I would have a tough time believing it. So I understand how a reader must feel when he reads my story. I can't expect him just to take my word for it. In my case, it's a phenomenon, and it's very controversial. I think it's important in this book to describe what is happening on the scientific side, under strictly controlled conditions, where trickery can play no part. And I think it's also important to show how the events have affected others besides myself and to present all the evidence, both from sceptical scientists and from ordinary people, that verifies the events.

What happened in England at the end of 1973 was strong evidence, because there was no possible way I could have faked anything even if I had wanted to. I am so convinced that there are great energies within us and above us we haven't even tapped yet that I want to explore them with others and help people realize they are there. I have other thoughts, too, about intelligences outside ourselves. And the more I can demonstrate these things, even though they might seem trivial and simple, the clearer I can make the deeper thoughts. Enormous energies exist within us. It's important to help people realize this.

* * *

The letter from the scientific consultant in England was startling because it demonstrated an impact that went even beyond what had happened in the many homes throughout England. His letter began calmly enough with general greetings and mention of my visit in England with him earlier. Then he came to the point:

'The aftermath of your rather meteoric visit to London has been an extraordinary psycho-sociological event to observe. At this stage, your name is a very distinct signature indeed in Britain's consciousness, and that such a thing could happen in a mere 48-hour time-span would have been predicted by few, if any, of us. No doubt you have many of the clippings and magazine articles. I myself, however, have been specifically concerned and interested by the impact of your visit on both the scientific and the policy-making level of the scientific and media communities.

'Throughout all levels, there has been a variety of interesting responses. As usual, there are the sceptics and the magicians—seeing them line up on the same bill, so to speak, makes one wonder if in the future the majority of sceptical scientists might not be more accurately regarded as really being threatened magicians!

'There have, however, been many more interesting responses, and these merit more attention and consideration. Perhaps the most dramatic of these has been the strong words I heard (from a source I don't wish to name as yet) to the effect that you may never again be allowed to broadcast *live* in Britain! Why? Because it seems that a number of very strange things happened to several important timing and radio transmission devices in Britain during your BBC broadcast. These devices were, it seems, *all knocked out simultaneously while you were on the air*.' I italicize those words because they were really a shock to me.

'The story I was told simultaneously with this involves a multi-million pound (£) project, in the area of "brain research," shall we say, and it seems so fantastic that I will have to check further in it before saying more. I will say however that the people involved have some rather interesting ideas about you. In discussing their reaction to your appearance, it seems that the simultaneous breakdown of important equipment is regarded as significant and a potential danger to the national security of Britain.'

This went far beyond the things that had happened in homes throughout the British Isles, unusual as they were. I had experienced something similar earlier, so it did not come as a complete shock: When I was doing tests at the Stanford Research Institute in Menlo Park, California, it was rumoured that the computers at a military project in the same building had gone haywire. This had never been fully confirmed, but it went through my mind as I read the letter from London.

From what I can tell about these energies, they always work for the good. I have never tried to do anything harmful with them and don't intend to, but the feeling I get is that they could never be used for bad ends or to create danger for others. That may have a Pollyanna sound, but I'm convinced it is true. I once tried to use the energy when I was in Las Vegas, and it wouldn't work at all. Not that such a use would be harmful, but it wouldn't really be honest. Whatever had happened in England, I am sure that it was not damaging. Of course, I don't know what other things have happened that I've never heard about.

It is almost as if these intelligences or energy forces or powers—whatever they are—are clowns out in the universe. They often do things I don't expect at all. When I am demonstrating and concentrating on a piece of metal, for instance, they are controlled. But things sometimes happen that seem silly.

I fly all over the world, and nothing ever happens to the planes. I'm as happy about that as the pilots are. But on three occasions, the film projectors in Boeing 747s simply let loose and spilled the film from their reels. Sometimes an ashtray will suddenly lift off a table and will next be seen dropping on the floor on the other side of a room. I know how ridiculous this sounds to someone who has never seen it happen in front of his own eyes.

The news about the effect of the BBC broadcast on important secret work aroused my curiosity, but there was nothing I could do to find out more about it. There were some rumours that the computers at the British Ministry of Defence had gone haywire during the broadcasts, but again this was not confirmed. I realized of course that, if anything like this were to happen, it could create a difficult situation. That was something I had no desire to do, which is one of the reasons why I want to do everything in the open. I do not want to work secretly with any government. I believe very much in the power of love and in people everywhere. I also believe completely in God, even though I don't observe any formal religious practice of any kind. And I believe very much that we must have peace in this world if we are to survive.

The letter from my friend in London had some other interesting things to say. He had talked with Professor David Bohm of the Department of Physics at Birkbeck College of the University of London, a famous physicist who had worked with Einstein in the 1950s, and also with Niels Bohr, one of the scientists who was responsible for the splitting of the atom. Professor Bohm was aware, my friend wrote, of the BBC broadcasts and the results they had produced in England.

'The thing about Bohm,' the letter said, 'is that he is not just another academic—on the contrary, he is both a brilliant and sensitive man with what seem like genuinely profound insights. In fact he is the first person I have spoken with about you who seems to both appreciate the significance of it all and offer some constructive thinking on a deep level. Since your visit I have had several more conversations with him and he has expressed a strong desire to meet and talk with you and, if you are willing, do some experimental work to be followed by a paper in *Nature*, which as you will learn is perhaps the most significant weekly publication in science. Many important discoveries have made their first appearance in its pages over the years.'

I had heard about *Nature*, even though I am far from a scientist. Someone had told me that the first paper on DNA, the Double Helix, was published there, and that it is supposed to be the scientific journal with the most prestige in the world. I thought it would be exciting to be included in its pages.

The letter continued: 'Bohm has indicated to me that he would first like to have a quiet meeting with you to discuss things generally. This would serve to establish some rapport and allow you both to mutually decide what you would like to do. Then if you agree, he could set up some work with you, aimed at trying to arrive at some theoretical understanding.'

This sounded very interesting to me, and so did Dr Bohm. It was of course also very flattering. I sometimes get nervous when I'm going through scientific tests, even though most, but not all, of them work out well. The more friendly and sympathetic the scientist is, the better results I get. If someone is very harsh and negative, I become so tense that I don't get very good results. I decided that I would like to meet with Professor Bohm soon on one of my trips to England.

In the meantime, other scientists were interested in further testings as a result of the effect of the BBC broadcasts. They included a group from the *New Scientist*, another important journal for scientists, and a group formed by Dr Bastin of Cambridge. He had observed some of the scientific tests I had made in the United States, and he had, in fact, brought several metal samples that I had worked on back to England and asked a Cambridge University metallurgist, Dr J. P. Chilton, to examine them in the laboratory.

I learned about the results of the lab tests when I was still in England. Dr Chilton said that 'close examination of the six hardened metal screwdrivers whose tips had broken off showed no signs of chemical treatment, heat distortion, or other indication of how it was done. These were normal fractures, achieved in a mysterious way.'

Of course, this was not the sort of laboratory test that could stand up officially, because the breakage had not happened under completely controlled conditions. But Dr Bastin had certified the conditions under which the screwdrivers were broken, and, at least informally, Dr Chilton said: 'Geller is either the cleverest magician of the century or he has something new. There is no halfway about it.'

Of course, I knew I was not a magician, not even an unclever one. I was groping as much as they were to find the real answer. I knew that I would want to work more with the scientists when I got back to England, but I was scheduled to return to the United States for more lectures, and there was nothing more I could do at the time.

Just before we left for the States, Professor John Taylor issued a statement that gave another indication of how seriously the British scientists were taking the phenomenon. He told the press that he wanted to set up a serious investigation in the light of the nationwide effect of the broadcasts: 'We may end up proving his powers are not unique,' he said. 'But if he will agree to co-operate with us he may help us make most important discoveries about the human mind.

'We are not thinking of another TV circus. What we have in mind is a serious, scientific investigation with a great deal at stake.'

I had no idea whether the results of the BBC broadcasts could be repeated when I continued the European tour. On the quick trip back to the United States, I was making only platform appearances, and no broadcasts.

One of the London papers was sending a reporter back to the States with me to keep the story running in the wake of the results from the British broadcasts. I was due to make a quick tour of colleges in the United States before I returned to

England, and then go on to the rest of Europe and Japan. Roy Stockdill, the reporter, was a pleasant fellow and like most people wanted to confirm my demonstrations with his own eyes.

Roy Stockdill stayed with me all during the lecture tour in the United States and saw what I am usually able to do. When we were on the plane, Stockdill asked me to bend his house key. I gently rubbed my fingers along it as it rested on the arm of the aeroplane seat. It immediately curled up. When we arrived in the States, he asked me to do the same with his hotel key, which was much thicker and stronger. I tried but failed. The key would not bend at all.

Stockdill had with him a very strong steel shaving mirror, which he tested by trying to bend it with his hands and of course was unable to. I tried stroking the mirror but had no luck. It seemed to be one of those times when nothing was working. I tried the hotel key again. Now, suddenly, it began bending. We watched it move up to a 45 degree angle.

This often happens—that is, the process doesn't work at first, and then does so on a second try. But there was something more amazing to come. Stockdill looked over at the mirror, which we had left on a nearby table. The mirror was bending visibly in the middle and rocking gently on the table as it did so. It kept on moving in front of us until it reached a V shape. This happens often too—it's a kind of delayed reaction. Or sometimes there is a simultaneous reaction; I'll be running my fingers over a fork or spoon, and several others on the table will curl up at the same time as the one in my hands. I honestly am surprised myself when this happens.

I went out to dinner with Stockdill that night at a restaurant where a film was being projected on the wall. We hadn't been at the table long before the projector suddenly began spilling the film all over the floor. Again, this was something I hadn't concentrated on at all. It was just one of those things that happened. Stockdill was startled, and I was too.

With Stockdill was a photographer, Michael Brennan, who had once been named British Press Photographer of the Year. We were staying at the Eden Roc Hotel in Miami Beach, where I was doing one of the lecture-demonstrations of the tour.

In the past I had sometimes been able to take a picture of myself through a solid black lens cover without removing or touching the cover. I asked Stockdill and Brennan if they'd like to give this a try. They were both interested, provided I would do exactly as they instructed. I agreed, and Brennan prepared his own camera, a 35-mm. Nikon F with Tri-X Professional black and white film, he told me.

They both moved very close to me and handed me the camera. I shot three rolls of film, holding the camera at arm's length and pointing the lens cap at my face. After each roll Brennan took the camera and removed the film, sealed it, and locked it in his camera case. I didn't touch the film at any time. When they got back to London the films were developed. Brennan was confident that any pictures taken would be totally blank. Two of the rolls were blank. But in the middle of the third roll, there were two pictures of me. Neither of them would ever win a photographic award, but they are clear and unmistakable. You can see them in this book.

On Sunday, December 2, 1973, the *News of the World*, with one of the largest circulations in the world, published the pictures, splashed all over the front page, calling them 'URI'S MIRACLE PICTURES'. Of course, they created a lot of controversy. The *Daily Mail* quoted photographic experts as saying that there was absolutely no way, physically or chemically, that the pictures could have been taken through a lens cap. Brennan and Stockdill stuck to their guns, swearing that no trickery was involved. As usual, I had to be satisfied with the knowledge that it had truly happened and ignore the controversy that raged about the pictures.

Roy Stockdill began his series of stories with these words: 'I still find it incredible, the mind-bending week I spent with Uri

Geller. A week in which seeing was not believing.' He ended the series by saying: 'Uri is something special. I've seen him at work, and there is no logical explanation for the things that happen when he's around. I certainly found no evidence that he is a cheat. A magician depending on the swiftness of hand, defeating the eye, could get away with some of his feats. But that doesn't explain how keys twist and spoons bend when he's nowhere near them.

'It will really take a clever team of scientists to reveal the whole truth about Uri Geller.'

By now some of the scientific journals were referring to the bending of objects as the 'Geller Effect'. This was very flattering but it didn't solve the riddle. At any rate, the broadcasts in England and the attention that followed them gave me more confidence in the face of my detractors, and they apparently made some scientists more open-minded.

My experience is that this is not easy to accomplish. But an editorial in *Nature* on December 7, 1973, showed that open-mindedness might be possible. Since this journal had so much prestige among scientists, it could play an important part in removing some of the controversy so that more progress could be made in exploring what was going on. The editorial was called 'Challenge to Scientists'. It said that the challenge 'will arise if investigations continue to turn up signs of psychokinetic powers, and with the present evidence this certainly cannot be ruled out. It would then be urgently necessary for the scientific community to come to terms with something totally beyond its powers of explanation—indeed something which in a religious context would be called a miracle. Just as the public wants scientists to validate Mr Geller, it would also want them to explain him and, however awkward this question may be, it should not be avoided. . . . The viewing public, shown a chest operation under acupuncture one week and an exhibition of knife-bending the next, is bound to ask searching questions about conventional scientific wisdom.'

Some of the scientists I met told me that it was almost unheard of for *Nature* to print an editorial like this, and they were very excited about it. The *New Scientist* also gave the BBC broadcasts a full-page editorial. It called for an open-minded investigation by a special scientific panel. My plans, of course, included a whole series of continuing tests with scientists, in between the lecture-demonstration appearances, but I was glad to see this new kind of thinking on the part of both scientific journals. For a long time, any scientist who took me seriously found that he was criticized by other scientists even for examining what was going on. It was good to see this curtain lifting, especially in such important publications.

After the experiences in England, I couldn't help wondering what was going to happen when I repeated the same type of programme in Norway. Flying there, I had time to think about what it all meant. It was unsettling to be in the centre of a controversy that some people thought would shake the foundations of science. I couldn't judge that as well as those who knew all the ins and outs of science. But those who did, and who had seen the demonstrations, kept pointing out that, if all the tests continued to check out, as they seemed to be, a whole new force would have been discovered.

My demonstrations had grown gradually into something almost too big to think about. The suggestion that machinery involved in the national security of Britain had gone haywire during the broadcasts was awesome and couldn't be ignored. The demonstrations themselves were interesting, but they were superficial. They represented something much deeper, and I had only very mystifying clues as to what it was and what it meant.

All along, my outlook had been maturing and developing, but I still hadn't got down to the core of it. By then I believed that the core had to do with some fantastic intelligence. I didn't know what to call it, because I feel that God is not reachable directly; but under God all these intelligences exist. Millions and millions of them. And one of them, two of them, five—who knows how many?—are trying to make some kind of contact with man.

I could be wrong. It could be so big that our human minds right now on earth can't understand it, because we have to stick to an ordinary time frame. And our minds will have to be expanded. For instance, I have a theory that some people think is far out. I am convinced that we are in the middle of a big map, a huge plan, that involves other civilizations and other planets, other solar systems, other galaxies. But somewhere down in the middle of the core, we are one. I see it as sort of a network, like a golf ball when you take the cover off and unwind it. It's rubber, rubber, rubber, and it seems never to come to an end. There's only one ball, but it seems there is no end to it. And there are infinite numbers of balls, but they still come from only one creator.

The things that happen when I do a demonstration are incredible—to me and everybody else—but they are still superficial, whatever they eventually may mean to science. I often ask myself, why does it have to be just watches and keys, and metals, things like that? Why can't it really be the things I want to see happening? Why don't these intelligences reveal themselves to me? Why do they keep throwing me nothing but symbols?

I don't think I've yet made even a dent in the core. I've only had a chance to see the thin tip of it. It will be a lot of work to find out. One thing I'm certain of is that these energies are somehow working through me, and that I can't ignore them. I think the controversy is good, because it helps make things known to more and more people. I can't help feeling that these forces, whatever they are, will come to be accepted just as electricity is accepted today.

They'll first be accepted as phenomena, I think, then as theories, and then perhaps as physical laws of science. The bending of the metals is easiest to see, because it's right there and can be observed clearly by scientists. The rest, like the telepathy, the way watches start up, the many strange things that happen without my consciously trying to make them—the answers to these will probably come later. One thing I know for sure is that I feel compelled to demonstrate these phenomena, not only in order to make a living, but because I know something important eventually will come out of all this, even if I don't know what it will be.

I went on national television in Norway on January 19, 1974. It would be the first time I had been on a broadcast on radio or television since the excitement in England, and I was curious.

The interview began, and we weren't far into the programme when the phone calls began coming in. It was the BBC situation all over again. The switchboard was jammed. Things were bending in homes all over Norway, exactly as they had in Britain. I had the same strange feelings as before. I was surprised, yet not surprised at the same time. Was this actually a new form of energy exerting itself? Was such a thing possible in the face of all the known facts of physical science? Something new had happened many years before, when electricity had been put to use. Radioactivity had hardly been around for more than a single lifetime. It was incredible that I could be in on the beginning of something new, but if I was, I had no idea why or how.

I finished the broadcast and headed back to the Continental Hotel. I would be continuing the demonstrations in Germany, Switzerland, Austria, Sweden, Finland, Denmark, and Holland. Would the same thing repeat itself through those countries? It was like a science-fiction story. Yet it is all on the public record, in the records of the Norwegian and British broadcasting companies, and in the front-page headlines of nearly every newspaper in both those countries. There were times when I had to look back at them to remind myself that this was real.

What still puzzled me was why many of the things that happened were so trivial. Like everyone else, I wanted to know when something with more meaning would be coming out of it all. I was producing something like a series of superstitious omens, but in the age of modern science that kind of thing seemed ridiculous. I wanted to *know* what was going on. This cosmic kind of energy was often as irritating and perplexing as it was incredible.

When I arrived back at the Continental Hotel, I went up to the desk to see if there were any messages. The clerk handed me a very official-looking envelope, and I opened it.

In it was a business card from Alv Jakob Fostervoll, the Norwegian Minister of Defence. On the back of the card he had written a note. It was urgent that he talk to me, and he was sending a car the next day to pick me up.

The first thing I thought of was the letter I had received from England with its implications about Britain's security. I went to sleep that night wondering what in the world the Minister of Defence for Norway wanted to see me about, and why he was taking the trouble to send a chauffeur to pick me up tomorrow.

CHAPTER THREE

THE NORWEGIAN NEWSPAPERS the next morning were filled with headlines about the strange events that had occurred all over the country while the TV show was on the air.

This kind of phenomenon, at long distance, which had begun with a small incident in Texas and mushroomed in England, was still new to me and seemed so much bigger than anything that had gone on before that I was more baffled than ever. Try to imagine how you would feel if such things were happening to you. You reach a point where you are both stunned and intrigued.

I had grown used to the simple things: keys bending and watches starting, because that had been happening ever since my earliest school days. But with the power being transferred across the airwaves to thousands of other people, either by television or by radio, I couldn't help being as surprised as everyone else. It increased my desire to find out more about the scientific reasons behind the phenomena and to make it a point not to let the magicians and others, who tried to explain it away as a trick, upset me.

No one could accuse the thousands of people who were reporting things in their homes of being liars or fakers, and the newspapers were full of photographs of them holding up bent keys and forks and spoons in every part of Norway and England. I guess a few of them might have offered their reports just to get attention and publicity, but surely not thousands of people spread so wide apart.

Also, what had happened could not be attributed to psychological factors or some kind of hypnosis or mass hysteria. The evidence was right there for everybody to see. But I realize that anything as strange as this has to be looked at from every angle. A reasonable kind of scepticism is a good thing. It is only when people refuse to believe what is right in front of their eyes that I am disturbed.

I didn't have much time during the day to think about the note from the Norwegian Minister of Defence, but I did wonder about it a couple of times. When a big black Mercedes arrived at the hotel later that afternoon to pick me up, my curiosity increased. It was an important-looking limousine with a place for an official flag, but there was no flag in it. Even though the short note on the back of the card had mentioned that the Defence Minister wanted to talk with me on a personal matter, I still wondered whether it wasn't something to do with the Defence Ministry, just as security questions had come up both in England and with regard to the Stanford Research Institute computers.

I have no way of being certain about this, but I started asking myself questions when we reached a long, grey government building with a high iron fence around it. It was late afternoon and just getting dark, and I could see quite a few antennae of various shapes and sizes. The chauffeur mentioned that it was a military headquarters building of some kind, but I couldn't get straight what it was exactly. What made me wonder was that he slowed down almost to a crawl and pulled over to the side of the road very close to the iron fence. There seemed no need to go so slowly—less than five miles an hour—because he had been driving much faster on roads that were in worse condition.

I couldn't help thinking that, if there were computers in the building, or radar apparatus, he might have been driving slowly to test for any effect on the electronic instruments. So many strange things had been happening, I had to be careful not to let my imagination run wild. My only guess was that something had happened to the electronics at the headquarters when I was broadcasting, and they wanted to check it further. But I never learned anything more definite.

When I arrived at the Minister's house, he asked me if I did psychic healing. He hoped, he said, that I could help his two sons, who were haemophiliacs. I said what I always say: that not enough is known about the powers to try healing. But he and his wife were so nice and so hopeful that I saw the boys. I was sorry to learn later that they had not been cured.

Back at the hotel, Gunner Moe of the Norwegian magazine *Now* interviewed me. He was extremely interested in the strange 'Geller Effect', but as in all interviews I had trouble defining it myself. He had brought with him a fifteen-year-old watch which he said had not run for four years. I held my fist over it and concentrated hard, and within a minute it was running. I gave it a few more moments of concentration just to make sure it would keep running. When we looked at the watch again, the minute hand had curled back on itself and doubled over, even though there was not enough room between the face of the watch and the glass to allow this to happen. Later, the reporter wrote about a clock that started up some time after our interview.

I get many reports about such delayed effects. One time I bent a key for some friends in Connecticut—Don Blinn, a commercial jet pilot, and his wife, Sally. They were soon going to leave for their summer house in Maine, and somehow I had the feeling that when they arrived there a few days later they would find that something had happened. I learned later that when they went into the house they found their extra door key —which they kept hanging on the wall—had clearly bent and curled since they had last seen it. No one had touched it since the previous summer.

After the first interview in the Oslo hotel, another Norwegian reporter talked with me. He was asking me about the various happenings, and I told him that I couldn't figure out why energies were sometimes very weak and sometimes quite strong. We were sitting by the window in the hotel room, which looked out over a large area of Oslo. There were a lot of street and theatre lights outside, and many illuminated signs.

I said to him: 'You know, sometimes these energies are so strong that lights can go out.'

I had no sooner finished saying my sentence than we looked out the window and noticed a big area of Oslo that had been brilliantly lit up had suddenly blacked out. The lights were still working in the hotel, and the reporter rushed to the phone and called his office to see what had happened. A report came back that a big section of Oslo was blacked out, and they were trying to restore service immediately.

It was a strange coincidence, and the reporter was excited about it. However, I am sceptical myself, and I have learned that I have to be careful not to jump to conclusions. For instance, in the United States I have heard many stories about people who plugged in electric razors or turned on kitchen lights or took out a single fuse at the exact moment the big blackout on the East Coast happened. There are many coincidences like this, and it is easy to jump to conclusions that are just silly. It does become interesting, though, when a series of these things happen one after the other, over a long period of time. But I always try to look for an ordinary reason first. If that has to be completely ruled out, then I have to accept the explanation that the energies are working through me. There is no other conclusion to make.

Some incidents are on the borderline. One occurred when two of my closest friends, Byron and Maria Janis, invited me to accompany them on a cruise from Bordeaux to Italy on the liner *Renaissance*. Byron is the internationally known concert pianist, and his wife, Maria, who is Gary Cooper's daughter, is a wonderful artist. It was a musical cruise. Byron was performing at the piano, and on board were the members of the Hungarian String Quartet.

After a stopover in Spain, we were sailing towards Italy when I got to joking with the orchestra members, who challenged me to do something big, like stopping the ship in the middle of its course. Quite a few people were on deck that day, and everyone was in a holiday mood. I was caught up by their spirit and said: 'All right. Let's all concentrate on stopping the ship.'

Everyone was silent for several moments. Then, to my complete surprise, the ship began slowing down. It got slower and slower and then came to a full stop. We were all really startled. In fact, some of the orchestra members were quite scared. We found a ship's officer and asked him what was wrong, and he told us he didn't know. This was one of those things that caught me by surprise but didn't *really* catch me by surprise. In other words, I half-expected it but couldn't quite believe it.

After a wait of an hour or so, the ship's engines started up again. Then the ship began moving, slowly accelerating back to normal speed. The crew finally told us what had happened. The main fuel pipe had suddenly bent and had choked off the fuel going to one of the engines. They had stopped the ship to make the repairs, which were not too difficult. Nothing like this had ever happened before, and they had no way of explaining how it had happened.

None of us dared speak of what we had done. And, in fact, it might have been just a coincidence. But this time my inner feeling was that we had carried the experiment a little too far. Thinking about it later, I couldn't help feeling that this was too much of a coincidence to be a coincidence, especially since it involved the bending of metal and the collected thought of a bunch of people concentrating with me at the same time. But you can see how puzzling and confusing this can be to me, because it happens so many times and in so many different ways.

To get back to Oslo, the electrical blackout that night was of course startling, but it didn't have quite the direct relationship that the incident on the ship did. I never did find out what really happened in the Oslo blackout, but it left the *Now* reporter baffled, as well as me.

I feel that all these things are just revealing themselves slowly, and some day they might add up to a big picture that will be more understandable than just a series of things that sometimes just look like jokes. There has got to be more to it than just what lies on the surface. I have other things to talk about later that will explain what I mean by this, at least partly. It's all still very fantastic.

After packing up in Oslo, I was off to Germany. Would the same strange mass phenomenon happen again? After two countries in a row, my inner feeling was that it probably would.

But I had learned that I could be surprised by anything, one way or the other.

The television tour had been lined up by my associate, Werner Schmid, so that, when I returned to give a series of lecture-demonstrations later in the year, more people in these countries would know about me and more people would come to see the demonstrations in person. I know that a lot of people think I should concentrate on the scientific tests alone and not give these lectures, because they seem so commercial.

They *are* commercial, but I do not agree that I should not do them. The more people know about the powers, the more quickly scientists will lose some of their understandable suspicion and look into them more seriously. In fact, it appears that the public has already stimulated science; *Nature* itself pointed it out when its editorial of December 7, 1973, said that the public sees some of these things on TV and, as a result, 'is bound to ask searching questions about conventional scientific wisdom.' If these energies were not being seen by so many people, scientists might be cautious about looking into them.

Then of course there is the fact that I still must make a living, and I don't feel I need to apologize about that.

I didn't have to wait long to find out that my television appearance in Germany would bring results as dramatic as in Norway and England. The switchboard was again flooded with phone calls reporting the same things happening in homes all over the country, and the headlines were bigger than ever, one of them reading, 'URI MAKES GERMANY CRAZY'. One German housewife, Barbara Scheid, interviewed by the German paper *Main Post* the next day, was photographed showing fifty-three pieces of silver that had been carefully wrapped in cloth and stored in a drawer; every piece had been bent when the programme went on the air. The family actually called the police to come and look at the silver. The newspaper *Bild-Zeitung* in Frankfurt had a front-page headline that read: 'ALREADY 7,000 *BILD* READERS REPORT SUCCESS'. The paper had asked its readers to place a spoon on a newspaper at the time the broadcast went on the air.

After I had left the country to continue to Austria, Switzerland, Holland, Finland, and Sweden, two popular German magazines took up the negative side, something that often happened. Both *Stern* and *Der Spiegel* said that I had used magic tricks and repeated the theory that I used chemicals of some kind to soften the metal. But they ignored what had happened in homes all over Germany, things I couldn't have done no matter how good a magician I was, and they failed to explain why my fingers had not burned off by now. The same events were repeated without fail in Austria and Switzerland. I now would have been surprised if the countrywide phenomena did not happen. But they did, with practically no change in the pattern: the flooding of the switchboards with reports of viewers who found metal bending and old, broken clocks starting up; the big headlines the next morning; and the press interviews to follow up.

Of course, there was an enormous amount of publicity, and of course it was commercial, but as far as I was concerned it did not take away from the serious side, which these energies seemed to be displaying in a very light-hearted way. I wasn't thinking in terms of a circus or a side-show, but with a sense of wonder and real excitement about the universe and these powers. I also knew enough to keep my feet on the ground and not let this kind of thing go to my head, because I knew I was just a channel, that others could share in this when they were triggered.

The TV programme in Sweden was to be taped in Goteborg and would be shown after my visit to that country ended. By now, my confidence was strong enough so that I would joke with the producers and engineers: 'Wait and see what happens!' Since I wasn't going to be in Sweden when the show went on the air, I too would have to wait and see. It would be an interesting test to see whether a delayed TV broadcast would produce the results on as large a scale as the live broadcasts had. If it did, it would add another mystery to the picture, a mystery that was growing stronger not only for me, but for the people in every country I visited.

While I waited to hear what might happen in Sweden, I went on to Finland, where the results were as amazing as ever. The phone company reported that all phone lines to newspapers and TV stations were tied up for hours in many places.

When I finally learned about the results of the delayed broadcast of the Swedish videotape, which went on the air about a month later, I found that the effect of it on the homes in the country was stronger than ever—in spite of the fact that it was not broadcast live. It was as if these energies could be put into a deep freeze and taken out later. How could this possibly be? I wish I knew the full answer, or at least something beyond the hints that I've received.

But it was in Denmark that I was to get my biggest shock on this tour. It is still hard to sift through the experience there and make sense out of it.

CHAPTER FOUR

I WAS WELL AWARE that the European events were not happening under the controlled testing needed by scientists to verify whatever forces were at work. And yet the happenings were later going to suggest to some scientists a way of approaching the 'Geller Effect'. When thousands of other people, and not just me alone, were involved, there would be other checkpoints for researchers to work on, to compare and measure, and to follow up with the controlled conditions they, as scientists, needed. Even if the broadcasts just triggered the forces in other people temporarily, they provided a chance for the scientists to carry their studies beyond me and to satisfy themselves that the 'Geller Effect' was not just some kind of trickery they were being skilfully fooled with.

On the way to Denmark, I tried to analyse the spreading of the effect. A theory began coming to my mind that I still haven't developed as far as I'd like. I was becoming convinced that everybody has some kind of hidden power deep inside him, and that it could be brought out in three possible ways: (1) psychologically, maybe by suggestion, (2) by actually seeing a demonstration of such power, or even by just hearing it described (as happened in the case of Texas and the BBC radio show), or (3) simply by developing a full belief in it.

I thought that many things might be able to trigger phenomena like those I was demonstrating. In adults, the power seemed to last only a short time. But children, I felt deep inside, could be stronger in reflecting these forces because they haven't accepted the negative attitudes that all of us pick up in life.

While the powers may be hidden in all of us, there has to be what you might call a cosmic connection that can be tuned in to. The main key, I think, is *believing*. It works like an ignition key to open up these energies in the body. Seeing or hearing about these unusual possibilities can establish, I think, a direct channel to this cosmic connection. I think that very few people go so far, of course. But when the belief is strong, a person might be able to click on to it.

I don't mean this in any arrogant way, but I believe that I'm tuned in to what I call the cosmic connection all the time. Why, I don't know. But because I'm in touch and cling to it, it gives me the opportunity to pass it on to others, even if only for brief moments. So when I go on a television programme or give a lecture-demonstration, it's a good way for me to connect with other people and help them make the connection with the forces outside ourselves. It's like exploring a whole new world, and it's very exciting.

There were to be three panellists on the air with me at the Danish television studio in Copenhagen. One was the head of the Watchmakers' Guild; another was a psychologist; a third was introduced as a businessman, but later I discovered that he was a skilled Danish magician named Leo Leslie.

What I didn't know and didn't learn until later was that Leslie had gone through elaborate preparations in an attempt to throw me off. First, he had obtained a chemical called mercury bichloride, which is supposed to soften metals. His idea was to bend a key on the programme with the chemical in a way that would match the way the keys bent when I concentrated on them.

In addition, he had arranged with the director for one camera to focus on my hands and never to leave them for even a fraction of a second. Further, he had the watch expert deliver five alarm clocks that were so tricked up that they couldn't start up under any conditions. In one, they placed a piece of cement; another was soaked with salad oil; a third was jammed with a paper clip, and so on.

Leslie had also prepared several nails and keys by nickel-plating them so that if I used a chemical—which I never do—the objects would resist it. There were other preparations as well, and I knew about none of them. I also found out when I arrived that the programme was to include a very frank discussion of sex, which I didn't want to be involved in—not that I'm against sex, but it had nothing to do with the type of demonstration I was going to do and probably would detract from it. They agreed to separate that segment of the programme from mine. I have to admit I was tempted when they challenged me to concentrate on the bra of one of the girls in the studio, which was held up by metal clips. She was gorgeous and beautifully built. Werner Schmid immediately said no to the idea and reminded me that the prank would be bad for my image. But I often wonder what would have happened if I had done that on the air. The Danes are very liberal, and it would have been interesting.

I was to appear with the panel on two segments of the show,

with an intermission in between. The show began, and they brought out the jammed-up clocks that couldn't run. Of course I knew nothing about what Leslie had had done to them, and I concentrated on them as usual, at the same time suggesting to the viewers throughout the country that they concentrate on their own watches or keys or whatever at home.

As I tried, nothing at all happened to the clocks in the studio. I was surprised, because certainly some of the five clocks should have started running. It was an embarrassing moment for me, as it appeared that I had failed completely. It made me uncomfortable. It's an awful feeling to sit in front of a TV camera knowing that millions of people are watching you fail.

I had better luck with the metals they had brought, because the energies have nothing to do with any chemicals or nickel plating. I felt very let down, though, still not knowing what was wrong with the clocks.

At the intermission, while the other part of the programme was on the air, I went into another studio with the panel. While we were alone there, I demonstrated several things for them, and they began to lose their scepticism. Meanwhile, the TV people told me that the switchboard was being flooded again with phone calls reporting the same kinds of things that had happened in England, Norway, and elsewhere on the tour *even though* the clocks had not started. As before, the switchboard couldn't handle all the calls. I began to feel a little better, and then Leo Leslie confessed what they had done to try to throw me off.

Sceptics in Austria had tried to block me once before. But when they told me they had used various tricks to block the movements in watches and clocks, I applied extra concentration and effort, and the timepieces began to work in some cases anyway. I told Leslie he should have let me know what he had done, but it was too late now to do anything about it because we only had a few minutes on the second segment. When we came back on the air, the psychologist, the watchmaker, and Leslie told the audience what they had done, and what had happened during the intermission. The panel told the viewers they were completely convinced that my achievement was not the result of illusion or magician's tricks, and we all had a good laugh about it. Meanwhile, the phone calls were still coming in from all over Denmark. So in spite of the tricks played with the timepieces, the programme was as successful as in the other countries.

Leo Leslie told me that he had tried the mercury bichloride to bend keys and spoons and other metals, but that it was utterly unable to produce the same type of bending effect, so they threw out that idea before the programme went on the air. It worked partially on aluminium, but how many keys are made of aluminium? He also told me that my hands were never outside the range of the TV camera especially set up to stay on them. Later, Leo Leslie was to write of this experience in a book. Even though he was a magician, he became one of my strongest supporters.

The Danish newspapers were as extravagant as the newspapers elsewhere. They described in detail the strange happenings all across Denmark, and one of them, the *Berlingske Tidende*, wrote: 'Now the doubters and the sceptics are beginning to give up. It has been clearly indicated that Uri Geller has talents which must be described as the greatest revolution in the history of man.' With words like these, I would have to watch my hat size, but I doubted that the doubters and the sceptics would give up so easily. Also, I always keep in mind that the forces or energies are not really mine; they are just on loan from the cosmic forces that have sent them my way.

Just before I left Denmark and headed back to England, a leading Danish magazine, the *Billed-Bladet*, asked me if I'd try an experiment with them like the one I had done from Paris to England: I would concentrate at a certain time, and the magazine would ask its readers to do the same.

I was very interested in this type of long-distance test, because if it worked it would back up the test that had been done across the English Channel from France. It would give a better idea of how widely the energies could operate, and I hoped it would increase the interest of scientists in learning more about them. If people all over a country would continue to give strong evidence that the forces could spread out over long distances, science just couldn't afford to ignore it, as the editorial in *Nature* had suggested.

Of course, I had no way of knowing whether it would work or not. I knew my critics would all say that it was a commercial promotion for the Danish magazine and for my future lecture tours. Well, it was. There was no doubt about it. If it worked, it would be good for the magazine, and it certainly would help my future lecture tours, and I'm not against that at all. But there was nothing tricky about it; it was perfectly above-board in every way. We set a time for representatives of the magazine to be with me in London, when I would concentrate on their readers, while the magazine readers would concentrate on broken watches and metal objects in their houses in Denmark.

When I got to London I planned to stay with friends in an apartment in a quiet residential area. By this time, the press was constantly following me everywhere, and it seemed I couldn't get a minute of peace and quiet for myself. I tried wearing dark glasses, but they always managed to spot me. They traced me to my friend's apartment and waited outside. One time, I had to go to another part of town, and I knew it would be impossible to slip away without their following me. We peeked out through the curtains, and the house was practically surrounded. My best friend, Shipi Shtrang, and Yasha Katz, who along with Werner Schmid were handling all the details of an eight-city lecture-demonstration tour in England, were with me. We decided they would pull coats over their heads, run to the large Land-Rover outside, and drive off fast. We hoped the press would follow them while I slipped off.

Shipi was photographed in dark glasses and was mistaken for me. It worked, and the next day the press told all about my 'vanishing trick'.

There were more serious reasons for me to stay as much out of sight as possible. We had received several threats on my life in the past, believed to be from an Arab terrorist group. We had to keep an alert watch on the mail. Werner Schmid had received another threat by phone the day we arrived in England from Denmark.

I constantly hope for peace, and in fact I've had a dream of being the first Israeli to give a lecture-demonstration in Egypt. I know instinctively that whatever forces or intelligences exist would never be able to be used for war. But there have been many jokes in this vein. One cartoon in a European paper showed two tanks locked together and tied in knots around each other. A commander is saying to his opponent: 'No—you bend it back.' Another showed a plane with its fuselage bent in half, and the pilot is saying to the co-pilot: 'So I said to this guy Geller, okay, smarty-pants, what else can you do besides bending spoons?'

It's probably all to the good that the energies can't work in a negative direction. I have been through war as a paratrooper, and I know its horrors. I was wounded in both arms and my forehead while raiding a pillbox in the 1967 Six Day War. After being wounded, I entertained the troops in the front lines. But there was a controlling force somewhere that didn't want these powers to be used for any purpose but peace, and never to harm anyone, apparently.

This latest threat sounded serious, and we immediately had a meeting to discuss what we were going to do about the eight-city tour. Werner Schmid got in touch with Scotland Yard, which immediately sent several men to us. A decision was made to move to a large hotel in London where security guards were set up while we tried to figure out what to do in view of the threats. The entrance and halls of the hotel were guarded.

Since the Danish correspondents, Torben Dahlvad and Ulla Ave, had arrived to observe the tests we had promised, we notified them of our change of address. They arrived while we were trying to decide about going on with the English tour or not. They were going to monitor the long-distance test and take some photos of it at the prescribed time.

We set up for the test in the hotel room just as if it were going to be a television programme. I was looking forward to it, not only because I was curious to see if the same things would happen again, but also because it was something to take our minds off the threats for a while, and the fact that we had to have security guards from Scotland Yard all over the place.

The Danish correspondents had brought with them from Denmark several broken watches and a big collection of knives, forks, spoons, and keys. They were all placed on a table, and I sat down at it and got ready to concentrate. I knew I would have to concentrate strongly if the test was to work at such a distance. At exactly noon British time, which was 1 p.m. Danish time, I began concentrating. I picked up one of the broken watches and squeezed it hard. Then I placed it lightly back on the table, and it began ticking away. I did the same with two other watches, at the same time sending my thoughts towards Denmark.

For some reason I don't understand, I can tell when the energy is high, and on this day it felt very high. After the third watch on the table started up quickly, I told the Danish journalists that I was convinced it was going to work, and already thousands of broken watches were beginning to run again in Denmark. Then, turning my attention to the forks and spoons on the table, I placed my hands over several of them. They soon began bending. A knife and a fork broke in two, one of them with a very loud crack. The Danish reporters and the Scotland Yard men were really startled by this. One of the reporters gave me the key to the main door of the magazine's office building. It bent quickly.

After about ten minutes, I told them that it was going to be very successful—fantastic, in fact. I had no sooner said this than the phone rang. It was the first report from the magazine office in Copenhagen. Its switchboard was already jammed with phone calls from readers, telling the magazine about things happening in their homes. In a matter of minutes, there was more phone traffic than it could handle. I was really happy, in spite of all the problems in England, with threats still coming in on the phone.

I put the success of the Danish experiment out of my mind, as Yasha, Shipi, Werner and I tried to come to a decision about the British tour. It was a hard one to make. But the climate in England at that time was very tense. A department store executive active in Jewish charities had been shot in the street, and the terrorist group had published a list of twenty prominent English Jews who it said would be assassinated. I didn't want to cancel, but Werner Schmid insisted that it would be too risky to go on with the tour.

It was some time later when the Danish magazine published the full report about what took place on that Sunday afternoon: 1,098 people phoned in, each describing fantastic experiences. One woman complained that nothing had happened when suddenly her metal glasses frames bent on her nose. Again, there were hundreds of reports about broken watches starting up. Lights went out in some homes or even began to blink on and off. A broken oil furnace suddenly started up. And remember, this was all without the benefit of radio or television—it was just me concentrating at the exact time that thousands, maybe hundreds of thousands, of Danes concentrated with me.

So it was not all my energy, it was theirs as well. One fact suggested to me that the people reporting were not telling their stories just for publicity: The magazine received reports from many people who refused to reveal their identities. One woman whose old watch restarted told the magazine:

'No, I will not divulge who I am. I am still shaking from the experience.' Another left Denmark that Sunday to visit her grandmother in Sweden. She brought a copy of the magazine with her and an old gold watch that hadn't run for years. She put it on top of the magazine, and it started going. So, apparently the test worked even outside the boundaries of Denmark. Mrs R. Smith of Glostrup, Denmark, forgot all about the test at 1 p.m. that Sunday, but an old alarm clock that she had put on a copy of *Billed-Bladet* started up anyway.

But the most startling occurrence was one I hadn't expected at all. A telephone call came into the magazine office in Copenhagen from a little island called Oro, in Holbeck Fjord. A seventy-six-year-old woman, Elisabeth Sorensen, who had just become a great-grandmother, was visiting her son-in-law, C. V. Brunn, and her daughter there. The family decided just for fun to try concentrating on the magazine and get a few old watches running again. Suddenly, according to the phone call, Mrs Sorensen found she could bend her knee for the first time in two years. Danish reporters went out to interview her and found that she had some kind of degenerative arthritis. Instead of concentrating on the broken watches, she had concentrated on her knee.

In this particular house, the watches did not start up, but to the surprise of her family, Mrs Sorensen got up and began walking normally for the first time in twenty-four months. When the reporters arrived, the little island was still talking about the event.

I was very happy that Mrs Sorensen seemed to feel better after the experience, but I have to repeat that, if her case was real, she herself was responsible, like those who concentrate on keys, spoons, and watches. I am far from being a mystical prophet, even though healing sometimes seems to be triggered when I concentrate. Sometimes I want to try to help people heal, and wish I could do better, but I know I'm not ready for healing yet. I do have a feeling, though, that such a day might possibly come, so I shouldn't be so surprised when I get a report like that one from Denmark.

Also, if and when I reach the point where healing can be done on a regular basis, I would want to develop it fully in a controlled and organized way, and I would want to work with doctors. Especially to prevent raising false hopes in people, I would want to work with this kind of thing openly, and only under medical supervision, just the way I'm working now with scientists at Stanford Research Institute and the University of London in trying to understand just what these forces are, how they work, and what they eventually might be able to do for the world.

Healing, I feel, is another form of these undiscovered energies. Any kind of healing that involves a new force should be done not as a challenge to medicine, but with it. It is not something to be played around with. I'm convinced that I must not deliberately attempt any kind of healing until a lot more experiments have been done in co-operation with scientists on the things we are exploring now—telepathy, psychokinesis, and clairvoyance. Then the healing could be explored the same way, with medical scientists instead of physicists and psychologists. If the scientific studies continue to show the same steady progress in verifying these energies that they are showing now, I'm sure that the results will encourage medical men to lose their fears about exploring and testing things that have been considered unscientific.

I'm convinced that we all could be healers of our own bodies if we knew how to find the key to unlock these powers. Somewhere there may be some way to open up certain cells in the brain so that they could be directed into self-healing, if the process could be found. Doctors have told me that for the most part it is nature that does the healing. They do everything they can for emergencies and to help things along, but the body processes really do the final healing. I think that nature and God combine to help us do our own healings and that we will some day learn how to hurry this along. I know it sounds far-fetched, but I believe it may be possible in the future for machines or computers to be designed that will trigger the necessary immunology systems in the body to bring about self-healing. Once that is developed, we will make even greater progress in medicine. Being healthy, I am sure, is within us.

But I also believe that love is one of the keys to health. If you have love deep inside you, it becomes an incredible power. I think it's the main key to curing things. A person in a hospital gets well much quicker when love is involved, but that is only a small part of what might be possible. I want to avoid giving anybody the impression that I think these healing energies are simple, easy, and available without slow development and without combining them with modern science. That would be a big mistake. The experience with the Danish test was unintentional and might be only a hint, and it was interesting for that reason only. It's a little bit like the reports you read of medical research in the laboratories, where they've had success with animal tests, but the new discovery is not at all ready to try out on humans. If some benefits come by coincidence right now, that's fine, but that's as far as it should go at the moment. I want to be always aware of my limitations.

With the lecture-demonstration tour in England called off, I was able to get some rest in the United States and had some time to prepare to go on to Japan for some appearances in that country. It gave me a chance to think over where I was going and what all this meant to me and to the rest of the world. What had happened in both the distant and the recent past convinced me that there was a plan behind it all, though its outlines faded mysteriously from sight at times. What was to develop in the next several months, however, was as much a surprise to me as it was to the scientific world.

CHAPTER FIVE

WHILE I WASN'T really aware of it at the time, things were building to something of a crisis after the Scandinavian and European tour. The controversy over whether what I was doing was real or fake was growing. I tried not to be on the defensive all the time, but it was sometimes hard. One of the reasons for the clamour was the long series of scientific tests I had gone through at the Stanford Research Institute (SRI) beginning in 1972, one year before the tour, and continuing in August, 1973.

The institute carries on some of the most advanced research in the world for both industry and the government. Some of its work involved complex computer research for the armed forces. After the first series of tests ended, back in 1972, SRI had issued a preliminary report saying: 'We have observed certain phenomena for which we have no scientific explanation. All we can say at this point is that further research is clearly warranted.'

Because SRI has such high prestige all over the world, even the preliminary announcement attracted a lot of attention. However, the results were not published in full right away, because the scientists who had conducted the tests had not yet placed their paper in a scientific journal, which I understand is a necessary step to having it fully accepted among scientists.

I had gone to SRI with Dr Andrija Puharich, who had brought me over from Israel after testing me there, and the Astronaut Captain Edgar Mitchell. The two scientists at the institute who conducted the tests were Russell Targ, a specialist in lasers and plasma research, and Dr Harold Puthoff, who specialized in quantum physics. Both are extremely interested in parapsychology as well and have done much study in that area.

I will have much more to tell about this later, but both Targ and Puthoff were determined in the early spring of

1974 that the report on the tests they did on me should appear only in the best scientific journal possible. Nearly everyone agreed that this was *Nature*, because it is so cautious and thorough about everything it publishes. *Nature* would spend months or even years checking out a scientific paper before publishing it.

At this time the Stanford Research story still had not been published, although it had been sent to *Nature* many months before. I had learned that nearly all scientific journals have kept away from studies on the paranormal, because this field had for so long been considered unscientific. If *Nature* accepted the SRI paper, then, it would be a major breakthrough. It might even silence the critics who were constantly trying to discredit me. I was hoping very much that the scientific paper would appear in *Nature* and relieve me of some of the ugly pressure that many magicians and some of the press were constantly putting on me. Surely, I felt, if *Nature*, with its high scientific standards, accepted the article after months and months of deliberations, the scientific world and the press would also accept it, and I would no longer have to face the constant controversy.

Even in the countries I had just visited, where the incredible phenomena had spread out from me to others by television and were repeated in thousands of homes, the controversy was continuing. I learned that a professor from the University of Wales had said that the whole business was 'rather ludicrous, and all that is needed is half an hour of properly controlled testing to unmask Geller.' What he and so many others with that attitude couldn't know was that the controlled conditions at Stanford Research were as rigid as they could possibly be. SRI had consulted magicians in setting up the tests, and Russell Targ is an amateur magician himself. They had isolated me completely, making any kind of collusion impossible. In the tests where I was to try to duplicate drawings selected at random for me, I was put in a shielded room called a Faraday Cage, which is built of wire mesh to block out any kind of radio waves or electrical or magnetic forces.

One of the developments after the British broadcasts was a real interest on the part of some scientists in following up with people who had had strange things take place in their homes while the shows were on the air. Among these scientists was Professor John Taylor. He believed that if he could study others who had had metal bend and watches start up in their homes, and compare them with tests that he planned to do with me, he could rule out any trickery. In other words, if he could pick a group of children and adults who obviously couldn't be masters of magic tricks, and if they succeeded in doing some of these things, it would go a long way towards showing that some new forces were being discovered.

A London newspaper had already invited ten of these people to lunch at a London hotel and asked them to try bending spoons or keys, or starting up or stopping watches. Although it was far from a scientific test, the results were amazing. In front of the reporters, two of the children were able to start up broken watches held in their hands. A seven-year-old boy named Mark Shelley concentrated on a row of forks and bent them all. 'I just think about a fork bending, and it does,' he said.

In the brief breathing spell I had before the trip to Japan, I had a chance to stop and think about the power. The energies or forces were showing themselves in many different ways. Some I could control by concentrating on them. Others seemed to happen without my giving any thought or attention to them at all.

I could control the bending of keys and metals, the starting up of broken timepieces, the producing of changes in things like compasses, magnetometers, and other laboratory instruments. And yet sometimes, while performing these acts, I would get results that went beyond the areas of my concentration. Often, I would be bending a fork or spoon, when another one nearby would curl up without my touching it or concentrating on it. The remote experiments, such as the one across the Channel from France to England, were only partially under my control, because I didn't know how many people would be affected or where they were. The same, of course, would hold true of the various things that happened during all the television broadcasts throughout Scandinavia and the rest of Europe.

Telepathy was another act I performed consciously. I could see hidden pictures clearly in my mind, and I could usually do so best in sympathetic surroundings where there wasn't a lot of negative feeling around. In some cases, I have even come up with a response almost exactly the same size and shape as the target. I also could fire a three-digit number or picture into the mind of somebody else by having him concentrate on a number or drawing I put down on paper without his seeing it. They tell me the chances against getting a three-digit number correct are a thousand to one. But it has often worked with ordinary people who showed no signs of paranormal powers before.

These forces also seemed to provide me with the power of clairvoyance. In one of the tests at Stanford Research I was able to tell eight of ten times what number was showing at the top of a single die, which had been placed inside a metal box and shaken by one of the experimenters. Twice I didn't get a clear picture of what number was showing, so I passed. They told me that the chances for these results were about a million to one.

The most puzzling ways the energies were showing themselves were those whereby objects materialized and dematerialized, transported themselves across a room, or dropped unexpectedly on a table or at people's feet. These are things I don't concentrate on. They just happen. I am as surprised as anyone else when they occur, and I can never predict them in any way. But they happen almost every day in front of many witnesses. I will have more to say about this later on.

I like to live a full, well-rounded life. I like television and films and sports, I like to date girls, to travel, and to meet people everywhere. I enjoy giving my lecture-demonstrations throughout the world. I like to play the piano, and I also like to write poetry. Poems come to me in strange ways, and I don't think I really write them myself. It's almost as if I'm in a trance, and I usually speak them into a tape recorder, as if the poems come *through* me rather than being composed by me. Sometimes I remember what I say, and sometimes I don't. And sometimes I'm startled when I listen to the words on the tape recorder.

I began doing this shortly after I came to America. One day there was a typewriter in the room where I was staying, and, even though I had never learned to type, I just sat down and began typing some poems. They are more like lyrics, because I feel music in them. Some seem very far out; they come from outside me. This one, called 'The Day,' is very much that way:

The day the wind grew yellow
The day the dust fell
The day they opened up the skies
The day the red was coming
The day the sun stood still
The day we saw the red
The day had come the day now here
The day I knew the end

The day the lift had begun
The day the red turned yellow
The day they lay

The day they lay
The purple went on yellow
It dripped and churned
And quiet, burned
The purple turned to green
The green became so white and silver
But silver turned to gold
And gold had dripped to rainbow colours
That coloured all the mist
The mist became so heavy sunken
Sunk so deep above
The colours dropped to nothing burnt
Again and sown the fields
The fields had grown these colours below
It began to sing

I was in a sort of trance when this came to me, and I dictated it on the tape recorder instead of typing it. When I first listened to it, I realized it was far out. I analysed it line by line. When I heard the words 'the day the wind grew yellow,' I remembered the storms I had seen in the desert, everything yellow with dust. It seemed to me that this described a huge catastrophe taking place, with the winds blowing all the dust from the desert, and the atmosphere coloured yellow because of all the sands of the earth. And then the dust fell. It started sinking towards the earth, and to me that meant something tremendous was going to happen. And 'the day they opened up the skies' seemed to mean a force opened up a hole in the sky, and it had to be an enormous power to do this.

The whole poem, with its colours and vivid images, pointed to something cosmic, something universal, so extreme that the people of the earth had to evacuate the planet. The purple seemed to reflect the infinite, and the green represented either a new evolution that had come to the earth, to start it growing again, or the discovery of a new planet. I could not understand it all, but it seemed to show that only after many evolutions could we understand, after we become part of God.

There were many other poems that came this way, some of them dealing with love or loneliness or sadness or cosmic intelligences. Some were short, some long. Here's a short one:

> Close your eyes and try to see
> The bright light that will be coming from above
> Try to control it by thinking towards the beam
> That will be transferred to your mind
> By means of evolution and understanding.

I know my poems are not polished literary gems, but I feel them deeply. When they come, a force seems to grab me. I feel it, strangely enough, in the middle of my forehead, a sort of light pressure.

When I showed some of the poems to Byron and Maria Janis, they liked them. In fact, Byron liked several so much that he composed music for them. They were also shown to Del Newman—who arranges for such leading rock singers as Paul McCartney, Elton John, Cat Stevens, and Paul Simon—and he liked many of them. Finally Yasha, Werner and I decided that we would make an album of song-poems, recording it in both England and Germany. I speak several languages, including English, some German, Greek, Hebrew, and Hungarian, and we decided to make several versions in different languages. Byron and Del would compose the musical settings, and I would speak the lyrics. Maxime Nightingale, who had been in the show *Hair*, would sing those songs that required complicated vocalism, with a choir backing up many of the numbers. The album would be called simply *Uri Geller*.

This was not out of character for me, because ever since

I was a kid I had always wanted to be a movie actor and performer. In fact, as I was growing up I would always try to push my powers or energies into the background because of this desire. I was, and still am, very ordinary, except for these forces.

The desire to be a performer, to be creative, is very natural to me, although some people think it conflicts with my work in trying to understand the unusual phenomena that are happening. I don't see it that way. I think the song-poems, especially, are all part of that picture, which is emerging so slowly. It's like a film when it is placed in a development bath. The picture begins to emerge slowly, not all at once. You have to wait for it to show all the details and the meaning. In terms of my own human feelings and emotions, there is a past, present, and future. But once I think about the deeper things, I know that actually there is no past, present, or future as far as they are concerned. Everything is really happening at the same time. I feel that we all have two channels, a cosmic one and an ordinary one, and that we can tune into them at different times.

In one of the songs in the album—the last one, in fact—I was hoping to discover just how much the energy forces can be transferred or triggered from me to others. I call the piece 'Mood,' and it goes like this:

Let us drift our minds to believing
And try with our thought powers to do something
That we never felt we could achieve
Let's pick up something
Maybe a fork, a spoon or a key
Now concentrate
Drift your mind into believing deeply
Want truly the phenomena to occur
Hold the fork or a key in your hands gently
And start repeating in your head and mind

'Bend . . . bend . . .'
Also run your fingers very smoothly
Up and down the object
Barely touching the metal
Stroking it tenderly
While repeating in your mind
'Bend . . . Bend . . .'
Now, if it's bending, just be happy
And want it to continue
You are part of a fascinating effect
That is really hidden in many of us
But if it didn't happen
Please don't be disappointed
Because it doesn't happen to everybody
Maybe it's not the time
Or the Mood is not right
Sometimes it doesn't even work for me.

It didn't take long to find out that the song-poems really worked. We had put on the back of the record jacket: 'All parties that have hitherto been involved take no responsibility for the experiments and their consequences.' This disclaimer actually was to cover contingencies both ways. If things bent as a result of a listener's hearing the album, we naturally did not want to be responsible. But also, we didn't want anyone to be disappointed if nothing happened. There was no way of telling.

Later, when the record did appear in Europe in 1974, it was played over the radio in Switzerland. Sure enough, the station received hundreds of phone calls from people reporting that cutlery and keys were bending in their homes, just as had happened previously with the BBC broadcasts and others. If this kind of reaction continues, it will be an important corroboration of the theory that there is a new force in the world, that it can be triggered in others, and that it should receive serious and immediate attention. That was why I had been so pleased about the news that Professor Taylor was planning a scientific study to follow up on some of those who had reported bending incidents in their homes during the BBC broadcasts. Here at least was something clear and verifiable that the critics couldn't try to ascribe to trickery.

There was a lot to do in getting ready for the album, and in the meantime I had several TV appearances scheduled for Japan in February, as well as a repeat tour of various Scandinavian countries in March. The reaction in Japan turned out every bit as spectacular as in Europe and seemed to show that the language barrier had nothing to do with the way the energy forces worked. Again, there were unusual happenings in homes all over Japan as the television show was broadcast throughout the islands.

But again, none of this did anything to silence the critics who wanted to discredit everything I did. This was perhaps why I was waiting rather impatiently for the SRI test results to appear in *Nature*, because only then, I felt, would the scales tip in the other direction. But, when I returned from Japan to the United States, the attacks were increasing.

Time magazine published what I thought was a really vicious onslaught against the whole field of psychic phenomena. The article tried to put down every effort being made in the field, rather than looking at it from a balanced point of view. I was shocked that a responsible magazine would print a story like this. The writers at *Time* apparently had made no study of what had happened during the British and European broadcasts over the previous months—or if they had they failed to acknowledge it.

But none of this should have surprised me. *Time* had launched an all-out attack on me a year before, when Stanford Research Institute had told the editors that they would have to wait until the tests were presented to the scientific world.

It seemed that most of *Time*'s position came from the faith it placed in a magician named James Randi, who claimed to be able to duplicate everything I did. Actually, he could give the illusion, by sleight of hand, of some of the things that I did, but he chose to ignore things that he couldn't duplicate.

What struck me as strange was that *Time* seemed to be saying flatly that a magician was more of an authority than the scientists—and even that I was more clever than the entire Stanford Research Institute. This was very flattering, but I don't see how anyone could buy it if they gave it any thought. Neither Randi nor *Time*, of course, gave any explanation of how watches and clocks that hadn't been working for ten to fifty years started up, or how things bent miles away from where I was, or how other people had these energies triggered in them. They remained completely silent about this, as if pretending that none of it had happened, even though it had been splashed in newspaper headlines all over Europe.

But apparently some interesting things did happen as the publication day for *Time*'s cover story approached. To give *Time* magazine credit, these events were described in the 'Letter from the Publisher' section in the front of the issue. The alarm clock-radio that *Time*'s science editor, Leon Jaroff, used to wake him up failed to go off three times in the week before publication, making him late for work each of those days. But more astonishing, as *Time* described it, both of the machines that print out *Time*'s computerized copy processing system stopped working simultaneously against what *Time* called 'astronomical odds,' just at the moment that the psychic phenomenon story was being fed into it. Right after that, the IBM computer 'in effect swallowed the entire cover story: it developed a flaw in its programming that sent the copy circling endlessly through memory loops from which it could not be retrieved,' *Time* reported. It took thirteen hours to get the story running again.

In contrast to *Time*'s negative approach, the *Daily Mail* of

Photo: Shipi Shtrang

Joker and I, in Nicosia.

My father and I, in 1967.

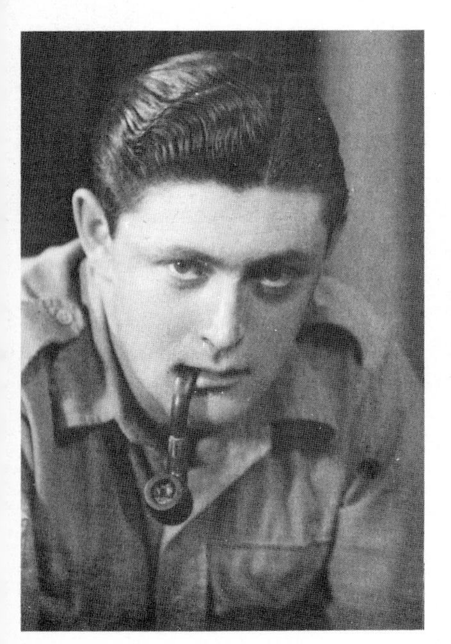

My father in the British Army, and I in the Israeli Army, each as a young sergeant at the same age.

London ran a poll for its readers about a week after the *Time* story. At that time, the paper was serializing parts of Dr Andrija Puharich's book about me, called *Uri*. On its front page, the *Daily Mail* ran a ballot to be marked 'YES' or 'NO' by its readers. In the ballot box was this explanation: 'Controversy rages around the Uri Geller story serialized this week in the *Daily Mail*. In America, scientists are split between those who regard Geller as simply a supershowman and those who believe he has superhuman powers. . . . So now it's your turn. Does Uri Geller have psychic powers? Mark your verdict YES or NO on the cut-out coupon, and send it to us.'

When I heard about the poll, I was pessimistic. If I had just read about these energy forces instead of seeing or experiencing them, I probably would have voted a big, black 'NO' myself. My guess was that not more than 20 or 25 per cent of the people answering would vote 'YES' although the preliminary results of the SRI tests were included in the *Daily Mail* story, and they were pretty convincing, even if incomplete.

On Friday, March 22, 1974, the results of the poll were published, and I have to admit I was astounded by them. The tabulation showed that 95·5 per cent of those voting believed I had genuine psychic powers, and only 4·5 per cent indicated they thought I was just using showman's tricks. In announcing the results, the *Daily Mail* said: 'Time and time again in the many letters sent to us, readers say that while they were sceptical at first, it was the Stanford Research Institute evidence which finally convinced them.'

But these were only incomplete, unofficial results from Stanford, and the publication in *Nature* still remained unannounced. The only news I could get was that the SRI paper was under consideration. It was now well over a year that this had been so, and the chances of its being accepted looked dim to me and to many others.

Meanwhile, I had completed my second Scandinavian tour and was working hard to get ready for the recording of the album, to be done in June. It was then that I learned that the Robert Stigwood Organization, the London production company that had produced both the film and the British stage version of *Jesus Christ, Superstar*, in addition to the film *Tommy*, had contracted for the film rights of my life story. I was pleased and enthusiastic about this, even though I guessed that the scientists who were studying me might think I should stick to the serious business of carrying out the scientific tests.

But I don't see any real conflict here. I have these two sides to me, the down-to-earth side and the far-out side that involves these energy forces. I want to be involved in both of them. I believe there are good reasons for my public demonstrations, for the television, the film, the music, the poetry, the album. In just over one year's time, I must have been viewed and heard by millions and millions of people on television and radio or in auditoriums. I think I have changed some of their thinking, opened up new horizons of the universe. You have to use energy to change something, especially the mind. I believe we all have to raise our consciousness, to look at these new cosmic things. I'm hoping the film, the record, this book, and my appearances will do more of this.

I honestly think that, if it weren't for all the public activity, science would be likely to ignore the energy forces. The public is interested, curious. It wants to know. And that in turn will stimulate scientists, even if it bothers them at times.

I'm convinced that it was the astounding results of the BBC broadcasts that helped University of London Professor John Taylor and other scientists there to plan the new series of tests, not only for me but for the people who had been triggered by the broadcasts. In fact, in May 1974 Professor Taylor wrote an article for the BBC weekly magazine *The Listener* about why he felt this kind of psychic phenomena should be studied. He remarked that the results of the broadcasts 'present a very serious challenge to the standard scientific understanding of the world around us.'

He continued: 'Reconciling these baffling phenomena with established science is difficult. Some scientists have been so disturbed by this that they have become very hostile: others have declined to watch Geller performing, so as to avoid any chance of becoming convinced. . . . Those who hope to understand the world as rationally as possible need not be completely downhearted at these developments. For, with the apparently well-developed powers, not only in the people I have mentioned but in others, too, it becomes possible to begin a careful analysis of how these phenomena actually occur. Once a causal explanation can be given, the rational view is saved.'

Professor Taylor knew that I planned to come to England in June to record the album there, and he wrote me a letter asking if I would be able to spend some time with him at the King's College laboratory to do some experiments. At the same time Dr David Bohm and Dr John Hasted wanted to know if I'd be willing to undergo some experiments with them. I arranged to do both, encouraged by the fact that all those involved were well respected in the scientific world.

Dr Bohm, I learned, had been honoured in the naming of the 'Bohm effect' in nuclear fusion after him, and all his work in nuclear physics was highly regarded. So I knew I would be dealing with first-rate scientists who would be listened to when they announced their results.

Curious results of the earlier tour in Europe and Scandinavia kept coming to my attention. A Swedish housewife from Jönköping, in central Sweden, had watched my broadcast there and wondered about how metal could be bent just by mental forces. She had successfully used an IUD, a copper contraceptive coil, for many years, and at the age of forty she counted on it to prevent adding any more children to the family. Just two months after my show had been on the air, her doctor told her that she was pregnant. Moreover, he reported that the copper coil was bent so much out of shape that it was useless as a contraceptive. At last report she had consulted a lawyer to see if she could sue me for damages.

Plans were moving along fast for the album and for the two series of tests at King's College and Birkbeck College of the University of London. It was going to be a hectic schedule, with long sessions involving a large orchestra and all the complications of a full studio recording. Werner Schmid was producing the record, which involved the scoring and orchestration of the original music by Byron Janis and Del Newman. I would be doing the new series of University of London tests in between rehearsals and recording.

Brendan O'Regan, a science researcher who had followed me closely over many months, had lined up the scientific tests. I learned that the experiments were being set up with great care and that the conditions would be completely controlled so that there would be little chance of ambiguity in the results. In addition, there would be more concentration on the actual physical effect on metals and instruments. I had done some metal-bending at Stanford Research Institute, but the research there had concentrated on telepathy, and the paper submitted to *Nature* dealt with that part of the study.

Dr Ted Bastin, who had followed many of the things that had happened with me and who had eagerly encouraged many British scientists to follow up on the research, felt that SRI was wrong to hold up release of the facts established in the tests. He thought that this served to increase the controversy and turned off many scientists who should be giving the energy forces serious attention. 'Stanford Research Institute has let us down in being so secretive about their results,' he said.

With some scientists still voicing negative arguments in the media, there was no question that something approaching an all-out war was on between those who accepted the new forces and those who rejected them completely. There was a lot at stake for science, and even the critics admitted this. *Time* magazine's attack on me had stated that, if what I was doing could be proved and established, 'it raises serious and disturbing questions for all of modern science.' *Business Week* had thoughts along the same line: 'To accept psychic phenomena would shake the foundations of science. . . . And it might even mean that man has a spiritual nature inexplicable to physicists and psychologists.'

My basic instincts told me that both scientific testing and communicating with the general public through appearances were important. I had to follow my instincts. There is no other way I can act. Maybe the trouble is that I'm a very down-to-earth person. Maybe I'm too human, and I cling too much to human needs. I love security, for instance. I would like to have a million dollars in the bank for that reason. I'm not selfish, I like to help people. I'd like my parents to quit working. I like to help people who work with me in my office. I like comfort, and I like luxuries sometimes, though I don't think I'm too concerned with them. But certainly I'd like to have a nice car and a boat and a house. Maybe this isn't good. Maybe if I weren't so down-to-earth, I would be operating at higher levels and would find myself in Tibet somewhere, wearing an orange robe and eating herbs up on a mountain. But I'm just not that way.

I know the importance of the science experiments, though, and the scientists lined up for my return to England in June 1974 were an impressive group.

At Birkbeck College, in addition to Dr David Bohm, there would be Dr John Hasted, head of the Department of Physics; A. V. Cleaver, who had been Director of the Rockets Division of Rolls-Royce, Limited; Dr Ted Bastin; and researcher Brendan O'Regan. They also had invited two important witnesses to the tests: Arthur Koestler, the famous author of *Darkness at Noon*, and Arthur C. Clarke, who wrote *2001* and many other science fiction books. There was no doubt that it would be an interesting group to work with.

At King's College, Dr John Taylor would be conducting

independent tests. Taylor, as head of the Department of Mathematics, would be working with a staff of engineers and other members of the faculty.

Even though I had overcome a lot of my edginess about scientists by this time, I was still a little nervous and always had that fear of failure. But this was something very important in history—to establish firmly the existence of a newly discovered energy force in the universe, and to resolve the warfare between the scientists who believed it existed and those who didn't.

If these new experiments succeeded, and if *Nature* finally accepted the SRI results after all these long months, then we could all get together and figure out what the new forces meant to the world and to mankind.

CHAPTER SIX

WHEN I ARRIVED in England in June 1974, I called Professor Taylor at King's College. He said that he had set up his experiments, was ready for me, and was looking forward to the tests. The recording for the album was all set, and I told Dr Taylor that when I finished it I would come over to his laboratories the next day. I felt that I should work with him first, because I had already met him and would feel more comfortable with him. Then I would go to Birkbeck College, where Professor Bohm was planning a different series of tests. In this way, I could work into the experiments gradually, because that nervousness was still with me a little.

The recording session went long into the night, and I didn't get to bed until four in the morning. I was very tired when I arrived at King's College. It was a large laboratory with all kinds of equipment and instruments. Dr Taylor told me that the most important thing he had to do was to rule out any possibility of fraud so the tests would be accepted by scientists; that was one reason for so much equipment.

I agreed with him, because many scientists were constantly bringing this possibility up. I knew no fraud was involved, but it was important that others be convinced too. As Professor Taylor told me, he had worked out instruments to check on any use of force by me in the bending of objects. Besides, every piece of metal had special markings on it to prevent the substitution of an already bent object for the original one. He also was prepared to check for the use of chemicals such as mercuric chloride. He told me these substances (which incidentally are poisonous and very hard to obtain) could sometimes distort metals, but they left easily identified markings.

He had carefully prepared many kinds of metal for the experiment, including copper, aluminium, brass, different kinds of steel, tin, lead, silver, and zinc. He also had single crystals of lithium chloride. The instruments used to check the metals during the experiments included a device to measure heat called a thermocouple, some special voltmeters, radiation monitors, special coating on the metals to measure ultraviolet rays, and another instrument to check infra-red radiation.

Professor Taylor and his associates had already completed many tests on children who seemed to have picked up the ability to bend metals after watching my BBC-TV broadcast, either by concentration or by touching them lightly. There were adults, too, who showed this ability, but he was most interested in the children, because they seemed better at it, and there was less chance of fraud or trickery with them. The fifteen children he had tested ranged from seven years old up to the early teens. Dr Taylor was pleased with the results of his tests with them because, he said, success in the experiments was repeatable, time after time, under controlled laboratory conditions.

Before we started the testing, Professor Taylor checked me completely for hidden magnets or chemicals and that sort of thing. That completed, the first test involved a brass strip about 10 inches long, which he had taped to a scale much like those used to weigh letters in a post office. Most of the brass strip was sticking out past the edge of the scale, so that I could run my finger lightly along it to try to make the metal bend.

The purpose of the scale was to show if I put any heavy pressure on the metal, which is of course one thing done by magicians in their sleight-of-hand work. The scale was very sensitive, and even the slightest pressure would show up on it. You could even blow on it and it would change. There was a needle on a dial of the scale to show how much pressure was being applied. If you just barely touched the metal, it would show about half an ounce of pressure, which of course wasn't nearly enough to bend the metal.

I began lightly stroking the metal bar on the top of its surface. The needle on the dial showed that I was putting enough pressure on it to read barely half an ounce. Professor Taylor was watching, carefully taking notes, and observing an automatic recording device that was attached to the scale for a permanent record. The needle never went over the half-ounce mark while I lightly stroked the bar.

Within a minute or so, the bar began bending. The staff was amazed to see it bending *upward*, against whatever light pressure showed up from my touching the bar with my finger. Then the needle of the dial that was recording the pressure began to bend. It continued to do so, very slowly, after I had finished stroking the strip of brass, until it bent to an angle of 70 degrees. It interested me that the bar, which I had touched, had bent no more than 10 degrees. I hadn't put my hand anywhere near the indicator needle. Professor Taylor later described the needle's bending as 'disconcerting to say the least.'

But this was only the beginning of a whole series of strange, incredible things that happened in the King's College laboratory that day. The next experiment involved a strip of aluminium. Embedded into it was a small cylinder covered by a diaphragm that was extremely sensitive to any pressure. The device would set up an electric current to record any physical pressure put on the aluminium strip, Professor Taylor explained. I was told that this tiny instrument cost more than $500.

I stroked the metal lightly, and the strip began bending. But suddenly the pressure device stopped recording, after the strip had bent only slightly. Professor Taylor immediately examined the pressure-sensitive diaphragm on top of the cylinder, and to our horror it began to crumble. A very small hole appeared in the centre and then dilated across the whole surface; the diaphragm had completely disintegrated within about ten seconds.

At the same time, however, the aluminium strip continued bending without my touching it for another 30 degrees. Everybody was completely amazed, and Professor Taylor said that the 'Geller Effect' had certainly been verified by the test—at the cost of $500 worth of equipment!

Next came the small single crystal of lithium chloride, which was sealed tightly in a plastic container so that it could not be touched. They asked me to hold my hand over the container without touching it to see what effect these energy forces might have on it. Keeping a gap between my hand and the plastic container holding the crystal, I held it there and concentrated on trying to break the crystal up without touching the crystal or the container—apparently an impossible thing to do from a scientific point of view.

Within ten seconds the crystal had broken into several pieces. In addition, an aluminium disc sealed inside another container buckled up almost double, while Professor Taylor held his hand between mine and the container. I could tell that Professor Taylor was surprised. He was becoming more and more amazed as the tests went on. And so was I, in fact, because everything seemed to be working so well in spite of the kind of conditions that can sometimes make me freeze up.

We went into another room where there was more apparatus. They had taken a strip of copper and glued a very thin wire to it that would record, with complete accuracy, any distortion in the metal. In this case, I tried to bend the metal without touching it, by just concentrating on it. I tried hard, just saying to myself, 'Bend, bend, bend,' which is what I usually do whether I'm touching the material or not. But nothing happened. We stopped for a minute, since it didn't seem to be working. Then, suddenly, it began to bend, and the thin measuring wire broke.

Just about the same time, Professor Taylor happened to notice that a piece of brass on a table on the other side of the laboratory had bent. He had placed it there just a few moments before and had checked that it was straight, because he planned to use it in another experiment. Neither of us had been anywhere near it during that time.

As we turned back to continue work, there was a metallic crash at the far end of the laboratory, at least 20 feet away. When we looked there, the same piece of brass had landed next to the door. Within moments a piece of copper that had been lying next to the brass left the table and landed at the door too. By now we were all astonished. Scarcely had these events jolted us when an iron rod inside a tube that had been on a far table landed behind Professor Taylor's feet. The rod, which had been straight, had bent as much as the tube would allow.

I was glad that I was in the laboratory of a prestigious university when all this happened, because I realize how hard it is for anyone to believe such things. In writing about the experience later, Professor Taylor said that he was completely startled and added: 'None of the flying objects could have been thrown by Geller, because he was some distance away from them, and would not have been able to get close to them without being spotted.'

Professor Taylor was right. I was nowhere near them at any time. As in many other cases, I was concentrating on something else, and I had no idea what was going to happen. It seemed that the energy forces were playing tricks on all of us, displaying their zany cosmic sense of humour. It was incredible, but it happened. Everything was there in front of us to verify that it took place. I never dreamt that so much was going to happen at once.

After we collected our senses, we returned to the planned series of tests, because they were the only ones that could be used in the scientific paper that Professor Taylor was preparing. They were somewhat like many of the informal preliminary tests at the Stanford Research Institute. In the presence of the Astronaut Mitchell, Russell Targ, Hal Puthoff, and many others, things like this would happen frequently. Some were reasonably controlled and some were not. The paper they hoped that *Nature* would use did not include any of these or any of the SRI metal-bending tests, because they wanted, as their paper said, 'to resolve under conditions as unambiguous as possible the basic issue of whether a certain class of paranormal perception phenomena exists.' It would be better to establish one firm part of the forces completely, the SRI team said, than to have any part of the experience challenged because of supposedly insufficient controls. As far as I was concerned, I knew the metal tests and everything else that happened at SRI were valid, but when they were dealing with such incredible events they wanted to be super-cautious. I can't argue with that. If and when *Nature* did accept their paper, though, I would be sorry that all the amazing things that had taken place there were not covered.

However, the King's College tests were concentrating on the physical part of the story, and I was pleased that they were moving along so well. The tests were startling, in fact. Professor Taylor's thought, he explained later, from his working with the children triggered by the BBC-TV broadcast and with me, was that without question matter was being changed in shape by entirely new ways. But since physicists didn't know what forces could do this, the problem was to find out what forces they were. So many strange things had happened to me in the past, I wasn't sure the forces could be analysed as part of regular physics or other fields of science. I knew that the experiments I was going through with the scientists could at least prove that they were real and not fake, which would be a good first step to clear the air for more serious scientific studies by scientists everywhere.

In other words, there was so much prejudice and resistance just to the idea of even examining these forces among practically everyone in the field that it was impossible even to begin to learn what was going on. But now a very small group of open-minded scientists was taking it seriously. It was a start.

In working with the experiments at King's College, I felt that professors like John Taylor and others were really risking a lot of ridicule simply by exploring these new phenomena. Ridicule is hard to take, for them even more than for me. And yet when something is really important, I guess that risk has to be taken.

Professor Taylor was willing to accept the possibility that metal was actually being deformed by new energy forces, because he was checking it at first hand under controlled conditions. And it was happening not only with me, but with the fifteen children as well. He explained that in some way there had to be a breaking of the bonds between what he called the 'metallic ions' and the metallic bonding of the electron gas flowing through these. He explained that it had to end up being known energy, because known effects resulted. If these effects came from unknown forces, it would be very bad for physics, Professor Taylor felt, because it would take the effects out of the area of known physics. He figured that if, after long tests, scientists could understand what was going on, they would then have to try to go beyond what was already set by the laws of physics.

But there were complications. If the effect came from the brain, for instance, science and medicine still didn't know enough about the brain to make much progress on the question, he said. He thought science had to learn what kind of patterns in the brain could send out radiations that would distort metal.

Two more experiments were performed with two associates there. One was a test with a Geiger counter. There is always a little bit of background radiation in every place on earth. But when I held the counter and concentrated on it, the machine clicked very fast, indicating up to 500 times the normal radiation in the background, he said. It went click-click-click-click-click so fast you could hardly count it. Then it would slow down to normal when I stopped concentrating, even though I still held on to it. Of course, the immediate thought of everybody on this test is that I was holding a piece of radioactive material somewhere. Well, in the first place, I would not be dumb enough to get near any kind of radioactive material even if I knew where to get it. And in the second place, I wouldn't have been able to make the Geiger counter start going fast and then stop and then start up again when they asked me to, if I had such material with me, on my hand or on my person. Even if I wanted to, I couldn't have cheated.

Another time, with two other colleagues present he tried me with a compass. Without touching it, I was able to make the needle move about 40 degrees. Then I allowed it to return to north when I stopped the concentration, so that they could check on any possibility of 'palming' some kind of magnetic material. Also, they pounded on the floor, tilted the compass, shook it, and did many things to it to see if any such action could have caused the results. It couldn't. It was uncomfortable having to be under suspicion all the time, but I knew that all this was necessary to verify the experiments. And since Professor Taylor and his two associates were serious and interested, instead of trying to debunk the whole thing, I was able to get good results.

Just as we were getting to the end of the experiments, we heard a loud click at the far end of the room, where the piece of brass that had flown off the table had been lying by the door. It had disappeared completely, and no one had been in the area since it had landed there. Later, Professor Taylor found it under a radiator on the opposite side of the room from where it had been.

Professor Taylor said afterwards that these events were almost impossible to comprehend and that he would have dismissed reports of them as nonsense if he had not seen them happen himself in the presence of witnesses. He said he could always take the easy way out, the safe line of thinking that I *must* have been cheating. But with what happened in the laboratory that day, which was checked and monitored on many different kinds of scientific equipment, he felt he could not take that path.

And there were also the experiments with the children to back up my tests. What impressed Professor Taylor strongly was that the experiments could be *repeated* time after time, both with them and with me. This, I know, is a big problem with many experiments in parapsychology; there was no way of making sure that the results would happen time after time. Not that I could get the same results 100 per cent of the time, but it was probably close to 90 per cent, and the same with the children he had tested.

I was as interested in the results Professor Taylor had found with the children as he was. It gave me a chance to look at these energy forces outside myself. I was able to see more clearly how people who had not personally witnessed these happenings could have a really hard time believing them and might place them in the screwball category. And of course it was amazing that the powers demonstrated by the children had been transferred or triggered over ordinary radio and television broadcast channels. But this was the way the children he had tested had been discovered.

The average age of the group he worked with was about twelve, half of them boys and half girls. As they stroked the metal specimens, Professor Taylor checked them with instruments, as he had checked me. An interesting thing, he pointed out, was that there were no temperature changes as the metal bent, except for the slightest increase, something like two degrees, from body temperature. This, of course, would not be enough to bend any kind of metal, or anything else, under normal conditions. The instruments showed that there was no electrical force involved in the bending. There was also no radiation detected. A thing Professor Taylor called static magnetic fields was ruled out, too.

He kept emphasizing what had made him take the 'Geller Effect' seriously. The children were reflecting what I was doing, which satisfied him that the critics' theory of magic tricks was completely wrong. To choose fifteen children at random and to train them as magicians so perfectly that they could foil a whole battery of scientific instruments as well as scientists is surely impossible.

Yet the results Professor Taylor got with the children were phenomenal. Many of his tests with them showed the metal bending upward *against* the light pressure of their fingers, as had been the case with me. One piece of metal tested this way bent right up to 90 degrees in five minutes of light stroking. One little girl held a copper strip about five inches from her forehead and concentrated on it. She didn't even stroke it, but it bent 10 degrees. Another little girl fractured a chromium-plated nickel silver teaspoon in three minutes by rubbing it very lightly.

I can't tell you how important this scientific confirmation of the children's abilities was to me. For the first time since these strange things had been happening to me, I felt relieved of the sole responsibility for events that could be described as—I really don't like to use the word—miraculous. The only reason I can say it is that I don't take any personal credit for creating these amazing powers or energy forces; I only demonstrate them. I'm hoping that the mystical side of them will be disposed of and that the forces will be accepted as a real phenomenon. Then, as scientists study them more and more, they can start putting theories to them and maybe change the physical laws of science to accommodate them.

At first, it will probably be like all the other phenomena of the earth. Some of them can't be explained, either. We really don't know what the universe is, after all. But we have to accept it because it is there.

So we will just have to accept this new phenomenon because it is here. I believe, though, that the explanation of the bending of a key without touching it or by barely touching it will be much easier than the explanation of the universe or other, more complicated, phenomena. I'm convinced there will be an explanation for these forces, and then we can start putting them to use for the benefit of humanity.

I believe that the powers I demonstrate are in everybody but that some people, especially children, have a much higher level of them than others. There is a superior intelligence that triggers this. If I can keep showing these energy forces to people, I think that great good will come of it, in spite of all the controversy they seem to bring about.

With everything working so well at King's College, I felt better about being tested in the laboratories at Birkbeck College, which I would visit four times. Brendan O'Regan met me with a cab at my hotel, and we drove to Professor Bohm's laboratories together. The group there was made up of high-ranking scientists, and on one visit Arthur Koestler and Arthur C.

Clarke would be important witnesses from the science-literature field. Arthur Clarke, O'Regan explained, would be particularly important because he was highly sceptical of anything paranormal. His position was that his books, like *2001* and *Childhood's End*, were pure science fiction, and it would be highly unlikely that any of their fantasies would come true, at least in his own lifetime.

Professor Hasted and Professor Bohm, the two physics professors in charge of the project, were both cordial and pleasant when we arrived. They took us to a conference room containing a long table with chairs around it. On one occasion, there were quite a few other people there, including Dr Ted Bastin, Dr Jack Sarfatti, an American physicist, and A. V. Cleaver, the man who had worked on rockets for Rolls-Royce.

I was excited about these tests. They were entirely separate from the King's College experiments, and if they worked out they would show that the process could be repeated, studied, and proved valid by more than one scientific group. Counting the Stanford Research Institute series, this would make three controlled test series by scientists, each of them, I hoped, confirming the others. It should help to cancel out the bad effects of *Time* magazine and the others, whose criticism seemed to be based more on personal bias than on an objective analysis of the facts.

The atmosphere in the Birkbeck physics conference room was good, which helped to calm my nervousness. I couldn't feel any negative vibrations there in the room. Everybody there seemed to be really eager to find out about the energy forces. They asked me to talk to them a little about my philosophy of this whole strange thing, and I did. They all seemed interested. Arthur Koestler, especially, was interested, because he had written on the paranormal in some of his books. The scientists were all very attentive, but I couldn't tell what they were feeling. I sensed that I really wasn't getting through to Arthur C. Clarke, however.

I thought that maybe, if I interrupted my talking and bent his house key for him, Clarke would feel differently. I asked him to hold his key out in his own hand and watch very carefully so that he would know that I wasn't substituting another key, or taking it away from his hand, or putting pressure on it.

Within moments, his key began bending. And he said: 'My God, my eyes are seeing it! It's bending!' I did the same for Dr Cleaver from the Rolls-Royce Rocket Division, and he was very impressed. Then we went out into the labs to do the real experiments. I felt very strong and confident that day, but still a little scared, as I always seem to be around scientists, at least at first.

Professors Bohm and Hasted led me around the lab to show me the sort of experiments they had set up. They included specially marked keys, metal objects, crystals and discs sealed tightly in glass tubes, spoons, Geiger counters, and even a laser beam they would ask me to try to bend. I asked them to let me try the Geiger counter first. I reached for it, took hold of the handle, and concentrated very hard. The whole group was standing around watching. There must have been eight of them, counting the technicians who had set up the equipment for the scientists. As I concentrated, the Geiger counter suddenly started clicking furiously, just as the other had done for Professor Taylor at King's College. It was connected with all kinds of instruments to record what was happening on both meters and charts. The background radiation had been checked out at half a count each second. There was a loudspeaker connected to the counter that amplified the clicking, and this in turn was put on magnetic tape to check later. Over a period of about ten minutes, the clicking went up so fast that it seemed to run together, like a 'prrr' sound, eight times.

Everybody was amazed. At one point, the count went up to 200 times the normal rate. Professor Hasted said that, if I was carrying radioactive material that strong, it would have been very dangerous for me. The clicking would go up fast, then die down again as I stopped concentrating. If I had radioactive material on me, the fast clicking would have continued over the entire ten minutes.

Neither Bohm nor Hasted suggested that the increase of the Geiger count came from a radioactive source. Because a magnetometer showed a deflection at the same moment as the counter, they speculated it was due to an 'electromotive force' across the metal case of the counter. Of course, everybody else in the lab tried to reproduce the same effect with the Geiger counter, but with no luck at all. Everyone was mystified—including me.

But they were more startled by an experiment with two thin crystal discs of material called vanadium carbide. These were sealed inside plastic capsules so that no one could touch them. To prevent any kind of contact with my hand, Professor Hasted held his hand over the capsules and asked me to put my hand on top of his for a few seconds. One of the small capsules moved slightly across the table, a little like a Mexican jumping bean. Professor Hasted said he could feel a very slight warmth as this happened. But more startling still, about half of one of the crystals was missing—it had actually dematerialized in the controlled test.

By that time, Arthur Clarke seemed to have lost all his scepticism. He said something like, 'My God! It's all coming true! This is what I wrote about in *Childhood's End*. I can't believe it.'

Clarke was not there just to scoff. He had wanted things to happen. He just wanted to be completely convinced that everything was legitimate. When he saw that it was, he told the others: 'Look, the magicians and the journalists who are knocking this better put up or shut up now. Unless they can repeat the same things Geller is doing under the same rigidly controlled conditions, they have nothing further to say.'

Clarke told me a little about *Childhood's End*. It's science fiction, of course. It involves a UFO that is hovering over the earth and controlling it. He had written the book about twenty years ago. He said that, after being a total sceptic about these things, his mind had really been changed by observing these experiments.

I could feel during the Birkbeck College tests that everyone was co-operating and interested in seeing that the experiments would work. In other words, I could feel the energy coming from them, especially from Arthur Koestler, who seemed to be most interested. He is such a beautiful man. I felt great calmness and peace with him.

The experiments went on for two days, and they were all successful except the attempt to bend the laser beam. I couldn't do anything with that at all. But, summing up his thoughts after the series, Professor Bohm said that it was his observation that these things that had happened, both through me and with the children tested, were mainly coming from the unconscious mind, and that the conscious mind sometimes became more of a hindrance than a help. He also said that conjuring tricks had to be watched for, and that they had taken great pains to check for all the usual things that magicians use. These included the use of a long hair attached to an object by beeswax; chemicals, like mercuric chloride; bending and flexing objects to a point of softness beforehand; and that sort of thing. All these and other tricks were watched for and prevented.

Bohm and Professor Hasted felt that they should approach the study of these new forces the way science had approached magnetic and electrostatic effects. These were impossible to account for given the state of knowledge at the time they were first discovered, but the effects were still noticed and observed.

In their summary they wrote: 'We feel if similar tests are made later, enough instances of this kind will probably accumulate, so that there will be no room for reasonable doubt that some new process is involved here, which cannot be accounted for or explained in terms of the present known laws of physics. Indeed we already feel that we have gone some distance towards this point.'

These were very strong words for prominent physicists. And I learned that Professor Taylor at King's College felt the same way regarding the results of my tests there. Hasted told a British reporter for the *Daily Mail* of London: 'It is time that scientists stood up and were counted on this issue. A series of things have happened when Mr Geller was in our laboratory. We have not only worked with keys and so on, but with single crystals and metal objects in capsules. We have identified the metal objects and controlled our tests very carefully. I am quite confident science will get to the bottom of it. Of course, science may be changed.'

He went on to say that the problem is not to ask whether the phenomenon can occur, but how it occurs. 'It is a very important phenomenon,' he said. 'It will tell us new things about human beings. The problem of understanding it will be one of the most exciting pieces of research of the next few years.'

Professor Taylor wrote out the strongest statement of all:

> I have tested URI GELLER in my laboratory at King's College, London University, with specially designed apparatus.
>
> The GELLER effect—of metal bending—is clearly not brought about by fraud. It is so exceptional that it presents a crucial challenge to modern science, and could even destroy the latter if no explanation became available.
>
> As a scientist I have been investigating some of the dozens of people to appear to have the ability to bend pieces of metal, first demonstrated so efficiently by URI GELLER. Some I have tested can even achieve this without contact, as can URI himself. Others only can do this when they hear GELLER or see him on TV.
>
> Results have been written up in two scientific papers and

two further papers are in preparation, as well as a book: *Super Minds: An Inquiry into the Paranormal.*

Both groups—King's College and Birkbeck—began working on scientific papers regarding the tests. They, too, felt that *Nature* was the best target for the papers because of its prestige.

Meanwhile, I was being swept up again in all the details of recording the album in Germany, followed by some time out with friends in Italy. I needed the rest because I had a long series of lecture-demonstrations lined up in South Africa. I had accepted this tour only on the condition that I could perform before black audiences there, as well as white. This took quite a bit of arranging, but they finally agreed because I would not make the tour there otherwise.

As I was getting ready to go from Europe to South Africa, the news that I had been waiting for all these months finally came. *Nature* was definitely going to accept the Stanford Research Institute scientific paper. This was the major breakthrough we had long been hoping for.

Little did I know at the time, though, how wrong I was to think that this would put a stop to all the criticism and prejudice that had built up over the years.

2. How It All Started

CHAPTER ONE

THESE STRANGE ENERGY FORCES go far, far back into my childhood, almost as far back as my first memories. Sometimes I see myself as a small child when I project the motion picture of my life on my mental screen. Usually the first scene that comes into my mind, one of the most beautiful I can remember, is an Arabic garden across from my home in Tel Aviv. There are beautiful old trees and a high, rusted iron fence patched with wood in some places. And there's a little pond near an old house. The garden has grown wild. No one has cut the grass for years. I might be three or four years old.

Some parts of the garden are dark, for the trees cut off the light in strange, mysterious patches. And I see myself there. Suddenly, starting from that scene, I see a total connection with the universe. I see the darkness of a deep, deep blue. And billions of stars, the Milky Way. And I see myself going through that universe. I hear strange voices and see brilliant colours.

Somehow, the film keeps going back to my early life, and I see myself growing up. I see my dog, my parents, my school. I see myself playing my own private games in the garden. One leaf alone is a huge tree to me. And all the grass is forest, forest, forest. The flowers are too big to be trees here. So I imagine they're a different kind of tree, on another planet. My father had brought me shiny bullet heads, sometimes copper ones. I would build a little round dune and put the bullet heads in it, pointing up towards the sky. Because they were rockets to me. They were pointed and looked just like rockets.

I would pretend they were taking off. They were rockets to the moon—or farther. I would hold the rocket in my hand and pretend it was soaring through space. It was a whole world in a little square of garden. I would squeeze myself through the fence—there was a hole just big enough to do that. There were birds, and the pond was filled with green water. And to me the smell was exotic, as if in another country, another world.

It was a magical, mystical garden, like a dream. There was no sound except for the birds and the wind in the trees. It was frightening at first, because people said there was a guy there who would eat you up. I felt courageous going there. But nothing ate me up, and I found peace in the garden. There was a big grey house, too, and the shutters used to hit the walls when the wind blew. No one lived in the house. I peeked inside once, and everything was covered with black cloth. It was the only time I dared approach it. And I heard the cry of a little cat coming from underneath the house.

It was the thin cry of a kitten, and, although I love animals, I didn't dare pick it up because the mother was there with other kittens, and I was afraid she might jump on me. I can close my eyes today and sense the smell, the cry of the cat, the mysterious house. I remember the full vibrations of that place. One day, as I was exploring the garden, I found what looked like an old rusty pipe in the bushes. When I pulled it out, I was overjoyed to find it was the barrel of a gun, in fact a complete rifle except for the wooden stock, which had rotted away.

This was a happy moment—to find and have a gun all my own. I took it home and rubbed it down and cleaned it as well as I could. My mother wasn't home at the time, and later I took it downstairs to play. It wasn't long before a police car came by, and the policeman saw me playing with it in the yard. The police immediately took the rifle away from me, and it broke my heart. I locked myself in my room and cried.

A few days later I decided to go back to the garden to find

another rifle. I knew in my heart I'd never find one, but I wanted to try.

And it was on this day that a strange thing happened—at that young age of three or four. Before I describe it, I want to make it plain that I know it sounds like a small child's fantasy, like something out of *Alice in Wonderland*. That doesn't make it any less real. It is more than real. I was very young, but my memory of the incident is now and has always been so clear that there is no question that it happened. I didn't know then exactly what was happening to me. I had to accept it the way it was happening. With a child's mind, I didn't ask questions of myself then, the way I do now. But it's important to remember what happened, because it might just possibly be a clue to the results of the tests I've undergone in university laboratories.

In that garden many years ago, it was late afternoon but still light. I had been playing all alone, sometimes dozing and dreaming in the garden during the afternoon. Suddenly there was a very loud, high-pitched ringing in my ears. All other sounds stopped. And it was strange, as if time had suddenly stood still. The trees didn't move in the wind. Something made me look up at the sky. I remember it well. There was a silvery mass of light. And I even remember the first thought that passed through my head: What happened to the sun?

This was not the sun, and I knew it. The light was too close to me. Then it came down lower, I remember, very close to me. The colour was brilliant. I felt as if I had been knocked over backwards. There was a sharp pain in my forehead. Then I was knocked out. I lost consciousness completely. I don't know how long I lay there, but when I woke I rushed home and told my mother. She was angry and worried. Deep down, I knew something important had happened.

I went back to the garden many times after that, hoping to see that brilliant, silvery mass of light again. It never appeared again, however, much as I wanted it to. My mother, of course, dismissed it as a childish fantasy, and I kept my thoughts about it to myself. But today, in the light of all that is happening with these energy forces, I think about it often. As I get farther into my story, I think you will understand why.

My life began against a background of violence, not in my home, where I was always loved, but in the world all around me. Perhaps that is why I pray for peace so much, why I feel we must bring peace to the world or we will all perish. I was born on December 20, 1946, in Tel Aviv. My father and mother had married in Hungary in 1938, on the eve of the terror of World War II. My father and mother had to flee from Hungary separately. My father, Itzhak, left Hungary in November 1938, escaped into Rumania, and sneaked aboard a ship bound for what was then called Palestine. The trip took four months, because the British shot at the ship when it attempted to land in Israel. It went to Greece, then tried again. Again it was stopped and turned away. The third attempt, made in March 1939, finally succeeded, with twenty dead refugees aboard the ship.

My mother, Margaret, had escaped from Hungary to Yugoslavia, where she was finally able to get aboard a ship named *Rudichar II*, which brought her to Palestine. When they were reunited, my parents first set up their home in Kerem Haa'teiman, on the border of Jaffa.

My father came from a very religious family. His grandfather, a rabbi in Budapest, brought the family up in a strict Jewish tradition and died at the age of ninety. My mother's family was not very religious. Although she was born in Berlin, her parents were Viennese. Their surname was Freud, and my grandfather, who was said to be a distant relative of Sigmund Freud, was fairly successful in the furniture business in Budapest. They had a big warehouse with all kinds of furniture and kitchen ware. But my mother's family was not rich. Neither was my father's.

My mother and father used to like to go out on a large lake some distance from Budapest in those long, thin racing sculls. It was known as a dangerous lake, and at times it could get quite rough. One time their boat capsized. My mother's foot was caught in the sliding mechanism of the scull, and she began to drown. My father swam under the boat and just barely saved her life.

I do not know if that is why they fell in love and married, but they did so in 1938. There are pictures of their wedding. It was in one of the biggest synagogues in Budapest, or perhaps all of Hungary. But their happiness would not last long for several reasons.

I know that when they settled in Palestine, which was ruled by the British then, things were hard for them. My father had to look all over for a job. He and a friend, who was a doctor, also a refugee, finally found work selling lollipops from a cart on the beaches. Later, my father worked as a cab driver, making dangerous trips from Tel Aviv to Lod. At that time, my father told me, it was very risky to go out of Tel Aviv, with constant shooting going on by both the Arabs and the British.

My father joined the British Army in World War II. He fought in the Jewish Brigade in Libya with the Eighth Army, under General Montgomery. He was in the tank squad, and at Tobruk his unit was surrounded by Germans for many weeks until they escaped by boat. It was so bad there, he told me, they had to drink their own urine. That was in 1941. He went back to Tobruk to fight again in 1942 and 1943.

When he returned to Palestine there still was no peace. He joined the Haganah, which was like a secret home guard. The Haganah did not engage in terrorism, but there was constant fighting among the British, the Arabs, and the extreme Zionist groups.

My very earliest memory is of a violent incident. Opposite the house where I lived as a baby was the railroad station. Behind the station was the British headquarters, a tall building.

There was constant sniping and fighting around us. I don't know how old I was, but I was still in a pram. My mother put me by a window, and one night a lot of shooting broke out on the streets. Suddenly, bullets came through the windows and right past my pram. I remember glass breaking, as young as I was. My mother rushed in and pulled the pram into the living room. I didn't have a single scratch, even though there was broken glass all over me.

Later, during the 1948 war and afterwards, there were always reminders of the fighting. When I was about five, I used to dig out bullets from pieces of wood and shutters with a pen-knife. Some were copper and some were shiny silver, and most of them were all smashed up. But to me they were always rockets to the moon and outer space.

I loved my father and mother very much. But it wasn't long before I realized that they were living separate lives. By now Israel was independent, and my father had left the Haganah and joined the regular Israeli Army. He was home only occasionally. And I knew he was seeing other women. In fact, he wanted me to meet one of them. I somehow felt this was bad, just by instinct. He was in love with her, though. And I'll never forget the day that she came to our house. She whistled up the stairs to my father. I was trying to make noise so that my mother would not hear it, trying to cover it up, because I knew my mother would be hurt.

Another time, my father was on the telephone when I was with him—not in our house, but an outside phone. We didn't even have a phone; it was a big thing. My father let me hold the phone and talk on it, and it was an exciting moment. When I got on the phone, I realized that I was talking to a woman my father was seeing. I didn't know what to say to her, because I really didn't accept this situation. I felt something very bad in my heart. I knew my parents' marriage would not be able to work, and I came to accept it.

But no matter what, I loved my father and I was proud of

him. He later became a sergeant-major in the Tank Corps—he was always in the Tank Corps after Israel became independent. Of course, I was closer to my mother, because I lived with her all the time.

My father would always do nice things for me whenever he did come home. One night he came home and said that he had a surprise for me outside on the balcony. I went out and found a little puppy. I don't think I have ever been so happy. I called him Tzuki. He was a funny little Arabic mongrel, light brown and white, with a little white heart-shaped spot on his forehead.

Tzuki and I were never apart except when I went to school, which was near my house. Tzuki would watch for me from the balcony every day, and I would look forward to seeing him.

It is hard to tell exactly when I began to notice anything unusual. My mother noticed some things first, before I did. She was working as a seamstress during the day, which was one reason why I had so much freedom for myself, although she arranged for a neighbour to keep an eye on me. Her main recreation was playing cards with friends, which she loved to do. But even when I was in first grade, as young as I was, I used to wait up for her when she came in from playing cards so that I could say good night. And somehow I knew whether she had won or lost, or how much exactly she had won or lost, in pounds and shillings. I don't know how I knew it, I just knew it. She was really surprised, because I was able to tell nearly every time. She didn't know quite what to make of it, so she shrugged it off.

And she noticed that I would often say things just before she was going to say them, as if I were reading her mind. She was often startled by this, but neither of us thought about it too much. I was a strange kid, there seemed no doubt about it.

I was very young, perhaps about six, when my father brought me my first watch. I was very proud of it. Now, from the very start I didn't like school much. I didn't like studying and classes, and I couldn't wait for recess, which I guess is normal, but I think I had a stronger dose of dislike than normal. Now that I had a watch, I would look at it many times to see when the bell would ring for recess. In some classrooms, but not all of them, there were wall clocks. On one particular day I remember, I kept looking at my watch, which told me that the class was over. But the recess bell wasn't ringing. Then I looked at the clock on the wall, and it showed that we still had half an hour to go. So I sadly pulled out the stem and set my watch back to match the wall clock. Then I suffered through the rest of the class.

But this was only the first time of many that the same thing happened. Time after time, my watch would jump a half an hour or so ahead of the school clock, and I would have to set it back. I finally told my mother about it, and we agreed that the watch was not working right. But it began misbehaving in a very strange way. The minute hand would spin four or five hours ahead, sometimes more. My mother said that there must be something really wrong, because no watch would jump that fast.

Finally, I left the watch home, and my mother checked it every day. Nothing unusual happened. The watch ran in a perfectly normal manner. It stayed that way for weeks. So I decided to wear it back to school. I was hoping to catch the watch moving, something I had never been able to do before. I took it off my wrist in the classroom, put it in front of me, and just looked at it. Soon I forgot about it, but later happened to glance down at it. Then I saw the hands going around faster and faster, as though the watch had gone crazy.

I shouted to the teacher: 'Look at this watch!' And I held it up for everybody to see. Then everybody in the class began laughing at me. I felt miserable. I realized for the first time in my life than I had to be very careful about what I said. People would laugh and make fun of me. As any child would be, I was really embarrassed.

I went home and told my mother how everybody had laughed. She asked me exactly what happened, and I told her. She finally said, 'All right, we'll get you another one.' It was months later when they finally did, and I never wore the old one again. I just thought it must have been a weird watch, and that was all there was to it.

I wasn't ready for what was going to happen next. I was wearing my new watch, and very proud of it too. At last, I thought, I had a watch that would run properly. And it seemed to. It kept perfectly good time. Then one day when we were all out in the playground, the bell rang to signal us back into the classroom again.

I looked down at my watch. To my amazement, the hands were bent. It was as if they had tried to bend upwards, then hit the glass, which held them back so that they bent sideways inside of it. I said to myself: 'My God, I don't want to show this to anybody!' I didn't want to be laughed at again. It was the last thing I wanted.

But one thing struck me even then. It always seemed to happen most when other kids were around. In the classroom. On the playground. In front of other people. But here was a practically new watch, and it was ruined. I didn't show it to the teacher or the other kids in the class, but I took it home with me. My father was home at that time, and I showed it to both my parents.

My father took the watch in his hands and looked at it. And he asked me one question: 'Did you open this watch?' I said: 'No, father, I did not,' because of course I hadn't. Then my mother told him of the troubles I had had with the other watch. Then they looked at each other, and neither of them understood what was going on. I never got another watch during my childhood.

In spite of the problems that my parents were having with their marriage, I was basically happy. My parents hadn't divorced yet, but my father was coming home less and less, and I did feel sad that my mother was working so hard as a seamstress. She worked at home and delivered the work when she finished it. I felt sadness at the way she felt, because I literally could read what she was thinking most of the time. I just seemed to have this very rich, imaginative mind inside myself. I was not really a loner. I had friends at school. But at that time, in the early grades, I didn't have any friend I was very close to.

I guess I realized that I was a little bit unusual even back then. My mind seemed to be drifting to other worlds, unworldly thoughts, quite a bit. I don't know if it was because of that brilliant beam of light in the garden or not. But that had made a tremendous impact on me. It was real, it was vivid in my mind. It was, I know to this day, no childhood fantasy.

I know I believed in God before my mother or anyone told me about Him. I knew that there was a superior power over me, over all of us. Nobody had to tell me. My mother wasn't very religious, but she too believed in God. I didn't, of course, attach any religious meaning to the bending and moving hands of the watch. That just puzzled me more than anything else.

Some time after my second watch was ruined, when I no longer had a watch of my own, another strange thing happened. One day at lunch at school, my classmate sitting next to me, who was wearing a watch, suddenly looked down and said: 'Hey! My watch just moved an hour ahead.' I was feeling daring that day, so I said to him: 'I did that.' He started arguing with me, saying that it was impossible. So I asked him to let me hold the watch, which he did. I didn't touch the stem or anything like that. I just looked at the watch and said, 'Move!' I said it two or three times. And sure enough, the watch jumped ahead some more. Then everybody gathered around, and I did it some more.

Now, instead of laughing, they all said it was the greatest trick in the world. And so I began to feel happier. But I soon ran into something I was going to encounter the rest of my

Concentrating on stopping the escalator in Munich, in 1971.
(Photo: Bernard Rudolph, *Bild-Zeitung*)

The cable car that stopped in Germany.
Below: An engineer and I in front of the console where the switch for the cable car flipped.
(Photos: Joachim Voigt, *Bild-Zeitung*)

life: everybody thought it was a trick. No one believed me when I said there was no trick to it.

I soon began to notice other things besides the hands of watches moving and bending, which made me feel more like a freak. One time my mother had made some mushroom soup. There was good white bread with the soup, and I dipped the bread into it and ate. Then I started eating the soup with my spoon. I'm left-handed, so I held the spoon in my left hand and took several sips of the soup. My mother was standing by the kitchen stove. I was lifting a spoonful up to my mouth, when suddenly the bowl of the spoon bent down and spilled hot soup into my lap. Then the bowl of the spoon itself fell off. I was left there holding on to the handle. I called to my mother: 'Look what happened!' She came over and looked at me, then looked at the spoon. And then she started laughing. 'Well, it must be a loose spoon or something,' she said. Now I knew that was silly. You don't just have 'loose spoons.'

I laughed, too. But then I started putting two and two together. Something was happening around me that was very strange, and I had no way of explaining it or knowing what to do about it. I only knew that, whatever it was, this kind of thing didn't seem to happen to anyone else. And it was not comfortable.

Try to imagine such a thing happening to you as a child of eight or nine. You have a spoon full of soup, and it suddenly breaks and spills the soup in your lap. What do you do? The first reaction is to jump back in surprise, then to get angry at the spoon. And if it happens again the reaction is: Wait a minute. What's going on here? What is happening? And then if it continues, as it did with me, up to thirty or forty times a year, it becomes disconcerting and worrying, to say the least.

The worst part of it was that there was no place to turn for help. Neither of my parents could believe what was going on, and I couldn't exactly blame them. I didn't want to talk to my teachers about it, and my classmates would either laugh or say it was all just a trick. I was too ashamed even to ask anybody about it, because I knew they would laugh at me.

Can you imagine having a problem that nobody can help you with? What do you do? The only thing I could do was accept it, try to overlook it, and live with it. My parents were kind, but they simply didn't know what to say or do.

My mother used to have coffee with friends in a coffee shop. Sometimes I would go along with her. I would be eating a piece of cake with them when suddenly several of the spoons on the coffee shop table would start curling up out of shape. I hadn't even touched them. My mother would be very embarrassed and never know quite what to say.

The waiters would come by, look at the bent pieces, and quickly replace them so that people wouldn't think the coffee shop was offering bent spoons. She would try to explain to her friends that this happened every once in a while when Uri was around, and they would all think I was a mischievous boy. I certainly had no way of explaining it. All I could do was continue to feel uncomfortable.

My mother gradually began to accept it, but only up to a point. When I told her of the things that would happen at school, she finally said that she didn't want to hear anything more. It's fine, she would say, it's interesting, but I don't want to have to take you to a doctor.

When my father was home, they did talk about taking me to a psychiatrist. They were hoping I would outgrow this strange thing. Since I knew there was no way to convince them that I wasn't causing mischief intentionally, I decided that the best thing to do was at least to stop talking about what happened at school. It was all very frustrating.

My mother seemed to accept it more than my father, because she knew how accurate I was in reading her mind, especially when I continued to tell her down to the last shilling how much she won or lost at cards and to anticipate what she was going to say, time after time. My father hadn't experienced any of this, so he was more inclined to take a harder line. One day he finally said: 'Look. Let's go to a psychiatrist, just to see what he says, Uri.'

And I got angry. I was thinking that my parents weren't able to get along together, that my father was going to leave with another woman, and here they were talking about taking me to a psychiatrist. I was only about nine then, but I blew up. I told them: 'I'm not the one who needs to go to a psychiatrist. Both of you are. You're not getting along with each other, you're going to break up, and you both need it more than I do. Why don't *you* go to him?'

That seemed to hold them off, and, though I didn't want to hurt them at all, because I loved them, I felt sure that a doctor couldn't do me any good. I wanted so much to forget all this. I didn't feel different from other children, I wanted to mingle with them and do what they did. I didn't have red eyes or mystic colours emanating from me. Or auras around me. I wasn't a bookworm. I hated to study. I played basketball and soccer. I wasn't a bad kid. I was free and very open. I just had this one big problem: crazy things happened when I was around, especially among other children. There wasn't any real antagonism because of this, from the kids or anyone else. I was just angry within myself, because there wasn't anywhere to turn, there was no one to confide in, because what was happening was something that no one, not even my mother, could understand.

Although I was very close to my mother, I was never a mama's boy. I was very independent, and she never tried to dominate me. Although I didn't see my father very much, we were close and understood each other most of the time that we were together. He was a handsome man, and women were always running after him. My mother understood this and came to accept it. Of course, she was hurt, and it was painful for her. But it was a fact of life.

I had my own dreams and hopes. From my earliest days, I always wanted to be a movie star, just the way a friend of mine wanted to be a pilot. And my mind continued to wander to other lands, far away. I always thought of exploring where nobody had ever been before. The unknown has always been exciting to me. I think every kid has this somewhere inside him—to go places that are dangerous, where anything can happen to you. I used to try to invent certain kinds of clothes you could wear that would protect you from any harm in adventurous situations. I even drew sketches and diagrams of my ideas.

Two important things happened to me in those early days that had nothing to do with watches, silverware, mind-reading, or anything strange. One time I asked a friend of mine to hold Tzuki for a moment while I went across the street. Tzuki wouldn't hold still for this and ran across after me—straight into the path of a car. It ran over him and killed him instantly. I saw it happen right in front of me. It was awful. Both my mother and I cried, that day and the next. Only then did I learn how much I loved animals. My father brought me another dog a few weeks later, and I named it Tzuki again. Maybe it was because I was somewhat different from the other children that I turned to my dog for companionship. Whatever it was, the sadness of that day stays with me.

I was in the third or fourth grade when I had the other experience. It was one of the worst incidents in my life, and I feel terrible even as I write about it now. I'll never understand why I did it. It was one of those foolish, immature things that happen when you are a child. One day in school the teacher asked the class to bring in their Torahs from home—those scrolls that contain the holy Jewish words. I didn't have a Torah to bring, so I came in empty-handed. When I saw all those beautiful Torahs, I felt very jealous. Everybody had a Torah but me.

When recess came my classmates put their Torahs under their desks and left the classroom. I then went back and stole one. It was somebody's Torah, I don't remember whose, a beautiful white one. I took it home. Then they found out.

That afternoon the teacher came to my house. When I saw her coming I knew they knew I had stolen the Torah. I was in a state of terror. I didn't know what to do. In a panic, I tore up the Torah and threw it in the wastebasket. My father was home that day, and the teacher told him about it. I'll never forget the way my father looked when she told him. He looked at me, and he knew I had stolen it. My father was never mean and never vicious, but he whipped me that day. He took me into the bathroom and really whipped me. And I realized I had committed two sins. I had not only stolen the Torah, but I had also torn it up.

There was a girl named Naomi in my class whom I secretly loved. After that incident, she didn't want to speak to me. I learned a lesson that day, and while it certainly wasn't the last I was to learn, it's one I'll never forget.

I was almost an outcast after that, which made it easier for me when my mother told me I would be going to school at a kibbutz, one of those collective settlements in Israel where everybody works and lives together. They weren't sending me there because of the Torah, but because the divorce was now going to come about, and it would be better for my mother to go about her work without having the responsibility of taking care of me full time.

I did not feel sad when they told me about the divorce. I knew the decision was better for my mother somehow. And I knew it was better for my father. I didn't cry or fight against the divorce. With my father leaving and my mother working hard every day as a seamstress, I would be able to keep well and have good food at the kibbutz. I would not be lonely and would be well taken care of. I knew they had made the right decision, although I felt a sadness in my heart at being away from my mother and felt terrible about leaving my dog behind.

But there was the excitement of going to a new place, a new

world. I had heard many good stories about what a kibbutz was like, that everybody's a friend there, that you're adopted by a family, that you can work, maybe drive a tractor, milk the cows, that kind of thing.

It would be a taste of a new life, and I was ready for it.

CHAPTER TWO

ALTHOUGH I WAS PREPARED for a new adventure, going to the kibbutz didn't turn out the way I had imagined it. I had never been away from home before. I was worried, because I had heard that the kids in the kibbutz didn't accept city kids very easily. I was tough in some ways, and I knew I could stand on my own feet. But it was strange to leave the city, and I began to get mixed feelings about the whole thing. I had to say goodbye to Tzuki, my dog.

The kibbutz Hatzor Ashdod was about 30 kilometres south of Tel Aviv. It was a beautiful place built on a hill, made up of little white houses with red roofs. There were trees and grass, a swimming pool, and a big dining room for everybody to eat in. And there were wide fields and orange groves where we worked. My mother took me to the kibbutz, and when she left I began to get the first small twinges of homesickness. I was taken to my quarters, which I would share with eight other boys and girls, and a teacher. Then I was introduced to my 'second family'. They were Hungarian, and they were nice people with children of their own.

It was awkward meeting the other kids for the first time, but they too were nice. However, the ones who had been born on the kibbutz were a little suspicious of me and the few others who had come from the city. I couldn't help feeling like a stranger. They had a word for city boys—*ironim*—and it immediately separated us from the others.

The routine at the kibbutz was simple and kept us busy. Everybody met in the morning for breakfast in the big communal dining hall. Then there would be school, work in the fields, swimming, and sports. The school work was light and not as hard as in the city.

We used to join our 'second families' around four in the afternoon for coffee or tea, then have dinner together in the dining hall in the evening. It should have been a happy and productive life, and I guess for a lot of people it was. I was nearly ten years old now, but I missed my home terribly. The homesickness seemed to creep up on me. I could feel it growing and gnawing at my heart, and in my stomach, too. I remember that when I went to work in the fields I would go alone, far, far away from the others. And from the hill I used to look to the north, because Tel Aviv was there, and that was home. At night, I used to look at the moon and the stars because I knew my mother would be seeing that moon and those stars at the same time.

And I was torn between two feelings. I was dying for my mother to come and visit, but I didn't want her to, because on her first visit the kids had made fun of her lipstick. She was dressed smartly, which was not the way of the kibbutz. I don't think they realized that she was a hard-working woman who dressed the way they did in the city.

Life in the kibbutz was run according to communal ideas that went against my thinking. Everything belonged to everybody, and I had to share everything. The only things I didn't share with the others were my thoughts, which I kept to myself. I had not thought much about the strange things that had happened with the watches and the bending of metals, and I didn't try to do anything along that line, although it sometimes happened when I wasn't thinking about it.

I think life in the kibbutz has changed now, but then I felt that, whatever I did, they would never accept a kid from the city. I slowly began to hate life there. I missed my dog. I missed my home. The routine went on every day without much change. We picked oranges. We picked bananas. We dug potatoes. We worked in the barn where the cows were. We worked in the dining room.

In the classroom, my marks were best in drawing and music. But the school work was easy, almost too easy. Even though I was not a good student, I had no trouble with it. I guess I liked that part of it.

I was so happy when my father came to see me. He would drive down in his jeep, and the kids forgot to tease me when he came. He would telephone me and say he was coming at such and such a time, and I would walk far down a long, dusty road to meet him. There were many cars that passed, raising the dust in the road, but I could always tell when my father's jeep was approaching, even though the dust cloud was far away.

He brought me all kinds of interesting things—pouches from the army, army boots, souvenirs. Then, towards the end of 1956, just before the Suez war between the Israelis and the Arabs broke out, my father came and said that the situation was quite bad and he thought there was going to be a war. Then the war did break out, and he was gone. I remember that you could hear the faint thundering of the artillery and the bombs in the distance. There was an air force base right next to the kibbutz, and at night we used to hear all the heavy American-made planes coming in with supplies. I used to want to be in one of those planes myself, to land and take off in them. My mind was filled with thoughts of both my father and mother. I would think: What is my father doing now? What kind of situation is he in? And what is my mother doing? What does she think of him now that they are divorced? Does she still care about him? Doesn't she care? I knew that somewhere out there my father was fighting for me, to guard me.

My mother had met a man she liked very much. His name was Ladislas Gero, and he was a Hungarian Jew who had gone to live in Cyprus. He was a well-built man in his fifties, a widower and a concert pianist. After escaping from Hungary, he and his first wife had formed a cabaret dance team and went on a tour to Cyprus. They stayed there in Cyprus and put together enough money to buy a small hotel. It was called the Pension Ritz and catered for the singers, dancers, and musicians who used to perform in the many cabarets of Nicosia. The artists liked to stay in his smaller pension, because they liked Ladislas and because his pension was more like home and less expensive than the big hotels.

When his wife died, Gero had gone to Israel and met my mother through friends of hers in Haifa. One day my mother came to the kibbutz with Ladislas and told me that they were going to be married. And even though I had mixed feelings, I was happy for my mother, because I knew she was going to change her life and that she would be able to stop working so hard. I was even happier when I learned that I was going to be able to leave the kibbutz and move to Cyprus with them. Ladislas was wearing a necktie when they visited. Some of the kids had never seen one before, and someone asked, 'What is that cloth hanging around his neck?'

Before I left the kibbutz, I got word that my father was alive and safe and on his way to see me. I'll never forget that day. He came in a command car, all bearded and dusty, and he was holding two rifles in his hands. It was one of my happiest moments. He told me that he was going to keep the rifles locked up and give them to me when I became eighteen. I had prayed very hard for him, and to learn that he was alive and well brought me great joy.

I returned from the kibbutz to Tel Aviv to get ready to go with my mother to Cyprus. It was an exciting prospect to be going to another country, another world, where everything would be new. All I knew was that Cyprus was an island in the Mediterranean not too far from Israel, and that we would be living in my stepfather's small hotel in Nicosia. I saw that my mother was happy about going, and this made me feel good for her.

I guess my spirits had been so low when I was at the kibbutz that nothing much happened there with the energy forces. I didn't even try to show them off, and when anything happened I kept it quiet for fear of being teased again. But in Tel Aviv, before we left for Cyprus, one unusual incident occurred that I remember very clearly. My mother had gone to Haifa, about 100 kilometres from Tel Aviv, and was expecting to return that night. I was eating at the kitchen table when I found I couldn't eat any more. Suddenly I knew that something was happening to my mother. She was sending me a sharp, clear message. I couldn't tell exactly what the message was, but it was very frightening.

I ran around the house trying to find the address she was staying at in Haifa. I couldn't find it. I was scared. I tried to go to sleep but couldn't. Finally she came home and found me out of bed. The first thing I said was: 'Mother, what happened to you?' She said: 'You knew, didn't you?'

She didn't say, 'How did you know?' She just said, 'You knew.' Then she told me that she had been riding in a taxi and that the driver had smashed into another car. Fortunately, she wasn't hurt, but I felt that impact from more than a hundred kilometres away.

There had been other incidents like that in my childhood. They might be put down as coincidence, but my feelings when they happened were so strong and so clear that I am reasonably sure that they were more than that. I went to the zoo one time with my mother a year or so before I went to the kibbutz. Originally my father was going to take me, but he was unable to get leave, and I was terribly disappointed and very sad. I had had my heart set on it. So my mother took me in his place.

Much as I had wanted to go there, we had no sooner entered the zoo than a feeling of terror came over me. I didn't want to say so, but I couldn't help myself. I said: 'Mother, I don't feel like being here today. We've got to get out of here.'

'But, Uri,' my mother said, 'you were sad all day long. Why on earth do you want to leave?'

'Mother, I have a very bad feeling. I can't describe it.'

'What do you mean, Uri?' she asked. 'How? Why?'

All I could say was, 'Mother, please. We've got to get out of here.'

Then she met a friend and stopped to talk with her. I started pulling her hand very strongly. I said, 'Mother, *please* let's get out.'

We started for the entrance gate. No sooner had we done so than alarm bells started ringing—a lion had broken loose from his cage. People were running and screaming, climbing trees, jumping into the pond. Panic seemed to be everywhere. The lion was running around slowly, but by that time we were right near the gate and got out safely. Fortunately, no one was harmed, and they recaptured the lion. The point was that I didn't usually react like this, and my mother had been very surprised when I insisted on getting out of the zoo.

Another time, my father was taking me for a ride in a big armoured car at his army base, a halftrack vehicle. I used to love those times when he took me around the army camps. He was showing me how it could manœuvre, and we started up an extremely steep test embankment. I wasn't afraid of this kind of thing. I loved it. But just as we started up, I yelled out to my father to turn the wheel and get off the bank. My father was startled, but my yell was so strong that he turned off from going up the hill. He told me the halftrack would take it, but turned back towards the garage. Almost immediately, there was a loud bang, and one huge caterpillar tread of the vehicle broke in half.

His face was white. If we had gone up the hill and the tread had broken the way it did, he said, we would have slid out of control and been crushed. I didn't know anything about telepathy or clairvoyance then, but there was no doubt in my mind that these things were not just luck or coincidence.

Since he was a long-time army man, my father was very orderly and neat in everything he did. He had a beautiful collection of medals he had won: the Africa Star, the King George medal, and all the ribbons and decorations that go with them. He kept them all together in a leather suitcase. At times I used to dig out that old suitcase and open it up to look at both the decorations and the pictures he kept there, all neatly packed. There were pictures of Tobruk and the Pyramids, and there was one special picture I loved—of a mummified pharaoh, partly eaten away. The picture had a morbid attraction for me. There were others of British generals and of my father at the time he was with Montgomery's army, posing near the Sphinx and riding in light armoured tanks.

I would look at these pictures of him and hope that I would look like him when I grew up, because he was so good-looking. It was always one of my dreams to be like my father and to be in the army—but the dream of being a movie star still stuck with me, too. That had begun back at the old school in Tel Aviv, when Naomi and I used to sneak away and go to see films of Tarzan and adventure and monster films—before that terrible experience with the Torah.

One day I was looking through the decorations and noticed that the two British decorations were gone from the suitcase. I had not taken them out, and I knew they had been in there the last time I looked. I didn't dare tell my father, because I was sure he would think I had taken them. But several months later he was home, and he came to me and said: 'Uri, did you take the two British decorations out of the case?'

'No, father, I didn't.'

'Are you sure you didn't?'

'No, father. I look at your things, and sometimes I play with them. But I have always put them back carefully.' I felt terrible, because I knew they were very important to him.

Then, in a way I can never explain, I had a strong, almost overpowering and unmistakable feeling that I knew where they were. I said, 'Father, I think they are up in the storage room.'

'What in the hell are they doing up there? How did they get there?'

I didn't know how, I was just sure they were in the storage room.

My father had to leave before I could get a ladder and climb up to look. When I did, I crawled among the old clothes and boxes and books to find the medals. I felt sort of foolish, because I knew I hadn't put them up there, and certainly neither my father nor my mother had. There were tins of food —my parents had stored extra ones during the war—and many other things that collect in an attic. In among all this I found an old kit bag, and something told me to open it up. Now, that was ridiculous, because there was no way those medals could be in that bag. I opened it up, and there was a bunch of old shirts and things, but I kept poking down to the bottom. I found both medals there.

I was really surprised, because I was just going on this strange feeling nothing else. I even began to suspect that my father had hidden them in the bag to protect them. Or maybe he had put them there and forgotten about it. But that didn't make sense either.

When my father came home again, I told him I had found the medals, way up in the storage attic, and deep down in the kit bag. He laughed and said: 'You didn't have to make up a story about it. You don't have to lie, Uri. I'm just glad that you found them.' This was the old trouble: no one believed me when I was telling the truth.

An even stranger thing happened once when I went to visit my father at his army camp. His office was in a sort of cage where they kept the guns and ammunition. I loved to walk around and look at the machine guns and rifles, all coated with grease for protection. This time he let me go out with him to the range as he sometimes did, and he brought along a small machine gun. He had trained me always to be very careful with guns of all types, but he let me fire a few rounds on the range on that day. I got a big kick out of that. He trained me never to point a gun, even though you thought it was empty, and never to wave it around.

After we had finished shooting, he showed me how to double check that all the bullets were out of the gun. He did this carefully, thoroughly, showing me the empty chambers and running his finger inside to double check. With the gun empty, I pointed it out to the range once more just to hear the click. When I pulled the trigger, the gun fired and a bullet came out. My father turned pale. He grabbed the gun from me, cocked it again, and checked it. There was great confusion on his face, and he was very upset.

Now I realize that there could be reasonable explanations for this. You could say that my father had not checked the gun completely to be sure there were no bullets left. As a matter of fact, this is what I would believe if somebody else told me such a story. But I knew, even if nobody else did, that the gun had been empty.

These incidents were important hints of the many strange and incredible things to come. At the time, I didn't realize that there must be a psychic force working; I had no idea of that. I was just puzzled and hurt because no one would believe me.

When we were getting ready to move to Cyprus there was again a big heartbreak that I would have to face. There was no way I could take my dog with me: I had to give Tzuki away. I remember the day that a friend of ours who lived on a farm came to take him. I kissed and hugged Tzuki, and I cried. Then I watched them take him down the street. But I knew he was going to have a nice home, and that made me feel better.

I had little time to think about anything else. I was about eleven years old, and moving was a big thing for me. In spite of the excitement, there were some things I worried about besides Tzuki. I worried about how I would get along with my new stepfather, and how I would get along in a place where they didn't speak Hebrew.

My mother had been to Cyprus to visit my new father and told me what a beautiful place it was. She said Ladislas had bought a nice dog for me. I looked forward to that. The day we left, my father drove us to Haifa, where the boat was sailing from. The port was full of people, American tourists, seamen, even Russians milling around. It was very exciting. A new Italian ship was going to take us to Cyprus. I began to forget whatever sadness I had about leaving. My father told me I would be coming back to Israel to visit. That made me feel good.

We went through Customs and boarded the boat. My father was allowed to stay on board until they gave the signal to leave. I saw him standing on the dock in his uniform as the boat left, and we waved to each other. I don't know what he was thinking then. Maybe he felt good also, because he knew that I would be secure and would have a nice place to live.

The trip was a great adventure for me. I went up to the captain's quarters and down to the engine room and all over the ship. I remember how Haifa disappeared into the mist, as if it had been a dream. The voyage took about two days, and I never got seasick.

For some reason, Ladislas was unable to meet us when we landed, so I went about helping my mother with the luggage. While we waited for a taxi to Nicosia, I saw a little kiosk. My first thought was to send a postcard back to my father in Israel.

Cyprus looked different, kind of Arabic to me, something like a movie set. Along the road to Nicosia I saw many little villages, and I learned that some of them were Turkish and some were Greek. The Turks and Greeks never mixed with each other. Fighting could break out at any time, I heard. In one village I would see the red flag with the white Turkish star, and in another I would see the blue and white flag of the Greeks. There were also British camps, with British flags flying above them. It was like an island of international villages.

The road was narrow and winding, and we dodged donkeys here and there as we wound up and down many hills and valleys. After less than an hour's drive we were approaching the outskirts of Nicosia, which is in the centre of the island and away from the coast. We pulled up in front of the pension, and Ladislas was standing outside waiting for us. And suddenly, seeing him again, I felt that I liked him.

He greeted us and started to take us into the hotel. There were about ten big stone steps leading up to it, and a big iron fence around it that reminded me of the Arabic garden.

The inn was quite large, with a red tile roof, a huge garden with a big oak tree in it, and a garage. It seemed to be a mixed English-Greek style. There were fourteen or fifteen rooms in it. I liked it. But the biggest thrill of all was that Ladislas had two dogs for me. Joker was a wire-haired fox terrier, and Peter a mixed-breed terrier. When I saw them I knew I'd be happy. They jumped all over me and licked me, and we played together even before I went into the hotel.

When we went inside, it was cool and relaxing, with thick walls and a big reception room with old but comfortable furniture. My stepfather took me up to my room, and there was another surprise waiting for me. It was a big box on the table. I ran to open it, and inside was a model of a beautiful blue Cadillac. I was so happy. I thanked him for it, and I knew that I was at home.

I would be at the hotel for a month or two, but there was a problem about school. My mother and father had spent a lot of time trying to figure out what would be the best thing to do. The schools in Nicosia were not very good, and my mother felt I should go if possible to one where I could learn English.

The best choice seemed to be a school in Larnaca, where we had landed, called the American School. I would have to board there and come home just to visit, and they would come to visit me. After the kibbutz I didn't like the idea, but there seemed to be no other choice.

It was a rather large school with old, crumbling buildings. When I arrived, I said good-bye to my parents and was led to a dormitory with thirty or forty beds in it. Almost immediately I felt lonely and homesick again, this time in a strange country with strange languages being spoken. It was an all-boys school, with mostly Greek boys, several of other nationalities, and only a few Americans, even though it was called the American School. Our classes were in a wooden shack that didn't look as if it could stand up very long. One other Israeli boy was there, but since he wasn't a boarding student we didn't become close friends. Most of my friends were English boys, and I began learning English fast.

We went to class and played tennis and other sports. Once a week they let us go into Larnaca to see a movie. I would buy ice cream at the same kiosk I had seen when we landed.

But I was still lonely and homesick. I seemed unable to shake that feeling. I remember one thing I used to do every once in a while. I would stand by the road going back towards Nicosia, watch the cars going that way, and wish I could go back there with them. I wanted to go back so badly.

I wasn't at the school in Larnaca very long before violence again surrounded us. It was now 1957. The Greeks on Cyprus were demanding union with Greece; the British had just deported Archbishop Makarios; the Turks wanted the island split up; and the Greek underground forces known as the EOKA were terrorizing both the British and the Turks. I remember we went to class one day and suddenly heard the sirens blowing. We heard ambulances rushing to the Greek hospital right next to the school grounds and machine guns firing in the distance.

It wasn't long after the fighting started that my mother and stepfather came to the school and said that because of the troubles they had come to take me home. I would go to school in Nicosia, closer to home. I had learned to speak English very fast there, which had been one of the reasons for my going to the American School. But even going to a school near my parents in Nicosia would be dangerous, for there were troubles there, too. (The fighting and the shooting were talked about as 'troubles'. Perhaps it was an attempt to make the situation sound better than it really was.)

So my mother and my stepfather took me out of the school at Larnaca and brought me back to Nicosia. I was very glad to go. When we got there, they finally decided that the situation in Nicosia was too dangerous for me to go to school right away. There was shooting everywhere on the island, and everyone was scared. Curfews were declared that lasted many days, and no one could go out. At the age of eleven I was seeing more violence and destruction, and it was a horrible experience.

At the hotel, singers, dancers, and even acrobats were stranded. I loved meeting them, and I used to pass the time by talking to them. They came from everywhere: Germany, England, Spain, America, Greece, Scandinavia. To a very few of them I showed the bending and the watch-jumping. I remember one couple, a British civil engineer and his wife, who was a dancer. He used to bring in stories about what was happening in the British camps and also bring back some meat from them, which was very hard to get. During some of the curfews there was a strange silence in the streets, and we would barbecue the meat in the garden of the hotel. At those times the performers would tell stories of their lives, and there would be singing with a guitar as the smell of the barbecue filled the garden. They were all waiting for the curfew to lift and the cabarets to open again. It was very strange during those beautiful, peaceful moments when the shooting and the fighting stopped. I got to like those curfew days.

There was a bicycle in our garage that my stepfather promised to give me as a bar mitzvah present when I became thirteen. I used to long for it, to be able at least to cycle around the big parking lot next to the hotel, where there were no cars and I would be close enough to the hotel to be safe. But there was a big combination lock on the bike, and I was not allowed to ride it.

But the temptation was too strong. One day, I said to myself: 'If I can bend keys and tell what my mother is thinking or has done, or move watches or clocks, I'll bet I can open that lock!' It was an exciting thought. I couldn't resist it. I tried the lock several times, but it wouldn't open. Then I concentrated very hard on the lock for about two minutes. I tried it again. It immediately opened. I still remember the feeling of pulling the lock open. It was amazing.

I sneaked the bike out of the garage and tried to ride it. I must have fallen fifty times, but I finally got the knack, and I had this wonderful feeling of freedom. Of course, it wasn't long before my stepfather found out I had opened the lock and was using the bicycle. He was absolutely amazed that I had found the combination for the lock. He didn't ask me how I did it. He just said, 'Well, I don't know how you opened it, but as long as you have, you can have the bicycle.'

I guess I was lucky to have such tolerant parents. This was perhaps the first time that I had put the powers, whatever they were, to what you might call a practical use, as mischievous as it was. There was much more of this to come—sometimes, as with the bicycle lock, when I tried deliberately to do something, and other times when I would have no intention of making things happen, but they would anyway. In either case, I would be reminded of the fact that things were happening that were very far from normal, and this was a condition that was to stay with me for the rest of my life.

CHAPTER THREE

THOSE WEEKS OF BARBECUES in the midst of the fighting were carefree for me. I had not returned to school. Then one day I found my mother and stepfather had disappeared from the hotel. They hadn't told anyone where they were going, and I didn't have any idea myself. I was worried. Something told me to go to a hospital. There were several, and I didn't know which. I started walking down the streets of Nicosia without any idea where I was going. After about a half-hour, I saw the big general hospital in Nicosia.

I hesitated a moment, then went straight through the main door, walked into the elevator, and went up to the fourth floor. No one had told me anything, but I didn't have any doubt as to where to go and what to do. I walked out of the elevator, turned left, and went straight down the hall to a room with an open door.

In the room I found my stepfather in bed and my mother sitting beside him. My stepfather had had a heart attack and had been rushed to the hospital. On arrival he had seemed in fair condition, but the doctors were taking no chances. After that, he had to take things easy and be careful of what he did.

It was a strange experience. My parents were absolutely stunned to see me. I didn't know what steered me in the direction of the hospital, or how I could possibly have known exactly what room and floor to go to.

As my thirteenth birthday approached, the question of my bar mitzvah came up. Of course, that was a very important thing for a boy in Israel, but in Cyprus, where there were very few Jews, it presented a lot of difficulties. With the constant fighting there was no place to have the ceremony. When the time came, we held it at the Israeli consulate. I had a friend named Peter who was about my age, and we had our bar mitzvahs together there. I received several books and a leather pencil case, which I loved. The combined ceremony was quiet and simple.

The time finally came when I had to go back to school. My mother told me one day, 'Look, we've found another boarding school that is not far away from the house, about a half an hour's drive. It's up on the hills near Nicosia, and it's a Catholic school.'

'What do you mean by that?'

'Well, the teachers are monks, and we've heard it's a very good school.'

'What do you mean, monks?'

She explained to me a little about Catholics and their beliefs, which I knew a little about from Scripture lessons at the American School. Being Jewish, I had been excused from many of the Christian religious activities, so I was pretty ignorant about the New Testament.

The school was on a hill, and the buildings were made of big yellowish blocks of what must have been sandstone. It had a beautiful entrance, and the garden was laid out nicely. (The first thing I noticed was that two sides of the garden were lined with bushes cut in the shape of crosses.)

I liked the way the school looked. It was new and clean, and the floors inside the buildings were made of marble. The dormitory was upstairs, a long room with about fifty beds in it. There were basketball courts, tennis courts, volleyball courts, and soccer fields. Surrounding the school were rocks and caves, with no other houses in sight.

The school, called Terra Santa College, was in some way connected to the Vatican. There were nuns on the staff as well as monks, working as both teachers and administrators. Father Massamino and Father Camillo ran the school. Then there were two other monks, both American—Brother Mark and Brother Bernard. I liked Brother Bernard very much. He was to have a lot of influence on my thinking.

Others on the teaching staff were laymen, not directly part

of the church. One tough, blustery teacher, Major Jones, who taught us history, had been in the British Army. Mrs Agrotis was an Englishwoman married to a Greek. I grew to like her very much.

I began to make good friends among the students there. A favourite of mine was Ardash, a chubby Armenian fellow who was a genius in mechanics. He was a day student who lived near the school. He used to collect all kinds of auto parts and rebuild cars. When I visited him, which was often, he would borrow his father's car and sometimes let me drive it on one of the dirt roads near his house. That was exciting. I also learned a lot about racing cars from him.

Gunth r Konig, a blond, good-looking German boy, was another good friend. He was extremely neat, got good marks, and was very clever in mathematics. I somehow had the feeling that his father had been a Nazi and that he was a little ashamed of this. There was also an American from California named Bob Brooks. Joseph Charles, whose father was Greek and mother was English, was probably my best friend, a very funny guy who was always making jokes and who boarded at the school with me. My other friends were all day students, and I couldn't see as much of them during the school week.

The rules of the school were strict. The Fathers wouldn't put up with any nonsense and wouldn't hesitate to deliver a sharp ruler across the knuckles if you strayed out of line. We ate in a big dining room, and I wasn't crazy about the food at all.

Gunther, Joseph, Bob, and I used to sneak out of the school grounds and explore the enormous number of caves that lay just outside the grounds in the hills surrounding the school. You didn't dare go into them without a flashlight and chalk to mark the path you took inside the caves. Otherwise, you would be lost and finished for good. There was a story about two boys who had entered one of the caves before the school was built and never did find their way out. Their bodies were found many weeks later.

When you entered from the hot, dry sun, it was like going into a refrigerator. You could go into one cave, find a little opening, squeeze yourself through it, and come out into another huge cave. This in turn would lead to another huge cave, which in turn would lead to another, and so on.

I used to like to enter one big cave alone, then slip myself into another hole. There would be a long tunnel, and I'd have to crawl on my hands and knees until I reached another hole that led into a smaller cave. From that smaller one, I would go through another slit, which turned into a tunnel sloping down, down, down. You could feel it getting colder and could see the wetness on the walls and the water dripping from them. Then, after about a five-minute walk, you would reach a point with four different ways leading away from it. You had to take the right path or you would be lost. I knew which one to take in that cave, because I used to go there many times. It led to a huge opening where the entire bottom of the cave was covered with a pond.

It was like another world. I could hear the water dripping in the pond, and I would turn off the flashlight and listen in absolute pitch darkness. I found peace down there. I wasn't frightened. It was just peaceful.

We got punished many, many times by the Fathers and Brothers, because it was dangerous and they knew it. They told us the story of the boys who had perished. I guess it must have been true. It could easily have happened.

One day I found another cave that was farther away from the school than any we had explored. I was alone that day and excited by the chance to explore an entirely new cave all by myself. I found that there were many caves inside after I entered. I decided to go into one of them to see where it led. I had my flashlight and my chalk with me. I marked my way carefully with the chalk, because I knew how dangerous it could be without these markings to follow back. As I went farther into the second cave, it seemed to have no end. After several minutes I decided that I'd better not continue alone in this strange cave. I had already come a long distance into it, and I figured I had taken as big a chance as I could for the first time.

I turned around to go back, and to my shock I couldn't find a single chalk mark anywhere. I pointed my light everywhere, but I couldn't see a single arrow. I was lost, completely. It is a terrible feeling to be lost underground in the pitch darkness. I was in a panic. I was getting cold. My sense of time had left me. I wondered how long the batteries could last in my flashlight. I started running. I had no idea which direction I was running in, and there still wasn't a sign of a chalk arrow anywhere.

I sat down and waited and prayed to God. I guess I must have prayed for an hour or more. I was terrified. There was nowhere I could go, nowhere I could turn. I had turned my light to every single section of the walls on all sides of me, looking for my arrows. It was absolutely hopeless. And then an incredible thing happened.

In the silence, I heard the unmistakable bark of a dog. I would have known that sound anywhere. I shone my light in the direction of the bark. There was Joker, as big as life. I was so happy. I grabbed him and we played together for several minutes. He licked me and scratched my chest with his paws. Then I held his collar, and he led me directly out of the cave. We walked home together, playing all the way.

My stepfather's hotel was on 12 Pantheon Street in Nicosia. It was at least forty minutes away by car from the area of the caves, if not more—and much more by walking or running up those hills. I tried to figure how Joker had known I was in trouble, how he knew where I was, how he found the cave, how he appeared there out of the blue. Things were to happen many, many years later that might explain it. At that moment in Cyprus, I could do nothing but wonder.

* * *

The troubles in Cyprus had not stopped. The school looked straight down on Nicosia, and we could hear the shooting and see some of the explosions from bombs. I didn't know quite what to think about it. The Greeks wanted independence, the Turks wanted the island divided in half, the British wanted to stay in Cyprus. I didn't know who was right.

On a visit to Nicosia I saw a horrible scene that still stays with me. A British soldier was walking down the middle of the street with his wife and carrying his daughter on his shoulders. I was idly watching this soldier when I saw a Greek sneak up behind him and shoot him in the back. I stood there petrified. The soldier collapsed, the daughter fell from his shoulders, and his wife screamed in agony. Everybody in the street ran and hid. There was nothing else to do. The shots of snipers could come from anywhere, from roofs, from doorways, from alleys. The British soldiers would walk up and down the streets carrying machine guns, looking to right and left, never knowing whether a bullet was going to come at them or not. Not only were the Greeks killing the English, but the English were killing the Greeks, and the Turks and the Greeks were killing each other.

Women and children were murdered and left in their bathtubs. Bodies were hung on meat hooks and left in the streets. At night you could hear the shots, the screams, and the sirens. It was there all the time, and there was no getting used to it.

In spite of the chance to make good friends at the school, I still felt lonely. From one point on the hill where the school stood I could look down on Nicosia and spot the area where my home was. I couldn't see my stepfather's hotel, but I could pick the area out. Loneliness would come over me at those times, and I would have to fight it. I kept wishing I could be a day student, the way many of my friends were, but of course it was too far to go back and forth, especially with the fighting and the troubles going on.

Being at a school with boys and teachers of various nationalities, I found I could pick up languages easily. I was speaking English without any trouble, and I picked up quite a bit of Greek. Of course, I could already speak Hungarian, Hebrew, and some German, because my parents used these languages. In my early years I thought in Hebrew, but now I usually think in English.

The strange energy powers continued to show up from time to time, but I didn't use them on watches. I still remembered all the teasing I used to take back in Tel Aviv, and I didn't want that to start up again. But I had some problems. I was not a bad student, but I certainly wasn't a good one. During some examinations, when I was stuck for an answer, I would wonder what to put down on the exam paper. I would stare at the rest of the class, and most of them seemed to be doing very well. One time, during a maths test, I looked at the back of Gunther's head. He was one of the best in the class. I suddenly saw his answers on the screen of my mind.

It was sort of like a television screen in my head. I was getting Gunther's answers on that screen, just as I used to get them with my mother when she came home from playing cards. I never feel these things. I see them inside my head. They appear in the front of my mind, my forehead. The screen is greyish. Now on that screen I get things. If someone thinks of a drawing, a number, or words, I see them in writing.

So on this screen I received Gunther's answers. I passed that exam with flying colours. Then I came to depend on it. I would pick the brightest kid in the subject, concentrate on the back of his head, and come up with his answers. I didn't think of it as copying then, but, of course, when you come right down to it that's what it was. The only trouble was that, as I continued doing it, I used to get the same mistakes the others were making.

The teachers began to suspect me of copying. I protested that I wasn't—which I thought was true. The teachers wouldn't listen to me. During examinations, they placed me at a desk in a far corner of the room where I couldn't possibly see the papers of any of the other students, and they guarded me personally to see that there was no chance of my copying.

But that didn't make any difference. I would just look at the best student in the class from a distance and get his answers. The teachers were baffled, because I was still getting the correct answers as well as the mistakes. They didn't know what to do, and I didn't have the nerve to tell them what was going on.

Mrs Agrotis, who taught English, got very interested in me about then. We all liked her. She was about forty, with a pretty face, and very good-hearted. She never punished or beat the children, as some of the teachers did. One time when she was guarding me during an exam, I began picking up her thoughts, in words, on this crazy screen in my mind. She seemed to be worried about something that had happened at the market the day before, and I forgot myself and asked her about it. She was taken aback. Another time she had just come from her doctor's office, and I asked her if everything went all right at the doctor's. She was shocked, because no one knew that she had been there. I got the thought by seeing the word 'doctor' on my screen, and then I also saw her in her doctor's office. This kind of information lasts only for a split second in my mind. But I can tell that I'm not making anything up, because what I see is not the least bit relevant to anything I'm thinking at the time.

Mrs Agrotis and I used to talk after class. She was sure that this wasn't something ordinary happening. I finally bent a key and a spoon for her, and she was really amazed. The word soon got around again, although no one teased me the way they had when I was very young. I showed some of what I could do to Gunther, Bob, and Joseph. They were very impressed.

Soon I became aware that the teachers were having

arguments about me. I would sometimes be asked to go to the stationery supply room, which was next to a room where the teachers gathered, and I could hear them arguing. One would say I had supernatural powers. Another would say that whatever had happened was nothing but pure coincidence. Another would say it was all tricks. Then each would tell the others what had happened in his class. I have to admit that I got a kick out of listening to them. They kept asking things like: What is he? What is he doing? What is he up to? Since I hardly knew myself, I couldn't have answered them.

After I had started two or three broken watches, one of the women teachers one day brought four broken watches, very old ones, into class. I passed my hands over each of them, and they all started working. This raised my stock with many of the teachers, which I didn't mind at all. The whole faculty was now really amazed and shocked including the Fathers and the Brothers.

I am still in touch with some of them today. One of the the Brothers is now in Chicago, and I had a nice talk with him about those days. Mrs Agrotis read about me in the British newspaper *News of the World* in December 1973, when so many objects had bent all over England after my television appearance there. She was still living in Nicosia. Not knowing my address, she wrote to the newspaper:

> Dear Sir:
>
> Uri Geller was a pupil of mine for five years in Cyprus. Even while so young he astonished his friends at the College with his amazing feats, i.e., bent forks, etc. The stories he told them of the wonderful scientific things that could, and would, be done by him, seem to be coming true. I for one do believe in him, he was outstanding in every way, with a brilliant mind, certainly one does not meet a pupil like him very often.

Please convey my best wishes to him when next you meet. I only hope I will be in the U.K. next time he appears on TV. I would like to meet him again and remind him of the happy years spent in Cyprus.

Yours sincerely,
(Mrs) Julie Agrotis

It was interesting to get a copy of that letter, so many years after those school days. It reminded me of how long the strange energy forces have been with me, and how they aroused controversy and disbelief even back in the 1950s, back in school. I also still hear from some of my friends there, especially Bob Brooks, who is in California now working with *TV Guide*. Joseph Charles also came to visit me in New York one time. Each had read about me and remembered all the strange things that happened back at the school in Cyprus.

There were others who remain in my mind. There was an old, very learned Turkish man who was the keeper of the large mosque in Nicosia. We all liked him, I think because he had a mystical quality about him. He would let us into the mosque during off hours and take us to look at the big pillars and the strange interior, with its spiral staircases and mysterious atmosphere. He used to tell us stories about the Turkish wars, and how brave the Turks were. But in the meantime I would be hearing elsewhere about how brave the Greeks were, and each side would be telling how important it was for its people to be independent. I would sometimes talk to the Turk about my belief in God, and he would point out that the Jews, the Muslims, and the Christians all had the same God; he believed that all men should not only love God but also love each other.

I wondered how we might really put ideas like that into practice. We really had to do it if the world was to survive. With all the terror and the horror in the streets of Cyprus, and with the Arabs and the Israelis at each other's throats, this seemed a long way off. Even then, back in Cyprus in the late 1950s, I was thinking that I would try to work for peace and love in the world, even though it seemed impossible. Each group was praising its own god, and yet that God was really the same for all of them. However, few of them were living up to their own faiths, which called for love and forgiveness. It seemed we were all lost in the dark caves, and there was no dog like Joker to come and lead us out.

One bright winter morning I was sitting in a classroom when Brother Bernard came into the room and told the teacher he would like to speak to me. This hardly ever happened. He took me out to the hall and told me that someone had come to the school to take me home. When I asked him why, he said that something had happened to my stepfather. And my first question was: Is my mother all right? I was very concerned. He reassured me, and I went down the corridor where I met a friend of my mother's. She told me that my stepfather was very sick, that he had another heart attack. Somehow I knew right away that he was going to die.

As the car started down the hill towards Nicosia, I burst out crying. While I felt badly about my stepfather, I never had such a deep personal feeling for him. My immediate concern was my mother, and what was going to happen to her. All kinds of emotions broke loose. I hated living at the school, and yet now that I knew I would be leaving it I felt bad about it, but glad at the same time.

At the hotel I found my mother sitting beside my stepfather's bed. His eyes were closed, and he seemed to be sleeping. He died that night. At the funeral, as my mother cried, I knew that she was both grieving and worrying about what we were going to do now that Ladislas was gone.

We were alone now, my mother and I, and I knew I would have to take on many responsibilities and try to help run the inn. I would say this was my real bar mitzvah, because I suddenly became a man that day.

I started going to school as a day student, which made me feel better. The hotel passed down to my mother, and we set about to keep it going. The property was only rented, my stepfather hadn't owned it, so we had to continue to pay the rent and try to make ends meet. My stepfather had also had a music shop in partnership with another man, and his interest there had to be sold while my mother and I tried to carry on the work at the hotel. The warfare was making things tough. Many of the cabarets were closing, and performers had always been our best customers. Everybody loved my mother, as well as her Hungarian cooking. All the guests who had stayed there before came back or planned to come back. Our problems stemmed from the times and the troubles.

Everyone at school was kind to me after the funeral. Father Massamino called me into his office, which was a very rare thing for him to do with anyone. He was a tall, powerful man with glasses and always wore a little cap. He called me over to his desk and told me he had been sorry to hear about my stepfather's death. Then he told me he wanted to give me a little present.

From under his shirt he drew out a chain with a cross on it, and near the cross on the same chain was a mezuzah, a Jewish symbol that I had never seen him wear. He said, 'I want you to have this.' And he took it off the chain and placed it in my hand, then closed my hand over the mezuzah. He told me that he believed in my religion very much. I had never talked to him personally before, and I was moved by his gesture.

With my stepfather's interest in the music shop sold out, my mother felt we were able to rent a newer and maybe larger inn. I was feeling the sense of responsibility very much now, so I got on my bicycle and rode all over Nicosia to look at every building I could find with a 'For Rent' sign on it. I guess people must have thought it was funny for a fifteen-year-old boy to come to the door and ask what the rent would be. But I was determined to find the best possible place for my mother. I came upon a nice, fairly modern villa with eleven rooms. It was on a quiet street and at one time had been a club. It was quite beautiful.

I went home and told my mother about it. After she had looked at it, she decided that it would be a good move. The rent was not too high, and we got ready to move in. The new responsibilities I was taking on gave me a sense of independence, of growing up. I made all the arrangements for the trucks and drivers to take the furniture from the old inn and did all the planning, down to tipping the movers.

After we got settled, I continued on in school, bicycling up the long hill from the town of Nicosia every day. Going up was terribly difficult, and I was practically exhausted when I arrived. But coming back I never even had to touch the pedals —that wonderful sense of freedom again. It was a strange time, this halfway period between boyhood and manhood.

I always had a good imagination, and I would have all kinds of future dreams and future realities planned. I wasn't afraid to talk about them to Mrs Agrotis, who had a sympathetic ear. I used to tell her the most far-out stories of what I believed in. I believed that there was definitely life outside of our planet, for example, and my instincts told me such a thing was not a myth or a science-fiction story. She listened and was fascinated. She would ask me to tell these fantasies to some of the younger classes she taught. I would tell them that I'm in a rocket, and I'm travelling at great speeds, and I'm arriving at very strange places with strange colours.

Mrs Agrotis wanted to know more about the telepathy that kept occurring during exams or other times, about how I could read teachers' minds. She sometimes used to give us a half-hour in class to write a fast composition. Joseph Charles sat at least five rows behind me. I never moved from my chair, and he didn't from his. Yet several times my composition was the same as his, almost word for word.

She would ask him: 'Joseph, did you copy from Uri?' He would of course deny it. And I would then look at his paper and say: 'My God, it's nearly exactly the same thing!' She kept asking: How did I do these things? And the only thing I could tell her was: 'I don't know. I just don't know.'

And I didn't. All I knew was that I sometimes knew what other people were thinking. It really didn't make life any easier. In fact, with all the doubts on the part of the teachers who thought I was deliberately cheating, it made life harder. It was something of a strain.

CHAPTER FOUR

MAYBE THESE STRANGE POWERS, my discomfort when people didn't believe me, caused me to go off by myself at times to seek adventure where no one knew me, to find out about the world around me.

One time a Hungarian pianist who was a friend of my parents bought an MG and wanted to try it out on the mountain roads. He took me along, and when we made a stop I decided to explore the mountains on foot. Before long I found myself on the ground staring at a rifle aimed at my forehead. I had stumbled on to a secret camp where a man named Grivas was directing EOKA guerrilla operations. There were many legends in Cyprus about Grivas and a big reward on his head, and the British were trying to track him down.

I was interrogated by a guard, then taken to see Grivas himself. He noticed that I spoke Athenian Greek, not the dialect of the Cyprus Greeks. He asked who I was.

I told him I was an Israeli.

'I have friends in Israel,' he said. 'You know what happened in Israel. You know how Israel got independent of the British.' Then he looked at me fiercely and said: 'Do you think we are right?'

I said that, as a matter of fact, Israel did the same thing about the British. I told him about my father, how he had fought with the Haganah.

He knew about the Haganah. We talked more, then he suddenly said good-bye in Greek. A huge sensation of relief came over me. I ran downhill as fast as I could and found my friend with the MG. He was worried to death. 'Where have you been?' he asked. I said, 'You're not going to believe who I met.'

I told him, and he didn't believe me. He said I was just making up the story. I couldn't resent this, because the story did sound unlikely. But I still wonder why I of all people stumbled into the EOKA hideout, and now and then I think of how close I came to being killed.

Like any typical boy, I used to go out of my way to find adventure. Cyprus is an island, and the sea always fascinated me. The sea around Cyprus is beautiful. I fell in love with it. It's so clear, you can drop a coin in water eight metres deep and see it on the bottom. I learned about snorkelling from a friend at school and became a fanatic. With the water around Cyprus so crystal clear, you could see all the beautiful patterns of the sea animals and plants, all of it an exciting new world.

I used to pack my things and take Joker to the bus station on a Saturday or Sunday. The buses were old and filled with pigs and chickens as well as people. They went to Kyrenia, the port city on the other side of the mountains. Outside of Kyrenia were beautiful beaches of pure white sand, practically deserted. I would change to one of the buses that went out to the villages, and when I saw a road that led to a beach I would ask the driver to let me and Joker off. I'd have a sandwich on the beach, play with Joker, and then dive into the water and snorkel for hours, until my back was black from the sun, while my stomach stayed white. People would laugh when they saw me, the contrast was so striking.

One day on the beach I met an Arab chap who wanted to sell me his aqualung equipment, with a tank big enough to last forty-five minutes. I scraped together enough money to buy it only because he was letting it go very cheaply. There was a little shop in Kyrenia where I could refill the tank, and I continued going out to the beaches alone with Joker. It's not the smartest thing in the world to skin-dive when you're alone, but I didn't think much about that. All I thought of was the adventure of diving in that crystal clear water and feeling that wonderful silence and beauty of another world. I would find places where the steep cliffs met the edge of the ocean. Every time I saw the underwater scenery, I wanted to go deeper. I always had a dream that I might find a sunken ship, or even diamonds and jewels. Of course, fish and shells were all I ever found, but I loved looking. I knew there were hazards, though, and I watched the time carefully. I didn't surface fast, and when the sea was rough I wouldn't go in. Some of the best moments of my life were spent diving.

Cyprus was also a land of wonderful contrasts. There was the sea around us and the tall Troodos mountains, such as Mount Olympus, where the snow fell and one could even go ski-ing. I never did rent skis and boots, but I liked to go to the mountains when it was snowing, just to explore and see what it was like. All this was squeezed in when the struggles of the Turks and the Greeks, as well as the British, permitted. You took what moments of pleasure you could between the curfews and sirens and shooting.

When I was nearly sixteen I moved into a period full of the little things that happen to every teenager. I had no idea that the mysterious powers and forces were to become such an enormous factor in my life or that they might turn out to be so important to science. All the crazy things that teenagers did were fun for me. I enjoyed them. I especially enjoyed my first taste of American life. There was an American Club in Cyprus, part of a military base, and one of my friends invited me to go there. You can't imagine what an impression it made on me. The PX store was like a dream come true. It looked to me as if Americans had everything they wanted; all kinds of shoes and clothing on display, every kind of pen and pencil, stationery supplies, a huge swimming pool, 7-Up, hot dogs, hamburgers, popcorn—everything that is taken for granted in America.

It was my first introduction to American abundance, and it blew my mind. I liked the kind of shirts the kids were wearing and the all-star basketball shoes. The basketballs were brand-new Wilsons, and the baseball gloves were real leather. There were American cars all over the place. Everything seemed practically free. The ice cream and hot dogs cost only pennies, and you could get a new basketball to shoot any time you wanted one. Or you could jump into the swimming pool any time of the day. There were jukeboxes and dancing, and any song you wanted to play, from Ray Charles to Chubby Checker.

It was a fairyland. Everything from America seemed top class to me. I asked my friends to get some American shirts and blue jeans, since I couldn't buy directly from the PX. They taught me baseball and let me play in the team. And since I was left-handed they had to order a special baseball glove for me from America. It was a great day when that glove finally arrived. I used to ask myself: If this is going on here, what is going on in America?

My friends invited me to the American Club often, even though I couldn't join it, and I went every chance I could. I joined a baseball team called the Barons and bicycled twice a week to a field at an English school, where we practised. One of the coaches had a daughter, Patty, who used to come and watch us. She was blonde, not too tall, slim, and very striking and attractive. She used to look at me, and I looked back at her. When I was up at bat, I always wanted to hit a home run just for her. When I hit a good one or made a good catch, I'd look over in her direction and feel very proud if she was looking. But being a teenager I was always too shy to speak to her. Then one day she came up to me at the field. She told me she liked the way I played ball and said: 'What are you doing tonight? Would you like to come to a movie at the American Club?' I told her that I sure would, and I was the happiest guy you could find.

I bicycled home and back to the American Club as fast as I could and met her there. She was wearing shorts, and so was I—nobody dressed up there. I can't remember what the film was, something with Alan Ladd in it. When we got to the post movie theatre, all the seats were filled, so we had to sit close together on one of the window sills. As the movie got exciting she put her hand on my leg. I put my arm around her, and I suddenly realized that I was in love. It was a wonderful feeling.

I saw her a lot. She lived quite a way out of Nicosia, and her father used to drop her off at the American Club. She was not only good-looking. She swam beautifully and could dance like a dream. We would dance all the time to the juke box, and our favourite song was *Sealed with a Kiss*. We used to kiss and neck, too, very innocently. We had hamburgers and hot dogs together and went bowling at the club. To me it was romantic and exciting. We saw each other for over a year, two or three times a week or whenever we could get free to be together. Being in love was something new.

But then a complication arose. It wasn't the first time I had conflicting feelings, but I wasn't sure how to handle it this time. Across the street from our hotel was a girl named Helena. She was Greek, but she spoke good English, because her family lived in America. She was just the opposite of Patty. She was dark and tanned, but she was lovely and intelligent too.

I would see Helena in her garden at times, or going into her house, but I had never met her and didn't quite know how to go about getting acquainted. One day she was in her garden, and I was playing with Joker outside the hotel, throwing a ball for him to chase. When I saw Helena, I purposely made a bad throw that bounced over the low wall and into her garden. I jumped the wall and apologized to her for letting the ball go there. I liked her immediately.

She was interesting to talk to, very spiritual, mystical, and quiet. I enjoyed seeing her. Being with her was less active and more peaceful than being with Patty. I had a little record player, and we listened to records. We used to read articles together. We talked about the troubles in Cyprus and other things happening in the world. She could not go to the American Club, but she told me of her visits to America, of all the big cars there, the buildings, the cities. America was like a mythical land to both of us. There were little things about it she liked—for instance, Jergens Lotion, of all things. I bought some at the PX for my mother, and Helena used it on special occasions.

It wasn't long before I found myself in love with both Helena and Patty at the same time. It was confusing. Although Patty and I kissed and necked a little, it never went farther than that. I didn't try. With Helena, I finally got up the nerve to try to explore farther, but she was very successful at stopping me.

Perhaps it was good that I felt strongly about Helena, because after about a year or so Patty had to return to America, and that's the last I heard from her. So my dilemma ended of its own accord.

At school, Mrs Agrotis continued to be interested in the energy forces. She liked to try experiments in telepathy. She put certain numbers in envelopes for me to guess. She was the only one I felt I could confide in about the watches, the keys, and the telepathy in any detail, because she was deeply interested and wouldn't laugh at me. She tested me many times on guessing numbers, and I could get them right nearly every time. She asked me if I had *any* idea where this power came from, and I told her no, I had just been able to do things like this ever since my early school days.

None of us at the school turned into angels as we grew older. We were always up to mischief, some of it pretty childish. We were lucky we didn't get caught at some of the things we did. I have a whole different view of it now. Not far from the school was a huge field full of abandoned military equipment: broken down army trucks, machinery, old aeroplane fuselages, broken tanks, and scrap metal. It was surrounded by a wire fence and guarded by men and dogs. We used to try to figure out ways of getting inside the fence and bringing souvenirs back to school.

Finally, a few of us got hold of a pair of wire cutters and started out on the big adventure. We made sure there were no guards or dogs around and found a place where we could cut an opening in the fence and crawl through it. We patched it back up so nobody would notice where we had cut through. We roamed all over the place, but whenever we saw a guard or dog we would scramble through the hole in the fence and push it back in place.

We were all trying to show each other that we were big men now, no longer fooling around with the kid stuff. One dare led to another. A gang of us discovered an old railroad wrecking crane on some abandoned tracks near one of the quarries close to the cave area. Part of the crane was closed in, like a boxcar, and we felt sure that there was some kind of treasure inside. When we finally forced the door open, we found it filled with old, dusty cases of beer.

We didn't know how it got there or whether it was spoiled or not, but we each drank a few bottles and tried to get drunk. None of us really succeeded. Later, we took the beer inside the caves, brought some packs of cigarettes, and continued proving to each other that we were really big men, very worldly about everything. We used to bet on who could drink the most beer and who could smoke the most cigarettes. I got a little high, but I couldn't get drunk, perhaps because the beer was so spoiled that none of the alcohol was left in it. Actually I hated the beer and the cigarettes. I don't use either of them at all now, and never really did. I tried smoking a pipe later, but that never caught on, either.

Our hotel was quite near the Israeli consulate in Nicosia. Although business was bad because of the fighting and the curfews, we sometimes had Israeli guests. One day a man arrived from Israel who told us he'd learned the name of our hotel from someone back home. He planned to stay quite a while, which was good news, because my mother was having a hard time keeping the hotel going. He left after a month and a half but said he would send us more guests from Israel. And he did, several of them. They'd stay a week or two and then leave.

One day a tall man by the name of Joav Shacham arrived from Israel. A powerful, well-built man, he seemed to be in his late twenties. He said his work had something to do with archaeology or grain-buying—I couldn't get it straight. I became friendly with him. He knew judo and offered to teach me something about it, and I learned a lot.

I used to collect stamps, and I noticed that his letters were coming in from all over, from many places in the Arabic countries, from South America—everywhere. They had beautiful stamps on them, and I asked Joav for the cancelled stamps. He told me no, he couldn't do that, but he would get me others. So instead of giving me the stamps from his letters, he bought me a beautiful album filled with all kinds of interesting stamps. I really appreciated this, but my curiosity was aroused. Wouldn't it have been easier for him to let me have the stamps he already had? I guess all the spy movies I had seen made me suspicious.

On top of that, I began to get definite impressions from his mind as he was teaching me judo. I could see all kinds of scenes on that screen in my mind. Many times I would see Joav shooting at targets with a pistol or working with documents and papers. Many things seemed to pass through his mind that could not have been normal for either an archaeologist or a grain dealer. I was almost certain that these impressions were not caused by all the spy movies I had seen or by my constant wish for great adventures.

My room in the villa that my mother and I had made into a hotel was a large storage area that was part of the attic. Originally there were no stairs to it, so we had some ladder-type stairs built and fixed it up for me to live in. That way, I wasn't using up space that could be rented to guests. A little door connected my room to the part of the attic that was directly over Joav's room. At times I would crawl through to look for an owl that was nesting in the attic and making strange noises.

One day while Joav was with us I thought I heard the owl, so I crawled into the attic to check it out with a flashlight. I didn't find any owl, but I heard voices coming from Joav's room. One of the electric wires in the attic passed through a hole in the floor to the room below. If you moved the wires just a little, you could look down into the room. I moved it and peeked through the slit. I could see Joav and a guest who had just recently checked into the hotel, an Egyptian in his fifties, perhaps, who lived in Israel.

They had all kinds of documents spread around, along with books, cameras, lights, and flashbulbs. Some of the papers were in Arabic, which was easy to recognize even through the peep-hole. I couldn't hear everything they said, but it included talk about the Egyptian Army, radio messages, agricultural equipment, Khartoum, and other things that strengthened my suspicion that they were spies for Israel. I was frightened and excited. I felt half-guilty to be in possession of such a big secret. I felt I couldn't tell it to anybody, not even my mother.

But the discovery was bursting inside me. I didn't know what to do. I liked Joav and wanted to protect him at any cost. I finally decided to level with him. When we were alone in the garden one day, I looked straight at him and said: 'You're an Israeli spy, aren't you?' Then I mentioned some of the things I had overheard.

I could see how shook up he was. He seemed to freeze for a moment, then said: 'How do you know?'

I told him how I had overheard his conversations and had looked down into his room. Then he said, 'Look, what I am doing is for the good of Israel. It is very dangerous for you to talk about it. I can get caught, and you can get hurt. You know a lot, but I can't tell you any more. You'll just have to believe that I'm doing the right thing.'

I told him I would keep his secret, and for the first time in a long while, maybe because I shared his secret, I wanted to share the secret of the powers with someone I didn't know too well. I told him that I had been able to pick up a lot of what he had been thinking even before I overheard his conversations from the attic. He naturally found this hard to swallow. So I asked him to think of a number. He did, and I guessed it. I had him think of others, four in all. Each time my answer was right. Then I asked him to concentrate on his watch with me so I could make the hands move ahead. They did so, immediately. He was shocked.

He said, 'Uri, how did you do this trick?'

I told him it was not a trick, and I could repeat it almost any time.

He thought for a moment and said: 'Uri, let's take a walk somewhere together. I want to talk to you.'

On the walk, I told him that I would like to work for the Israeli Government, too. He told me that I was too young, that I still had to go to school, and then into the Israeli Army when I reached eighteen. But he ended up by saying: 'You could help me.'

This was wonderful. It was part of my dreams and fantasies to work as a spy—probably the next best thing to being a movie star. I was young. I was enthusiastic. I was just crossing the bridge into being a man. Joav told me that he would be leaving soon and that there would be many letters with Arabic stamps coming to him at a post office box. When they came in, I was to take them on my bicycle to the Israeli consulate and give them personally to a man he named there.

All I lacked was a code name. I would pick up the letters, put them in a plain envelope, seal it, and deliver them by bicycle to the consulate. It was an exciting business for me then. I had to work on my own and not tell another soul about it. The intrigue added to the excitement.

Every once in a while I used to wear a little blue and yellow insignia on my jacket that my father had won for meritorious service in the army. Nobody in Cyprus knew what it was; I just wore it as a souvenir because it reminded me of my father, and I missed him. We wrote back and forth quite a bit, and twice I visited him in Israel during the years in Cyprus. We were close, and we have always stayed that way. He came to visit me in Cyprus once and stayed at the hotel for a little over a week. My mother and father were on fairly good terms by then.

I happened to be wearing the little insignia one time when I delivered the secret mail to the consulate. I brought the envelope in, and the man I delivered the mail to asked: 'What's that you're wearing?'

I said, 'Oh, that's a decoration my father won in the Israeli Army. He's a sergeant in the Tank Corps.'

He was interested. He wanted to know my father's name, exactly what unit he was in, and that kind of thing. I guess in his business they had to check everything out right down the line. When my father returned from Cyprus to Israel, he wrote me that a strange thing had happened. His house had been turned upside down, all the drawers pulled out, everything a mess. But nothing was stolen. My guess was that the Israeli Secret Service was checking him out because of the work I was doing—but I couldn't tell him anything about it.

I saw Joav several times off and on as I continued the work as a courier. I grew to like him very much. He told me he was going to marry a girl named Tammi, and once she came over with him and I met her. He took a real interest in my future and offered to help me in every way he could. When I finished my tour in the army, he said, I was to tell him, and if I wanted to I could resume working in the Secret Service.

I was eating like a horse in those days and putting on a lot of weight. In fact, I was getting almost chubby, even though I played a lot of basketball, which was one of my favourite sports. I used to practise on some of the courts in Nicosia, which had been put up on the bottom of the broad moats that had once surrounded the city. Joker and I would go down there, and I practised for hours at a time. I had a pretty good hook shot. It intrigued me that, when the ball rolled anywhere on the rim, it would inevitably drop in if I concentrated on it; it would also seem to vary slightly in its course if I concentrated. I dismissed this then as my own imagination. Now I wonder if it was just imagination.

Along with the rest of my schoolmates, I continued to try to prove my manhood in many ways. I got enough money together to buy a motor bike, which is a regular bicycle with a motor added to the back wheel. This took the agony out of climbing those steep hills on the way to school from Nicosia. Later I was able to get a motor scooter, and Joker learned to ride between my legs on it.

It became apparent as I was growing up that I liked to take action on impulse, quickly and decisively. Whenever a problem came up, I had a tendency to bulldoze through all the obstacles. For instance, before my stepfather died, he had rented a piano to a big hotel in the Turkish section of Nicosia. As the months went by it became obvious that the hotel was no longer going to pay the rent on it; we never received any money. When I talked to my mother about it, she said we might as well forget the piano, because it's on the other side of the barricades and barbed wire, there's shooting going on there all the time, and the whole Turkish quarter is guarded by United Nations troops. No trucker from the Greek section could go in there without being shot, she added, so it was impossible to retrieve. I told her: 'Now look, Mother. Just leave it to me.'

I found the rental documents for the piano and went to the Greek police station that was near the Turkish quarter. The police didn't have anything to suggest, so I went to United Nations headquarters, which was nearby.

I told an officer on duty that we owned a piano in a hotel in the Turkish sector and that I wanted to take a convoy in to bring the piano out. Can you imagine anything more nervy? I was surprised at myself. I showed him the papers, but he said there was absolutely no way, that I would have to talk to higher authorities. Even then he didn't believe anything could be done about it.

I said, 'What do you mean, higher authorities?'

He said he meant the colonel in charge, but he was all tied up. The officer said he himself wouldn't be able to arrange anything like this, and he doubted the colonel could arrange it. I thanked him and went up to the second floor. There was a whole row of doors marked Major this, General this, Colonel this. I picked one of the colonels' doors, knocked, and walked in. I decided I would have to take the offensive, so I told the colonel about the piano and said: 'What is the United Nations for? This is our piano, it's worth about one hundred pounds. We rented it to the hotel in good faith, and they have not paid us for months. We need the money or we need the piano. Can't you help us get it back?' I was surprised at my own determination.

The colonel was so knocked over that he laughed. He

seemed to like me. He asked how old I was, and I told him that I was almost seventeen. I explained that my stepfather had died and that we needed the money. So he finally said, 'Let's see what we can do. Do you have a phone?'

I gave him our number, and he said he would call back. He called about three days later. 'There are four Land-Rovers going into the Turkish section,' he said. 'Can the piano fit in a Land-Rover?' I told him I was sure it could.

I'll never forget that day. They let me ride with the convoy, with the papers for the piano. There were four Land-Rovers, an armoured car, and a semi-tank. We drove slowly into the Turkish side of Nicosia, through the barricades, past mines, past gates and barbed wire. There were broken bottles everywhere, and sandbags on window sills with guns pointing out between them.

We got to the hotel, and I went to see the manager. I showed him the papers and told him we had received no rent for the piano for many months. Surprised at my own firmness, I told him I wanted both the money and the piano. He said, 'Well, I can't give you the money. I just don't have it.'

I said, 'Okay. We'll waive the money, but I'm taking the piano.'

He didn't know quite what to say. We were standing at the entrance of the hotel, and he saw the convoy with its armoured car and semi-tank along with the Land-Rovers, and he saw all the U.N. officers standing around with their blue berets. He finally said okay, so we hauled the piano out and brought it back to the hotel. We were able to sell it shortly after that.

I became very conscious of my approaching manhood when Eva and her sister Ingrid checked into the hotel. They were dancers with a large company that somehow had the courage to brave the fighting and curfews of Cyprus to perform. Eva was really beautiful. She was Austrian or German, if I remember right. She had short black hair cut in a French style, and she had a wonderful perfumed smell around her.

One late afternoon when my mother was away, Eva seemed to be well on the way towards getting drunk. I was watching television, and she sat down and joined me. She drank beer after beer. It was a very hot day. We watched TV for a while, and then she said it was so hot she was going to her room to change into her bathing suit. She got up and went towards her room, weaving a little as she walked.

After a few moments I heard her call for me through her closed door. I got up, knocked on her door, and went in. She was standing there in a sort of mini bathing suit. She said she was having trouble getting the bra part closed and asked me to help her with it. I was embarrassed and my heart was pounding. I walked over to her and took hold of the two ends of the bra to try to figure out how to hook them together. I didn't have the slightest idea how to do it.

Suddenly she turned around and ripped the bra off her shoulders. She threw her arms around me and pulled me to her. Then she fell back on the bed, pulling me down with her. My heart really started beating now. I tried to act very experienced and worldly, but all I knew about this was what I'd learned from pictures and the movies.

I was awkward. When we were through she said she was sorry she did this, and all I could think of to say was: 'Don't tell my mother about it.' I had become a man, but my emotions were those of an adolescent.

CHAPTER FIVE

THE AFTER-EFFECTS of my experience with Eva were naturally strong. I couldn't help thinking how nice it would be if Helena and I could do that. I loved Helena, and it would be wonderful for both of us. But Helena remained firm, and I was left with a feeling of wanting to explore more in this exciting new territory. I felt like the inventor of something, as if no one had ever made love before. I couldn't have been more proud if I had engineered the whole thing myself, and I couldn't stop telling the guys at school about it. Ardash was all excited. He had never had the experience, and he was determined now to do so.

That's why Lola came up. Everybody knew Lola. She was Greek, with gorgeous blonde hair, in her mid-thirties, and she drove around in a red German Taunus car. She was a prostitute, but she had class, according to the stories. We had heard that she was licensed, checked by a doctor, and that sort of thing. I don't know if Lola had ever had customers arrive at her establishment on bicycles before, but we pedalled to her house determined to be the most worldly and sophisticated teenagers in Nicosia. This seemed a very necessary follow-up on my initiation into the big mystery of life.

After we parked our bicycles, I began to feel nervous. We rang the bell and were met by an old lady in black, the costume widows wear in Cyprus. When she asked us what we wanted, we got the nerve up to say we wanted to see Lola. That didn't bother her. She led us upstairs to a little room with four bright-coloured chairs and a little table with flowers on it. A certificate hanging on the wall reminded me of a doctor's waiting room. The old woman asked us if we wanted some Turkish coffee. We said yes, and she brought some immediately. I was so scared now I could hardly keep the cup from shaking. I kept saying to myself: 'What am I doing here? What the hell am I doing here?'

I couldn't tell how Ardash felt. He didn't show any emotion. In about ten minutes an older man came out of another room. He walked right by us and never looked at us, never looked left or right. Now my heart was racing so fast I couldn't count the beats. I said to Ardash, 'You go first.' He answered, 'No, you go first.' And I finally said, '*Please* go first, Ardash.' All my worldliness seemed to have left me.

Finally the old lady led Ardash out of the room we were in and I waited another ten minutes. I felt like getting up and running away. At last Ardash came out, and he was beaming. He said everything was great, fine. And I finally got up the nerve to go in.

Lola was very blonde and beautiful in her white robe. My knees began to stop shaking, and for the second time within a few weeks I learned about life.

The experience cost only ten shillings, but I felt guilty about it. With the war intensifying very fast, money was hard to come by. Every hotel was losing money as the fighting went on, and ours was no exception. My graduation would be coming along in several months, and my mother and I had begun to think about returning to Israel. I would have to enter the Israeli Army when I reached eighteen, and there was no way my mother could run the hotel without my help. Very few entertainment people were arriving. Even the number of Israeli visitors had started to diminish. My mother had many friends back in Israel who would help her get work there, where she knew the language well and would be on familiar ground. The decision was made that after my graduation we would return. My mother made a visit to Tel Aviv, and with the help of friends who lent her some money bought a little apartment so that we would have a place to go when we moved back.

Getting ready to close things down was complicated. The furniture in the hotel was rather old and worn, but we arranged to sell it for a small sum of money. Whatever was left, we packed up and got ready to go. I said good-bye to Father Massimino, Father Camillo, and Brother Bernard, along with all my other friends at school. They gave me something called a General Certificate of Education. All our heavy goods, including my motor scooter, were shipped to the port city of Limassol, and we prepared to go by car with just our suitcases. A girl named Rose, who was living with us and was devoted to my mother, went ahead in another car with Joker.

The complications came thick and fast. Although we had checked the big baggage on the ship, the Customs people for some reason took so long to examine our personal baggage that the ship actually shoved off without us but with Joker and Rose aboard. My mother began crying. I tried to comfort her, telling her that Rose would take care of everything, including Joker, and that we could phone my father who was going to meet us with a truck to take our luggage from the port of Haifa to Tel Aviv. I said, 'Come on, Mother, let's laugh about it. Let's go back to Nicosia and get the first plane, then we'll drive back to Haifa and arrange to pick up the baggage.'

But there was no plane going to Tel Aviv for two days. The new owner let us camp out in the empty hotel until we could finally take off for Israel.

Here the complications continued. When we finally arrived at the docks in Haifa and met my father, we discovered that they had not let Rose take Joker or any of the baggage from the ship. We found the baggage, but there was no sign of Joker. No one seemed to know where he was. They wouldn't allow us on the ship.

I was in a panic. Joker was nowhere on the docks, there was no sign of him anywhere, no one knew anything. I slipped on to the ship, which was practically deserted. I finally found an officer and said to him: 'Listen, my dog was left on the ship. Where would you keep him?' He said to try the upper deck, where there were cages for animals. Joker wasn't there, and another sailor said to try the stern. There was no sign of him there either. On the way back to find the officer, I passed a small metal door, one of many, and suddenly felt Joker would be inside. There was no reason to believe this, but I was absolutely sure. I tried to open the bulkhead door, a thick metal door, but it was locked. I pounded on it and called 'Joker! Joker!' But there was no sound, no bark. I hit the door again and called, 'Joker, don't worry. I'm here. I'll get the door open.' But there was still no sound behind the door.

I found the officer again and said: 'Please come and open the door. I *know* my dog is in there.' He said the door led down to the engine room, and the dog couldn't be there. He finally opened it for me. I went down some steps, and there was Joker, smeared with black oil and tied up with a chain. He gave me a look that seemed to say, 'Look what they did to me!' I felt so sad for him. I grabbed him in my arms, kissed him, and hugged him. I was furious, but there was nothing to be done about it. At least I had found him.

Our new apartment was on the ground floor, opposite a famous cemetery in Tel Aviv where many well-known Israelis are buried—foreign ministers, composers, poets, war heroes. The apartment was very small and cramped after the hotel in Cyprus, but it was the best we could do. My mother went back to sewing, this time making beautiful neckties for some of the shops in Tel Aviv. I got ready to go through the army physical and tests and to wait for induction. It was kind of dreamlike, returning to Israel, like going back to the past.

It was a good thing I had brought my scooter, because I got a job as a messenger for an architects' copy machine service while I was waiting. I was able to help my mother financially while I kept busy driving the scooter all over the city. I got £350 a month and gave most of it to my mother. I ended up doing routine work inside the architect's office, which I found through Landau, who had served under my father and who now worked there. Landau was in his early twenties, and we became friends.

He played on a basketball team in his spare time. I told him how I used to concentrate on the ball so that it would often go into the basket. He didn't understand at all what I meant, so to demonstrate I asked him to concentrate on one of the several architectural plans he had worked on that day. He did, and I drew it for him almost exactly as it was. He was astonished but was convinced it was a trick.

Landau asked me to try out for his basketball team, and I

joined it. In practice and warm-ups the concentration worked very well, so well that people talked about my 'golden left hand'. In the fast action of the games it didn't work as well, but my hook shot was very effective, with or without the chance to concentrate on it.

After the army check-ups, X-rays, blood tests, and all that, I found I had about four months to kill. I was offered a job as a desk clerk in a vacation hotel on the Red Sea, which I took for a while. There were hippies and lots of girls at the resort. It was a wild, swinging time.

As the time for my induction drew near, my father asked if I wanted him to help me get into any type of service. I asked him not to, because I wanted to work it out for myself. I tried to make my mind up between trying to be a frogman, a pilot, or a paratrooper. I knew that I eventually wanted to get into the Secret Service because I liked Joav so much. I hadn't heard from him in a long time. I wondered where he was.

It was a new feeling, getting ready to go into the army, but a good feeling. There was an excitement about it, an anticipation of what was going to happen next, a sense of challenge. On the day of induction I went by bus with a crowd of eighteen-year-olds to Jaffa, where we would be processed. It was a varied mixture of recruits. There were Israeli boys from Polish, Hungarian, and Russian families, along with Moroccan, Egyptian, and Yemenite groups.

We went through the long, routine classification interviews and tests and ended up in a boot camp called Tel Hasomer, about a half-hour's drive out of Tel Aviv. The first thing I saw when I got there was a platoon running back and forth to a 'hup, two, three, four' count, yelling out a slogan to the effect that they were paratroopers. There were tents spread out all over the place, and every tree was painted white at the base. Every stone was in place, and the ground was clean enough to eat from. The sergeant-majors, with big moustaches, were running up and down with the troops. We lined up to get uniforms along a counter, and they threw the stuff at us: green shirts and pants, black boots, underwear, soap, comb, toothpaste, dog tags—all of that. Eight of us were assigned to a tent, where we began making friends and wondering where we would all end up.

There were different bunkhouses for the different types of service you could volunteer for—infantry, air force, navy, paratroopers, and so forth. I was still trying to make up my mind exactly what I wanted to do. When I passed the paratrooper office, I stopped and looked at a poster of a guy stepping from a plane into mid-air. I looked for a minute and said to myself: 'Uri, you can't do that. You can't jump out of a plane. Come on. Forget it.' Then another voice inside my head said: 'Uri, why don't you try it and see if you can?'

I went back to my tent and thought about it. I was thinking to myself: 'Look, if you sign up there, there's no way out.' Then I thought some more, and said: 'Ridiculous. If I don't want to jump out of a plane, nobody can push me out. I mean, if I change my mind, I change my mind—and they'll send me back to boot camp.'

So I went back to paratrooper headquarters and signed up. They put me through more tests. The doctor hit me on the back and on the head, checked my spine, made me jump three or four times, things like that. There was a lot of enthusiasm about going into the paratroopers. You got special boots with thick crêpe soles, a different kind of shirt from the regular army, and a green beret. These symbols set you apart from the ordinary troops and gave your morale a boost. If you got through all the required jumping and training, you would get a red beret.

My father surprised me with a visit the next day, and he asked me what I finally decided on. When I told him it was the paratroopers, he said: 'Well, Uri, it's going to be very tough.'

'I know, Father,' I said, 'but I've played a lot of basketball,

I've run a lot in my life, done a lot of swimming and diving. I'm sure it won't be too tough.'

'We'll wait and see. And I'm proud that you went there. But just promise me one thing. I want you to become an officer. I'm a sergeant-major, but I want my son to become an officer.'

I told him that I wanted that myself, that I'd do my best to become one in the paratroops.

They shipped the paratroop recruits by truck to a special camp an hour out from Tel Aviv, near a place named Natanya. There were some engineering recruits with us, and we stopped at another camp to drop them off. One young engineer started flipping out when they told him to get off. He was shouting, crying, cursing, and yelling: 'I'm not going to get off! I want to go home! I won't get off!'

We all sat and looked at this terrible scene. They had to push him and drag him off. It was as if he was going to his death, as if he was going to be executed. It gave me a bad feeling. I was saying to myself: 'My God, he's just going to the engineering corps, and here we are volunteering for the paratroops!' Our camp was about ten minutes farther on. It gave us all a lot to think about.

When we pulled up to the paratrooper camp eight of us were left in the truck. I was chewing my gum fast. We jumped down to the ground, and suddenly we saw a sergeant coming towards us. He was a mean-looking guy. He shouted: 'Get into line!' Then he came up to us, one by one: 'What's your name? Where are you from?' Right down the line.

When he came to me, he shouted: 'Are you chewing gum when you're talking to me?' I was so scared I swallowed the gum. I told him no, I wasn't, because by now it was no longer in my mouth. But he yelled: 'Spit it out!' I insisted that I didn't have any gum in my mouth. He yelled again: 'You're chewing it. Spit it out, damn it! I want to see it on the ground.'

Then I told him I couldn't, because I had swallowed it. He

seemed to want to burst out laughing, but he controlled his face. When he got to our tent, he told us: 'Listen, you guys volunteered for this service, and you don't know what's waiting for you here. I'm going to tear your arses apart. You're going to work here like you never dreamed, ever in your life. For a beginning, you're going to run around camp now, and I'm going to show you where things are. Now put your kit bags on your backs and follow me.'

It's one thing to run, but it's another when you have a forty-pound bag on your back. We were supposed to follow him in a line, but we fell all over ourselves. I was thinking to myself that I was a good runner, but what was he doing to us? He took us all over camp, to the dining room, to the synagogue, to the place where they stored the weapons, running every inch of the way. Then we learned that for the first three months we could never walk anywhere. We had to run in the camp whether we wanted to or not. If we were caught walking, they'd wake us up in the middle of the night and take us for a long run.

We had long runs blocked out for us every day. At first we ran without guns, then with them, then with helmets. They kept building it up. If you fell back, they pushed you. Some of the recruits would faint, and we'd have to carry them, like the wounded. I gradually became better at it as we went on to the courses where we had to crawl through obstacles, jump from high places, climb ropes, go through barrels, and go under barbed wire—all in three minutes. If you couldn't make it in three minutes you had to do it again, and again, and again. But as the training got tougher, your body got tougher. I still hated it, even though I began to get more used to it. The long marches were the worst, even worse than the running.

Then the big day came. We were going to make our first jump from a plane. We were all waiting for that moment, really, because we didn't know exactly what was going to happen. We had had practice jumps from a parachute tower and jumps from dummy planes. But this was going to be it.

We had a big breakfast and then went to the airfield. It was hot, and I was feeling awful. We buckled on our parachutes. The plane taxied towards us. I had a funny feeling in the pit of my stomach. We climbed into the plane and sat parallel to each other, after they clamped us on to an overhead wire. We were yelling hey yo, hey yo, hey yo, hey yo to drown out the noise of the plane and keep up our spirits. The plane took off and headed towards the fields. It took only a few moments to get there, and the green signal light went on. That meant to get ready. The commander yelled: 'E call. Get ready.' On the command we stood up, as the red signal went on.

On that first jump I didn't really feel anything. The door opened, and the wind burst into the plane. The engines roared louder. I saw the first guy standing in the door, then all of a sudden he was gone. It all went so fast. I found myself in front of the door. And bang, I was out. Automatically my eyes closed. There is about 50 metres of free fall before the chute bursts open. You have to count in your head, 21, 22, 23. The chute should open. If it doesn't you're in trouble, and you have to pull the reserve chute.

Suddenly I felt the pull, and I yelled out: 'Yeah, I did it! I did it! It's easy!' I was telling myself, 'It's not scary, it's nothing.' You fall pretty fast, even when the chute is open. You see the land coming closer, closer, closer, and you have to get ready for it.

I fell beautifully, I did the right turn, I didn't get hurt, perfect. I couldn't do a better jump. But that was the only time I fell correctly.

The next jump was one I'll never forget. I was never so scared in my life. My stomach was banging in me. A fear was building up. The feeling of stepping out of a flying plane. 'What am I doing here?' I kept thinking. I started cursing myself. What the hell did I go into the paratroopers for? And then I got really scared.

My knees started trembling. I could hardly get up. I had to

pull myself up on the wire. But there was no choice. There were people behind me, people in front of me. And I jumped. When the chute opened on this second jump, I saw the ground getting closer and closer. I panicked. I really smeared myself. I didn't make the right turn, I landed with a terrible crash, and I got hurt.

We had to make seven jumps before we got our red berets. Another jump was called for very early in the morning. We were to leave camp about 4 a.m., fly out over the Negev desert, and jump there. The night before, I had a dream in which I jumped out of the plane and the parachute didn't open. In the dream, I was killed when I hit the ground. That really scared me until I thought, well, anybody in the paratroops could have a dream like that.

I was still disturbed by the dream as I jumped into the truck to go to the airport in the morning. Suddenly, out of the back of the truck, I saw a white dog run out on the road behind us. The truck behind us hit the dog and killed it instantly. It was almost like an omen, and it put me in a deep depression. I thought of Tzuki, my first dog, who had been killed that way. I thought of Joker at home, and I thought of my dream again. Then I said to myself: Something is going to happen to me on the jump. But I couldn't say anything about it to anybody. For some reason, I wasn't even afraid. I just knew that something was going to happen to me.

We boarded the plane. It took off. We flew out over the Negev to the jumping area. I got up in line and proceeded to the open door. I pushed myself out. But I guess something made me hesitate in the doorway for a second before I jumped. I didn't jump strongly enough. As I left the door of the plane, the wind hit me back against the side of the plane and made me spin. The cable released the chute as I was still spinning, and the cords spun with me. I counted 21-22-23-24-25-26-27, and so on up past 30, which is about eleven seconds. The chute didn't open. I was in what is called a candle fall, because that's just what it looks like. It usually means death if you don't open the small parachute. In those eleven seconds I had to do many things.

I had to release the sack that held the weapons, because if you don't, you break your legs. Then I had to press open the reserve chute. I released only one side. The other side wouldn't release. And I was falling. I saw the ground coming up, and I knew this was it. I felt I was still in the air, but suddenly everything went pitch black. And I thought: This is death. This is what death is. But I could feel myself. I knew I was alive, but I felt I was still spinning.

What I didn't realize was that, as soon as I pulled the reserve chute, the big chute opened up. The little chute had blown up over my face, and my eyes were completely blacked out by it. I grabbed the harness and tried to see the ground, which is very important to avoid getting hurt. But I couldn't see a thing. I knew I must be near the ground and was trying to brace myself for hitting it when suddenly, without warning, I did hit it. I saw stars. It hurt me terribly. I prayed to God that nothing like this would ever happen again. It was a terrible experience.

Well, we all got our red berets, but it was no piece of cake. As soon as they gave us our wings, we had to put them back into our kit bags and start off on a 110-kilometre march into the Negev. We were reminded that our training was mostly on the ground and not in the air.

Meanwhile, not much had been happening in the psychic or ESP part of my life. I kept it to myself anyway, as I usually did unless someone I liked was really interested. We were starting out on a programme to get our corporal stripes, which involved a lot of military manœuvres. My assignment was to be a heavy machine gunner, using the large Browning machine gun, which is very, very heavy, something like 80 pounds. There are three parts involved, body, legs, and ammunition. I was number one on the team, and it was my job to carry the heavy, main part of the gun. Number two carried the legs, and number three carried the ammunition. I had never jumped with the big Browning machine gun before. I had heard stories that this was the toughest thing in the world to do, because of its weight. Most of the weight was inside the main part of the Browning—the barrel, another heavy tube, and the mechanism that fed the ammunition through.

The plan for the new operation was to go by truck with our kit bags to a base camp, make a jump with our heavy Browning equipment, and march back about 10 kilometres to the camp, carrying it by hand all the way.

I came up with an idea that was pretty stupid, now that I look back on it. Since we weren't actually going to use the gun on the first day, I made the brilliant decision to take out the very heavy parts of the Browning barrel and stow them in my kit bag at the base camp, where they'd be ready for use the following day when we really needed them. After that bad jump, I was really worried about jumping with all the weight, and I figured this would give me some practice as a warm-up. I was a damned fool for doing this, because I could be hung up in the stockade for a long time if I was caught.

I closed the heavy parts up in my bag and left them in my tent. We went out to the plane. The shell of the Browning machine gun was strapped to me. Even that was heavy enough. The jump went well enough. The gun was tied with a cable about 5 metres long so I wouldn't hit myself with it when I hit the ground.

I landed successfully and immediately got myself organized, packing up the chute, picking up the machine gun, and getting together with the others to begin the 10-kilometre march back to the camp. I slung the Browning, zipped up in its canvas bag, on my back. Usually you have someone else carry it for you, it's so heavy. But I knew if I did that I'd give away my secret.

A friend insisted on helping me, because everybody was

saying, Look at Geller, he's carrying that damn thing alone. I let my friend carry it up the first hill, a long haul. He told me that this was unusual, he never before could carry the gun more than a few hundred metres alone without rest. Now, he said, it was a lot easier. He felt he was getting stronger. I would have thought that was funny, but right then I saw a jeep pull up to where we were resting. There was a general in it, and I knew immediately what was going to happen. I grabbed my forehead and said to myself, 'My God, they're going to put us through a manœuvre!' This happened every once in a while, when high staff officers arrived for a surprise exercise during a routine practice. We would then go through an exercise just as if the enemy were really attacking, using our guns with live ammunition.

They told us to spread out. We were ordered to set up the guns, ready to fire. There I was with an empty Browning gun, with no barrel inside it and no firing pin. I didn't know what to do. I didn't want to take the canvas off, but I did. I could look through the open tube of the gun, and I could see daylight through it. The number two man came up with the ammunition belt, and I fed it into the empty outside casing and cocked the gun, knowing that nothing would happen. I wanted to bury myself in the ground. I knew that the penalty for this would be many months in a prison camp. I knew it would ruin my army career.

The general's jeep came up behind us. We were high on a cliff, standing by for the order to fire at the imaginary enemy. I opened the lid of the Browning and looked again. There was the bullet, just hanging in the belt and flopping there with nothing to fire it. I heard the sergeant-major yell: 'Group A, open fire!' They started firing as we stood by. I was trembling and just about in shock, with the generals standing behind us, all their insignia shining in the sun.

I figured that maybe if I took my small gun, called an Oozie, and put it next to the big one, it would make some kind of noise, even though it made a sharp, high bang compared to the Browning. Then the order came for us to fire, and I pulled both triggers.

What happened next is something I can hardly believe to this day, even with the many things that have happened to me since. I know anyone will have trouble believing it. All I can say is that it happened; there is no question in my mind that it did. It is not a fantasy, not a daydream, not anything that I made up in my imagination. I would have no reason to make this up, because what I'm about to tell strains my credibility with anyone reading about it. But it is a clear, hard fact.

When I pulled the triggers *both* guns started firing. The Browning was firing, firing, firing. The bullets were flying out. I couldn't believe it. How could it be? I had looked inside twice just moments before, and the inside of the gun had been vacant. I was shooting steadily, and the ammunition box was emptying fast. There wasn't a bullet left in it. I thought about God immediately. I said, thank you, God, for doing this for me. One of the officers behind me tapped me on the helmet and said: 'Good shooting, soldier.'

There were no more bullets left when the firing was over. There was a whole pile of empty cartridges from the Browning lying around. The gun was dripping black oil from the shooting. I put my hand on the Browning, and I kissed it. I couldn't understand how it had happened. I didn't even want to understand. It was a mystery like the machine gun incident with my father years before. I put the gun back in the canvas and zipped it up, and we marched back to the tent area.

When we got there, I rushed to my kit bag and opened it up. The barrel was still there, and so were the other parts. I ran back to the Browning and looked at it again. It was still empty. And now the most shocking part hit me. I drew out the barrel from the kit bag and looked through it. It had been clean as a whistle when we started out on the manœuvre. Now it was dirty, covered with grime, exactly the way it would have been after firing. I mean, I had to clean it. That barrel had been fired. There was no question about it—yet I had left it in the kit bag and definitely had not opened it until after our return to camp.

This experience anticipated others that came along when I was older. I didn't understand it then, and I don't understand it now. But that is true of many things that have happened since.

As I was cleaning the gun, I was still in shock. I couldn't talk to anyone. I was thinking back to Cyprus, to my teacher and the telepathy we had done together, the bending of metal objects, and the starting up of watches that were broken. I was just thinking to myself: Was it all just one thing going on here? Or was it a new phenomenon every time? Because I knew it was a phenomenon. I didn't blame it on anybody. I knew nobody was tricking me.

I couldn't tell anyone. I had to keep it in my own head, because who would believe me? I had to accept it as a miracle, and it scared the hell out of me.

CHAPTER SIX

EVENTS PILED UP one after another. I became a corporal after eleven months of brutal training. I went home on a few leaves, saw my mother, played a lot with Joker, and went out on dates to a few discotheques. I was one of the five in our group chosen for officers' training school, and my father was very proud of me.

This was a new life. It was tougher than ever, because not only did the manœuvres continue, but we had to cram a terrific amount of knowledge into our heads in a short time. During one field exercise in a blinding rain, I was setting up my tent when I saw a jeep parked nearby with an officer inside.

I had to look twice before I realized it was Joav. I knocked on the canvas door, opened it, and yelled his name.

He was startled. He yelled: 'Uri! Get in!' I jumped in, and we embraced. It had been so long since I had seen him. I told him, 'My God, Joav! I didn't know you were an officer in the paratroopers.' He was happy to hear I was in officers' training and told me to be sure to call him when I finished the course. He asked if I still did the telepathy and said that it could be put to good use some time. I was happy to see him and looked forward to seeing him again.

Shortly after that, two tragedies struck. I went home on leave and found Joker so sick he could hardly move. He was over ten years old now, and I knew it was natural, but that didn't make me feel any better. He lay on the floor and could do no more than wave his tail. I knew he was dying. It broke my heart. I took him to a vet, who told me what I expected: Joker would have to be put away. I kissed him and held him, then left him there.

I can't express how terrible I felt. I was crying inside. I couldn't cry tears; I was a paratrooper, and I didn't want the vet to see me. I wanted to get away, but I seemed unable to leave. When I got to the street level, I stopped in the doorway and waited. I must have stood there about twenty minutes, then I heard the shot. I burst out crying, openly. I couldn't stop it, and I couldn't leave the doorway. What would it look like to see a paratrooper going down the street crying? I finally went back to my mother's apartment, and she cried too.

When I got back to officers' training camp from leave, the second blow struck. I picked up the newspaper to read about a border raid by an Israeli task force in Jordan. Only one Israeli officer was shot. It was Joav, a bullet through his head. That, combined with the loss of Joker, made my world crumble. I seemed to lose all incentive to do anything. I just went through the motions at officers' school.

One night on a manœuvre I was in charge of five men in

the field. In the exercise, a red flare would be fired, and we were to shoot our weapons, then run back to where the rest of the platoon was stationed. It was a long wait. We all fell asleep waiting. A kick in the back woke me up. An officer was standing there telling me to wake up. I knew right away that I would be thrown out, and the next day I was.

For some reason, I felt great relief. It was a different day, a different morning. A huge responsibility was lifted from my shoulders, and I actually felt good about it. I knew I would be going back to the regular paratrooper unit as a corporal again, but I didn't mind. The big strain was over.

I went back to Tel Aviv briefly to help my mother move into a new apartment, small but nicer than the older one we were in. My mother had taken a job as a waitress in a little coffee shop, and I hated to see that. I wished I could make more money so my mother could stop working, but there was nothing I could do until I got out.

Back at the paratrooper camp I re-entered as a driver of a new type of armoured vehicle they were experimenting with. At other times I drove a command car. I wasn't back in the routine too long before I went down with pneumonia, and the next thing I knew I was in the hospital with a high fever and feeling terrible. It was now 1967, and the situation in the Sinai desert and at the Suez Canal was getting bad. Even in the hospital, I could tell that everyone was getting ready for war, especially when they began taping all the windows and setting up emergency operating rooms.

I stayed in the hospital for nearly a month. Then the complications cleared up and I was sent to convalesce at an army station called Resort No. 3. The food was good there, and all you had to do was rest and recuperate. Movies, games, and a piano helped to make everything very pleasant. One day I was playing the piano—I had picked up quite a bit of music by ear—when one of the girl officers who helped run the place came over to listen. Her name was Yaffa, and she was

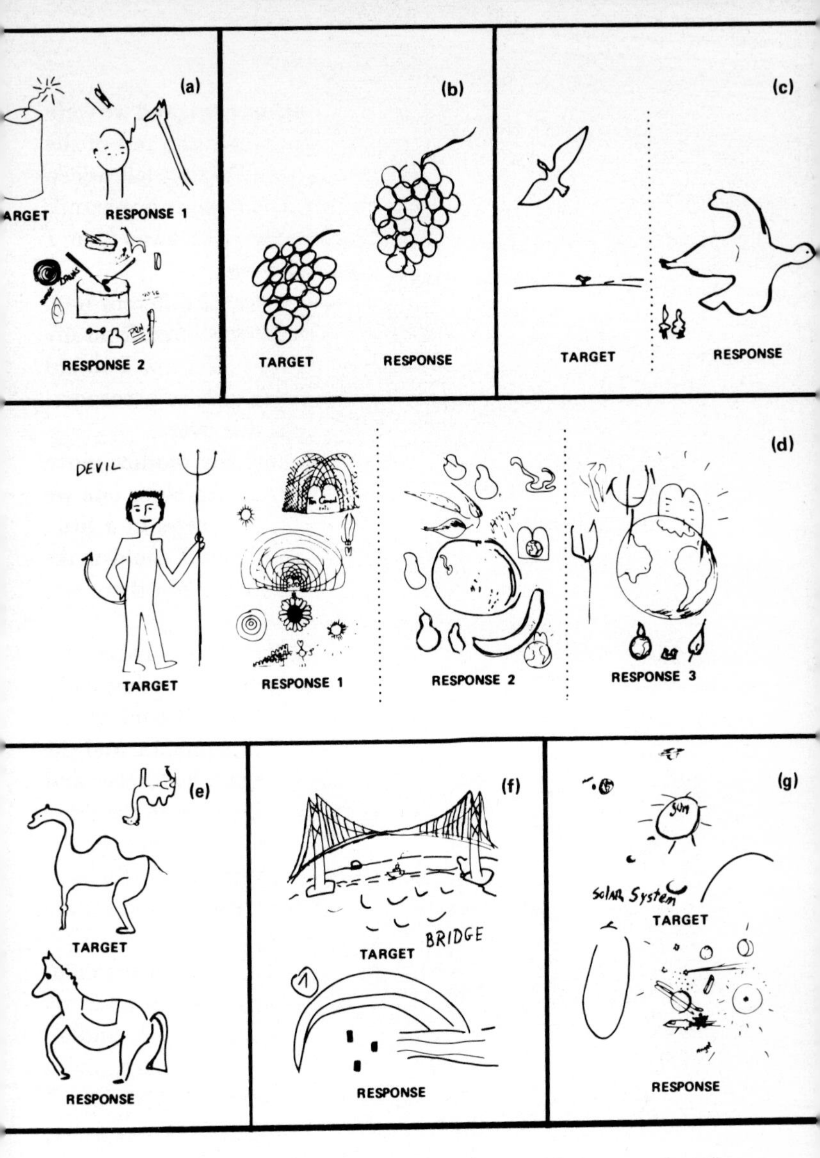

A sample of the results of the telepathy experiments conducted under controlled conditions at Stanford Research Institute, Palo Alto, California, and published in *Nature* magazine.

Iris Davidesco and I, in 1972.

On right, above: Trying to photograph myself through a sealed lens cap. (Photo: Michael Brennan) Underneath are the two frames that actually came out absolutely beautiful. I looked at her and she looked at me. I think it was one of those rare instances of love at first sight.

I was suddenly so in love with her I couldn't think of anything else. She was tall and had black hair, green eyes, and a beautiful body. She was quite intelligent. I went to her room and we slept together. I experienced a full feeling of love that I had never known before.

The next morning I felt I was in paradise. We saw each other every moment we could. I never had felt this way before, not with Helena, not with Patty, not with anyone else. I told Yaffa I loved her, that I couldn't stand the thought of having to leave her. She told me she loved me, too.

But she had something very serious to tell me. No matter what she was about to say, she still loved me. She said she was engaged to someone else and loved him too, but in a different way. I was so let down I didn't know what to say. I couldn't accept it. I told her that I was completely hers and couldn't understand how she could love anybody else at the same time. I thought back, though, to Patty and Helena, and remembered how I had once felt that way myself, loving two people at once. But that didn't make it any easier to take. She tried to explain that each love was different, that she loved me and the man she was going to marry in different ways.

I had only another week left at the rest station. One day we went up to Mount Carmel and looked out over Haifa. It was like being high. She was in my arms, and it was painful to think that something of her belonged to someone else. She confessed that she had a better time with me and was more physically attracted. But she had known the other one since she was thirteen. She didn't feel she could break the engagement. It was a terrible feeling, terrible. I was heartbroken.

She gave me a list of all the places she would be over the next months, and we swore to see each other whenever we could.

I went home for two days before reporting back to my unit.

I was miserable. I tried to forget her. Meanwhile, the international situation was getting tense, unbearably tense. News came that the Egyptians had closed the Suez entrance to the sea and had mined it. There was talk of war everywhere—in the streets, in the coffee shops, in the camps.

The morning I was to return to my camp, the sirens blowing all through Tel Aviv woke me. They were the sirens of war. The practice sirens would stop and go. These were steady. It was announced on the radio that the Israeli forces were proceeding deep into the Sinai desert. It was a full-scale war.

I rushed to get dressed, said good-bye to my mother, and drove my scooter as fast as it would go back to my unit. I was worried. What if my unit had already gone? My hand never left the horn of the scooter, and I went through every red light. I located my unit, with armoured vehicles standing by, packed and ready to move out on command. Since I had been away so long I wasn't allowed to handle a vehicle. Instead I was put in charge of eight men in a command car that followed the light armoured vehicles.

I assigned them guns and helmets, put on my camouflage suit, and we were ready. By now it was late afternoon, and we had no word on where we were to go.

I kept looking at the room where all the senior officers were. We were ready, but still nobody knew where we were going. Some said we were going up to the Golan Heights. Others said to the Jordanian side, or to the Sinai desert. Nobody really knew, not even the officers. All our ears were stuck to the transistor radios. We got news that many Arab villages had been taken in the Sinai and that our troops had reached the Suez Canal. The war was under way.

I was thinking a lot about Yaffa. Then very strange feelings started coming over me. I knew something was going to happen to me. I remembered the lion in the zoo, I remembered my mother's taxi accident, I remembered my dream before my second training jump in the paratroopers. I was frightened because I was convinced that all those premonitions had come true. Oddly, I knew I wasn't going to be killed. I would just be hurt or wounded. I put my hand to my forehead and prayed to God that I wouldn't be gravely wounded, that everything would be all right even if I were wounded.

Evening came, and there was still no word of where we were going. We slept awhile, very restless. Early in the morning, about three, the word came. We were going to Jerusalem. By the time the sun was up we were on the road. We stopped, waited, and started up again on the road as new instructions kept coming in. Many tanks passed us. Fighter planes were constantly flying overhead in the direction of the Sinai. Helicopters were whirring elsewhere.

I thought of Yaffa again, I thought of my mother, I thought of Cyprus, I thought of getting wounded. We moved slowly, with all the starting and stopping. Night was falling again. We kept asking the officers what the story was, and they kept saying they didn't know. There was no word from headquarters. We were to wait where we were.

At night we received orders to stand by for moving out in the morning. I told the eight men under my command to fuel up the armoured vehicles and to return the empty jerry cans to the command car, where they would be filled again from the big tanker that was following us. I grabbed a can and went up to one of the light armoured vehicles to fill it. I yelled to a soldier on top of it to open the hatch. He turned out to be Avram Stedler, a friend from my old platoon. He said: 'Hi, Uri. Fill her up.'

I looked Avram in the eye, and he looked at me, and I knew that he was going to die. It was a horrible feeling. I stopped pouring gasoline a moment and asked him what his job was. He told me he was manning the armoured car's cannon. I asked him how he felt. He said fine. I didn't know what to say. I wanted to figure out a way to save him. But I couldn't. I finally said: 'Avram, can I shake your hand?' He said: 'Why?'

I said: 'Just shake hands with me, please.'

We shook hands, and I turned and walked away. I didn't look back at him. I went back to the command car and sank into the seat. I said to myself, 'God, I know these things so suddenly. I know things that nobody else knows, and I don't know why. Is there any way I can save Avram?'

But I didn't know how. I couldn't sleep that night before we went into action. I thought a lot more about Yaffa, about how it would be if we were married, and about what she might be doing right now. Was she thinking of me? Dawn broke, and the rays of the sun lit the sky and the hills above. We took off down the highway that led to the Jordanian border. We could already hear far away the shooting and blasts of cannon and tanks. We knew a war was going on.

We were proceeding towards a place called Ramala, which was several miles from Jerusalem itself. We heard that one unit of Israeli paratroopers was already in the city. Our job was to close down the road from Ramala to Jerusalem so the Jordanians could not bring in supplies. Suddenly, without warning, shooting started coming from all over. We seemed to be boxed in by firing. My command car had no armour protection, so we had to drive behind and beside an armoured vehicle. The command came over my walkie-talkie to let the Sherman tanks hit the hills first. They started firing.

There were many of our planes, even fighter planes, in the skies, diving at the hills. I saw one of our own planes drop a napalm bomb on one of our vehicles by mistake. It was such a big mess, with all the shooting, bombs exploding, planes diving. We didn't know exactly where the enemy fire was coming from. We knew only that it was coming from the general direction of the hill in front of us. We soon learned that there were Jordanian tanks firing at the road, trying to block us from proceeding to Ramala. We were told to take cover behind rocks and wait. I ordered my unit out of the exposed command car and behind a graveyard wall that was near us. We had only light arms, which wouldn't do us any good right then.

As we ran to the graveyard, I stumbled over the bodies of Arabs. One of them was covered with a blanket. I thought, is this guy sleeping, or what? I pulled the blanket down, and it was the body of a Jordanian, all shot up. I covered the corpse up again and got my men behind the graveyard wall. The noise of the machine guns, the tanks, the planes, the screaming walkie-talkies was indescribable. We were spread out and pinned down behind the wall by the fire coming from the hill. We were partly exposed there. It didn't give much protection.

I was at the entrance to the graveyard checking out the men. I had no cover there. Suddenly I felt my hand spin away from me. I didn't realize what had happened. About twenty seconds later I felt wet and looked at my hand. My shirt was covered with blood. I was really scared, because I thought I was hit inside my body. I jumped over the wall and started screaming, 'Chovesh!'—the Israeli word for medic. There was none, but a soldier ran up and tore off my shirt. Blood was dripping from a hole in my left hand. The soldier took a bandage from his first aid kit and tied my hand up. I didn't feel any pain. There was just a lot of blood. It began to stop bleeding, so I just stayed in charge. The Jordanian tanks were zeroed in on us, because our vehicles were all around us shooting at the hill.

There was no safe place. We were in the hands of God. Our tanks were moving up the hill—we called it French Hill—and battering the Jordanian positions. But the enemy's Patton tanks were shooting at us and trying to push our forces off the hill. I saw one of the Jordanian tanks in an open field only about a quarter of a mile away, shooting at us. One of our armoured vehicles drove in front of us on the road in front of the graveyard, moving towards the Patton tank. I knew immediately that it was the one Avram was in.

I saw the whole scene. It was like a movie, not reality. The guns of both the Patton tank and Avram's armoured vehicle were silent for a moment. Our captain had his head out of the hatch and yelled 'Fire!' I couldn't see Avram, but I knew he was manning the cannon, and he fired. I saw the shell blast about 4 metres short of the Arab tank. Nothing happened. I saw the captain look down the hatch and yell 'Fire!' again. But it was too late. The Jordanian tank fired. I heard a loud bang and saw Avram's vehicle tilt and shudder. There was no smoke, no fire, just a strange rattle. I saw the captain slip back down the hatch as if he were hit. Then I heard a rumble like an explosion deep down inside the vehicle.

Everything became quiet. I knew they were all killed. I knew Avram was inside there and that he was dead. I was stunned and silent. All kinds of thoughts flashed through my head. The Patton tank of the Jordanians was moving closer to us. I yelled to one of the soldiers near me: 'Let's get over there. Let's see if anyone's alive!' We leaped over the graveyard wall and started running to Avram's vehicle. The Patton tank was getting closer to us, but we ignored it. We got to the vehicle, and I touched it. It was red hot. I had to pull my hand away.

Suddenly I saw someone coming out from the other side. It wasn't Avram, but the driver. His leg was nothing but meat, and he seemed half dead. We started to haul him away. The Patton tank was now very near. But then we heard another loud bang, and the Jordanian tank exploded. The shock wave knocked us off our feet. When the smoke cleared, it sat there silent, burned to death. Nobody came out of it.

We got up and dragged our wounded driver to the road, then carried him farther away. He was conscious but very pale. He just kept saying, 'I'm hit. I'm hit.' He asked me: 'Where am I hit?' I looked, and it seemed as if one of his legs was practically blown off. Then he said: 'My God is my thing all right? Is it still there?'

I opened his trousers and looked. Everything was blown off. I just took a deep breath, I remember, and got my strength together. We got him to a little Arab house, where we found stretchers, and put him on one. He said: 'Are there helicopters coming?' I grabbed a walkie-talkie nearby, but it had bullet holes in it and wasn't working. I pretended to call into it anyway. I said to the dead microphone: 'Hey, can you hear me? You're on the way? Good. We're waiting for you.' And I turned to the wounded guy and said: 'The helicopters are on the way. Hold on!'

I saw his face relax a little. I was certain they would really send a helicopter soon if he held on. Then some big blasts hit right close to us. There was a big Jordanian truck filled with jerry cans of gasoline not too far away. Three Arabs behind it and others behind some rocks were shooting at us. My men started shooting back. Next to them was an Israeli soldier with a bazooka, but he seemed to be in shock and wasn't shooting it. I hadn't been trained to handle it, and I yelled for someone who knew how to fire it. Two Israelis came running up. They grabbed the bazooka from the guy who was in shock. I told them to keep cool and aim at the truck. There was so much shooting around us that nobody could keep cool.

But they fired on command. I saw the missile head straight for the truck, I saw it hit the Arab truck, I saw the truck burst into flames. Farther up on the hill, I could see a pillbox firing at us and pinning us down. I decided to take several of my men and attack it. We started sneaking up the hill to one side of the pillbox. Two of my men were behind me.

Suddenly an Arab jumped out from behind a nearby rock. He shot at me twice and missed. I don't know why he didn't hit me—it is another mystery in my life. He was about 30 metres away. I looked at him and pulled up my gun waist high. I just shot from the waist. As I was shooting, I looked him in the eye. I saw his face. He had a moustache. As I fired, I was thinking of Avram's vehicle when it was hit, and the driver who was dying, and all the wounded lying around. I didn't have time to think much. I guess I didn't have any feelings.

I knew there was a war going on and it had to be fought. I knew that if I didn't get him, he would get me. The man fell.

The guys behind me were also shooting. Somehow the whole scene looked like a big motion picture studio again. It looked like a story or a dream that any minute I was going to wake up from. It was all unreal. But my left hand reminded me that it was no dream, because it started to hurt. The smoke and the bullets hitting all around were real enough, too. But one side of me thought, what if it's a dream?

It was at least a nightmare. We started back towards the command car. There were explosions and bullets hitting all around us. I don't know where it came from—a shell from a tank, a grenade, or what—but I felt a blast, something hit my right arm, and something else hit the left side of my forehead above the eye. Everything went completely black, and I lost consciousness. In that fraction of a second before blacking out, I thought: I am dying. I was more convinced this time than during the parachute jump. I said to myself: So this is death. There was no terror, no panic. I was surprised that death was so easy.

When I came to, I was in a bed. Everything was clean. Both my arms were bandaged, and there was a bandage around my head. I looked at my body and saw that I wasn't hit anywhere else. I was in a hospital. I didn't think of anything but Yaffa then. I thought to myself: Does she know what's happened to me? Then my thoughts wandered to my father and mother. I looked around and saw many other wounded soldiers there.

I was able to phone my mother and let her know I couldn't come home, but I didn't tell her I was in the hospital. I knew my father would be in the fighting, maybe in the Sinai. I didn't know where. I got Yaffa on the phone and didn't tell her where I was, either. She said she had to see me and wanted to know where I was. I wanted to see her so much that I had to give in and tell her.

I stayed in the hospital about three weeks. I was lucky. The wounds were not serious. The bullet or shrapnel had just creased my forehead above my eye. The wounds on my arms and hands were bad, but not bad enough to make me lose the use of them. Two days before I was to be released, Yaffa came to see me. It was lovely being together with her again, but very brief. She had to go back to her camp at Haifa, and I had to go through a big medical check-up.

Of course, I could think of nothing else but getting back to Haifa to be with her. But then I said to myself: This thing with Yaffa can't go on. She couldn't love two people for ever, and she had said she had to stick by her decision to be married. I resolved to be strong, to manage without seeing her, to try to forget her.

I talked to her on the phone, and she repeated that she was going to get married but still loved me. She said she was being torn apart. I was too, but then I was torn in other ways—seeing my friends die, the whole awful scene of the battle. Every time Yaffa came into my mind I was depressed. I would say to myself: 'Look at those other guys. They didn't even make it. They're dead. They're in the ground now. There's no love, nothing. They're in another world. They're in the ground now.' I was lucky. I was alive.

I had three full months to recuperate. I had nothing to do, so I started looking for work. A girl I knew in Tel Aviv, just a friend, told me she was going to be an instructor in a resort camp for children and wanted to know if I wanted to work with her there. I told her I'd be happy to. I would get paid, and the camp was near Tel Aviv. My left hand and arm were in a cast, but my right arm had healed. Only the scars remained. There was still pain in my left hand, and when they took off the cast I would have to go through therapy with it. The doctor said it would be a long time before I could stretch it out, and maybe I would never be able to stretch it out fully. But after seeing what had happened to my friends—some of them with no legs, no hands, no eyes—I knew how lucky I was.

Looking back on it, going to that children's camp was the biggest turning point in my life. It was there that my whole career of demonstrating the strange energy forces really began. The camp, called Alumin, was about an hour's drive out of Tel Aviv. It had palm trees, a swimming pool, grass everywhere, and accommodation for about 200 children at a time. A new group would come in every three weeks. I was a counsellor, not instructing in anything particular but keeping the kids busy and happy.

In one of these groups was a kid named Shimshon Shtrang, about twelve or thirteen years old. His nickname was Shipi. We used to sit on the grass with about ten kids for storytelling periods, and I used to tell them about the caves in Cyprus and some of the imaginary stories I had told to the kids in Mrs Agrotis's class back there.

Shipi was always pressing me for more stories, and I finally got around to telling him about some of the strange things that had happened to me off and on, over the years.

I decided to try some of the telepathy I had done with Mrs Agrotis, and I noticed that the experiments I tried with Shipi were absolutely incredible. They worked both ways. I would write numbers down so that he couldn't possibly see them, and he would get them exactly right time after time. Or the other way around. It was so consistent that I was shocked. Sometimes he would go upstairs in a building and draw pictures and seal them in envelopes, while I would be out on the grass drawing the exact same things he had drawn. I tried it with other kids, but it didn't work nearly as well.

Then I decided to try bending things. This worked with nearly everybody, but with Shipi it far exceeded anything that happened with others. He brought some keys from home, and within half a minute they would bend up to 90 degrees. With others the bend was there, but it usually ranged from 10 to 45 degrees. I kept asking myself, why does it work so well with him?

As the days passed, we performed these experiments for longer periods of time whenever I wasn't taking care of the kids. We'd sit together and bend nails with just the lightest touch, move the hands of watches, and so on. He told me about his background. His father was German, his mother was Russian. He had two sisters—Hannah, who was nineteen, and Shoshanna, who was about twenty—who were due to visit the camp soon. I looked forward to meeting them and wondered if the forces would work as well with them as they had with Shipi.

As it turned out, I liked Hannah very much. She is not what I would call a beautiful girl, but her face is good-looking in an unusual way. Her green eyes reminded me of Yaffa. I told her about the things that had happened with Shipi. I tried some experiments with her, but they didn't work very well. Then Shipi and I demonstrated some phenomena for her. She found them fascinating and unbelievable.

When Shipi left the camp, I took his address and promised to look him up. In the meantime, I got word that I couldn't return to the paratroops because of my wounds. Actually, I was pleased about that. I had about eight more months to finish out my service, and I wanted to spend it in the regular army, in as much peace as possible. The war was over now, and I was glad. Before long I was back in the army with the job of tracking down deserters. I got sergeant stripes soon after that.

My job consisted of going out into the small villages on a motor-cycle, which was fun, and locating those who were avoiding the service. When I did, I got them to sign a paper saying that they would present themselves the next day to an army base. I went all over the countryside, up to Jerusalem, all through the rocky hills, the irrigated fields, the Arab villages that had been occupied. It gave me time to reflect. I thought about the war, the friends who had been killed, how peaceful life can be, and how deadly things can become in contrast. I couldn't understand how our human minds can destroy so. I remembered the useless killings, and I was very sad. I wished it had never happened. The pictures of the really badly wounded men came back to me, soldiers turned into monsters, blinded, with no sex organs, no hands, the guys in wheelchairs for the rest of their lives. Can you imagine it? Suddenly you cannot make love. Maybe when a guy dies young, God needs him up there. For some reason, maybe God needs him the way he is, and takes him that way.

I was able to see my father much more often now. He was living in an apartment in Giva Taim, which is near Tel Aviv. He had found a girl he liked very much, and she was living with him. She was quite a bit younger, but he was still handsome and didn't look his age. I used to bring my dates up to his apartment, and we kept in close touch.

One day I was driving back from my father's and was amazed to see Shipi on the street. I had never kept my promise to look him up. We were excited to see each other again, and I discovered he lived close to my father. I visited Shipi and his family the next day. His parents turned out to be really kind and intelligent people. It was good to see Hannah again. Their father told me that all Shipi could talk about when he got back from camp was those strange powers that worked so well between the two of us. We all enjoyed each other so much that I almost became part of the family. I got to know Hannah better and started dating her. It was an unusual relationship. I loved Hannah in a different way. She was fragile and a good girl, and we were very close.

We got along wonderfully, all of us, and had lots of good times together. Shipi was getting ready for his bar mitzvah, and I was invited to it, of course. During that period he told me he had been telling his teachers at school all about the things that had gone on with the telepathy and the other experiments, and none of them believed him. However, the school administration had told him there was a little fund to pay outside speakers at some of their Sunday meetings. Shipi said that, if I could come over and demonstrate some of these things, they could pay £36. He was sure the teachers and the pupils would enjoy it.

I thought that would be a great idea. I was still in the army and could use the extra money. So I went to the school. I entered a hall full of children, with the teachers sitting up front. When I stepped on the stage, it was the first time in my life I had ever been in front of an audience. I must be a natural-born ham, because I found myself enjoying it. What they were about to see that afternoon, I announced, I had no explanation for at all. They would just have to judge for themselves.

I was just playing the demonstration by ear. I started with telepathy, using the blackboard, turning my back to it without peeking and guessing what different children had drawn on it. Shipi had already asked the teachers to prepare drawings sealed in envelopes and to bring in any broken watches to see if I could make them start up again.

Everything seemed to work fine. The show went on for more than two hours. Nobody wanted to go home. They kept clapping their hands, never stopping. It was wonderful. They wanted to see more and more.

I observed all kinds of reactions. Some just plain didn't believe what they saw at all. Others wanted to see more and more, as if just one more experiment would help them figure out what was going on. I thought to myself: All these things are happening; there aren't any explanations. Anyway, the audience loved it.

The teachers asked intelligent questions. They wanted to know when I first found out about this. Whenever that was asked, I remembered that light in the Arabic garden when I was very young. But I never said a word about that. It was too strange. I did tell about some of my early experiences at school, what happened in Cyprus in the classroom, and that kind of thing. It was a successful demonstration. I was fascinated with the reaction of the audience and gratified by the interest of both teachers and children.

Though I didn't realize it at the time, I had set the stage for a big part of my future life. I had no idea of the complicated directions it was to take, the controversy it was going to create, or that it was going to make my name known to the public throughout the world.

3. The Search for Meaning

CHAPTER ONE

I HAD ENJOYED performing in public. I was surprised at how well the demonstrations worked in front of so many people. The experiments had worked nearly three out of four times. Having an audience even seemed to help. But I had no ideas about going back on stage with more demonstrations. I had other things on my mind. My military service would soon be over, and I had to decide how to make a living.

With Joav no longer alive, I lost my desire to join the Secret Service. I made a stab at applying, but my heart wasn't in it. Then as now, I always wanted to meet people, see people, talk to people. Work in the Secret Service would have to be hidden, and I'd have to keep everything to myself. I wanted something exciting that would involve meeting people.

When I got out of the army late in 1968, I ran into a friend from my unit whose father owned a textile factory. They were looking for someone who could speak English, and who would learn the business so that eventually he could set up meetings with customers in Canada and America and describe the company's products in English.

There would be a long training period first, handling export orders and that kind of thing. It seemed to be just the right job at the time, so I took it. The work was near Shipi's family, and I would often have lunch with all of them. Hannah and I were close friends, and Shipi and I practically became brothers.

Shipi was so happy about the first demonstration that he arranged more appearances in other schools and for private parties. Young as he was, Shipi was a great manager. We were able to make only about seven dollars an appearance, but the performances were fun to do. I still wasn't taking it seriously; I was surprised that the phenomena worked most of the time.

Yaffa had married. But we were still in love with each other. We would meet several times a month in out-of-the-way places. I knew it was hopeless, and so did she. But we could not stand the thought of not seeing each other. I dated other girls, of course, but I wasn't able to feel about any of them as I did about Yaffa.

One day I was waiting for a friend in a coffee shop when I noticed a beautiful girl sitting at the next table. She looked about nineteen or twenty, with blue eyes, brown hair, and a little nose. Her complexion was white and creamy, and she looked so tender and lovely. We kept looking at each other and finally started talking. I couldn't help telling her how beautiful she was. Before I knew it, I had asked her for a date that night. Her name was Iris Davidesco.

Iris was someone I could express all my feelings to. We sat in a coffee shop for hours on that first date, talking about everything under the sun. As we got to know each other, we would play games, guessing what other people did, whether they were millionaires from Texas, school teachers, vegetarians, or whatever. We even stopped people to check, and many times we turned out to be right.

I started seeing Iris a lot. Then I found out that she was only fifteen years old. I was surprised; she looked and acted like someone twenty-three or so, which was my age at the time. I was really embarrassed and incredulous. And I had been on the verge of falling in love with her. The time we spent together meant so much to me that we kept on seeing each other as usual. Hannah knew about Iris, and I could see that she was a little hurt. But Hannah and I were close in a different way, more like brother and sister.

Iris had won a couple of beauty contests and was modelling

for an advertising agency. One day she asked if I would model with her in one of her ads. I would be able to make some extra money to add to the £500 a month in starting pay I was earning at the export company, which really wasn't very much.

I posed with Iris for a beer advertisement and got a big kick out of it when it came out. There's no doubt about it, I have a very healthy ego. This fed it, even though it was only an ad for something I never drank.

Word was getting around about the demonstrations. Shipi was working overtime. The number of appearances increased week by week, and now we were taking in quite a bit of extra money. Together with the money from my job and from other modelling work that came my way, it added up to quite a bit. Finally I sat down, figured things out, and realized that my mother could stop working. I told my mother I had always hoped this day would come. She had kept me alive through all the years of struggle, kept me well, and kept me fed. It was wonderful that I could take care of her. That was a happy day.

Meanwhile, just about every newspaper in Israel was writing up our demonstrations. Suddenly many different managers and promoters were calling and asking me to sign with them. Shipi, who had really started me off, was in school and much too young to work on a full-time basis. I tried one manager without signing, but that didn't work out. I was very inexperienced.

I finally signed with a big professional manager, not knowing exactly what this business was all about. The next thing I knew, I was being booked into big theatres all over Israel and playing to large audiences. I bought a secondhand Triumph sports car and felt very prosperous in spite of the fact that a huge percentage of my money went to the manager and to income tax, and very little stayed with me.

The demonstrations hardly changed at all since that first one at Shipi's school. I had no set plan but improvised as I went along. I would do telepathy while members of the audience wrote or drew things on a blackboard; pass thoughts directly into people's minds; describe what people were wearing without looking at them; start up watches that hadn't run for some time; bend keys and other objects they brought in; and then have a question-and-answer period. All the experiments would work about 75 or 80 per cent of the time. It was a simple, informal routine, but the audiences enjoyed it.

One day the manager came and told me I was doing great, but there ought to be more to the act. It should last longer, so people would feel they were getting more for their money. He said I should add tricks to fatten up the act. I told him that was ridiculous, because everything I did was real, and people accepted it. But he had thought of a way I could make it even bigger. He would watch people get out of their cars and write down their licence plate numbers. Then he would have them ushered to selected seats as they came into the theatre. He'd give me the numbers before I started the demonstrations, and I would point to these people and tell them their licence plate numbers. Unless I did this, he said, the demonstrations would start failing. I'd be unable to make a living any more.

By then I had quit my job with the textile firm and stopped modelling, because I was doing shows almost every day. It was very hard and tiring work. After the demonstrations in the big theatres, practically everyone in Israel knew about me. I was invited to a party to meet Abba Eban. Golda Meir addressed the country at the New Year about all its problems and its future. An interviewer asked her what she predicted for the coming year, and she said on the air: 'I don't predict. Why don't you ask Uri Geller?' I didn't predict either, but it was an indication of how well known I had become in so short a time.

When the manager urged me to add the magician's trick to the regular demonstration, I didn't know what to do. He was very persuasive, and I was young and inexperienced. He insisted that everything was going to fail unless I added the trick material. I figured, well, it won't last much longer anyway. We'll soon cover all of Israel, and that will be it. Maybe I'll be able to save enough money to open up a coffee shop or something like that. I really didn't have any conception about the gift that had been given to me. I didn't know that this power, this force, this unknown energy was going to be taken so seriously by the scientific world. I never even associated it in my mind with science.

It was a far cry from the simple way Shipi and I had started out, but I finally gave in to the manager's pressure. I felt I was wrong the minute I agreed. I didn't realize, though, how big a mistake I was making, one of the most crucial mistakes of my life. After all, the more I became known all over the country, the more the controversy would grow as to whether what I did was real or phoney. I added the trick to the legitimate demonstrations and I hated myself every time I did it.

I had become a good friend of Amnon Rubinstein, who was dean of the law school at Hebrew University and a very learned man, well known in Israel. I had met him at a party in Tel Aviv. I had shown him how the energy forces seemed to work. He believed in me and was taking my side in the controversy, which was getting more intense as I became better known. The papers were saying that I must be using a laser, or chemicals, mirrors, accomplices—things like that.

Shortly after giving in to the manager's pressure, I went to see Dr Rubinstein. I told him to forget about me. I said that I had been using a trick in the demonstrations, and that I was no damn good. It hurt to have to tell him this, because I liked and respected him. He took hold of my shoulders and shook me. He said: 'What do you mean, Uri?' I get goose pimples when I think about this even now. He said: 'You've done things that neither you nor I can explain. You don't need to add any tricks to it!' Then he added: 'I don't believe what you're telling me now.'

I told him how the manager was forcing me to do the licence plate thing. Dr Rubinstein said: 'All right, that's a trick. But how did you do the things with me? The bending of my key with just a touch? The drawings I did, and kept out of your sight completely? The drawings and the numbers that you fired into my head? How did you do those things?'

'I just don't know.'

'Of course you don't know. It's some unknown force. That's just it. You must stop thinking that, just because your manager forced you into this, it's the end of the world. You've got to stop it right away, of course. And you must never do it again, ever.'

Then he really shouted at me. He told me that I had to give myself over to scientists to show that these forces do exist. He believed in me, and that helped. He knew that, aside from the things I was talked into doing, the rest was real. I put a stop to the trick after that and decided to stand or fall on what was really happening, even if the demonstration didn't run long enough to suit the manager. I also started thinking about working with scientists, although that idea scared me.

Dr Rubinstein was one of the few people I could talk to openly. Yaffa, Iris, and Shipi were others, because as my closest friends I felt I could share everything with them. We all decided I should look for a lawyer to see what could be done about terminating the contract.

After the talk with Dr Rubinstein I started thinking seriously about the powers for the first time in my life. What was really behind them, and why did they have the effects they did? I asked myself: Why did it seem no one else had them?

I was in the army reserves after my service. When I became well known in Israel, I was assigned to a unit that entertained troops all across the country. It was a lot different from being in the army. I got to know many high-ranking officers and generals. Demonstrating to the soldiers at their stations was enjoyable. Doors were opening to me all over.

I hadn't lost my taste for exploring and adventure. Shipi

drove with me one time to Eilat, where I was scheduled for an appearance before an armed forces unit. When the navy people learned I was interested in scuba diving, they offered to lend us some underwater gear. So Shipi and I took off the next afternoon to explore an area where the desert meets the sea. We found a lonely spot on a rocky beach that looked like a good place to dive. After wading out, however, we found that a long coral reef blocked us from getting out to the deep water where we could dive. It was impossible to climb over the reef because the surface was sharp and cutting, and there were spiky sea urchins all over it. After about ten minutes, we found one narrow slit that opened to the sea. We slid through it carefully, making sure not to hit the equipment. I made a bad mistake right then. I forgot to leave a marker to show us where that slit was so we could return to shore later.

The area was so deserted that it looked as if no one had ever dived there before. That added a little excitement to our sport. The waters were deep and blue, perfect for diving. We had been swimming quite a distance from the reef, when I suddenly saw an enormous blue shark beneath us. I swam immediately to Shipi and tapped his mask, pointing down to it. The shark was coming closer and beginning to circle us. He looked as if he were going to attack. I took off my mouthpiece and let some bubbles rise, which is supposed to scare a shark away, but the big fish didn't pay any attention. All I could think of was getting back to shore as fast as we could. I tried concentrating on the huge, ugly fish. That didn't do any good. I could see one of the small eyes on the side of his head as he was circling us. It looked horrible.

We had about twenty minutes of air left, but we would have to surface slowly, which would take time. Not that surfacing would help us any with the shark. My compass showed that we were heading in the right direction for the reef, but now the shark was between us and the reef. He was moving faster and coming closer, about 15 metres away. We had spearguns, but I was sure all they would do was wound him and enrage him. I was scared. I thought about how this monster could tear the limbs off our bodies in seconds. Shipi's parents had given me responsibility for him, and that made the matter all the worse. I was shouting in my mind: Get away, get away, disappear.

Now he was only about five metres away and was coming straight towards me. I felt as if I was in the door of a plane, about to jump without a parachute. I did the only thing I could. I aimed the spear gun at him and pressed the trigger. I involuntarily closed my eyes. I figured that if I felt a hard pull on the spear, which was attached to the gun by a line, I'd just let the gun go, and maybe that would turn him away.

But I didn't feel any tug on the spear. I opened my eyes and saw the spear sinking slowly below me. There was no sign of the shark. I looked everywhere. I couldn't understand it.

We swam for several more minutes, and there still was no sign of the shark anywhere. We came to the reef and surfaced slowly, being careful to breathe correctly as we did. When we got to the surface, we told each other how lucky we were. It was a terrifying experience for both of us. But we had another problem that took our minds off the shark. It was now late afternoon and beginning to get dark fast. We didn't have any idea where the slit in the reef was.

With all the equipment we were wearing, it was impossible to cross the razor-sharp coral and the sea urchins, both of which can give painful infections. We had little air left, and the waters were getting dark. We had to find that slit in the reef. I started to concentrate again, and something told me to start off to the right. We started diving along the reef, then came up and swam along it, trying to swim on the surface with the tanks on our backs. It was almost impossible. By now it was so dark I couldn't even see the car on the beach to give us a heading. Trying to grip the rocks and pull ourselves along, we cut our hands badly. Just as total darkness fell, we found the slit. We got to the beach and rested on the sand. I lay there, looked at the sky, and thanked God or whatever it was that had sent the shark away and told us to go to the right when we reached the reef.

Back in Tel Aviv, things were even worse between the manager and me. I found I could not easily break the contract with him even though some evidence pointed to his dishonesty. While my lawyer was trying to figure out a way to establish it, some appearances in Italy were arranged to see if the demonstrations could succeed outside of my country. I had appeared before so many Israeli audiences that I would soon run out of people who hadn't seen me.

The appearance at a big club in Rome seemed to be a disaster. The interpreter was poor, so no one could understand him or what was going on. The demonstrations worked, but nobody seemed to believe them. I was depressed. When I got back to Israel, I decided I ought to look for another way to make a living. I thought: Well, Geller, you've got to go back to Israel, it's the only place you can work.

However, a few people in the Rome audience that night had found the demonstration impressive. One of them was an older, well-dressed Italian man who spoke good English. He said afterwards that he thought the demonstration was fantastic and had a very important matter to talk over with me at lunch next day, if I were free. I was curious, so I agreed. He picked me up at the hotel in a Silver Shadow Rolls-Royce, pointed out many things of interest around Rome as we drove along, and then told me at lunch that he could arrange a large number of appearances for me in America, especially Las Vegas, if I should decide to go there. He wanted me to think about it. He put much quiet but urgent pressure on me and asked questions. Of course, the idea of going to America was appealing. Whether it was my imagination or not, something about the man suggested the Mafia to me. I decided the next time he got in touch with me just to tell him that I had commitments in Israel. Maybe in the future if I came back to Italy, and if I wanted to go to America, I would look him up. I didn't want to involve myself with someone I didn't know, especially in view of the problems I was having with my manager.

The next day, as I was getting ready to check out of the hotel to go back to Israel, a message from the desk told me there was an envelope for me. I went down and, to my great surprise, inside the envelope were all the papers and the keys for a brand new car in my name. The desk clerk told me the car was outside. I went out and looked; there stood a brand new Alfa Romeo Spider. The anonymous donor, of course, was obviously the man I had talked to the day before, and the last thing in the world I wanted was to put myself under any obligation. I crossed out my name on the papers, gave them back to the clerk, and told him to return them to whoever had brought them. There was a telephone number on the papers, and I told the clerk to call that number to tell someone to come and get the car. There was something mysterious and scary about the whole thing, and I didn't want to be mixed up in it. I never heard from the man again.

I returned to Israel depressed and upset. I still was forced to work with my manager because of the contract. My lawyer had discovered that many times the manager would arrange for an appearance for £800 and enter it as £500. The missing £300 would never appear in the records. My lawyer was collecting the facts and preparing to take the case to court so that the contract could be cancelled.

Meanwhile I was scheduled for more appearances in Italy, at better places this time. Other Italian managers had seen my demonstration and understood that the real problem had been between the interpreter and the audience. My manager now had a new publicity man working for him who arranged for me to meet and talk with Sophia Loren when I returned to Italy. He figured that this would be great for publicity and that a picture of Miss Loren and me would attract attention in the Israeli press.

I still had my dreams of being a movie star, and the idea of meeting Sophia Loren appealed to me. I had heard that she very rarely gave interviews and was extremely hard to see. It would be a wonderful experience for me, and I welcomed the idea.

When the time came to meet Miss Loren, there were troubles. She had recently returned from New York where her hotel suite had been robbed. She was upset about the robbery and didn't want to see anybody. We talked with her husband, Carlo Ponti, who explained all this and offered his apologies. After talking for a while longer, however, he agreed that we might drive to her villa outside of Rome.

The villa was huge and beautiful. Miss Loren was charming in spite of her recent setback. She and I talked alone for about a half-hour. I told her what I thought was coming from her mind, and she was impressed with the accuracy of my reading. When we rejoined the others, the public relations man asked if he could take a picture of her and me. Miss Loren said that her own photographer took all her pictures. He wasn't available.

We thanked her and left. The publicity man was upset. The picture was extremely important for future publicity, he said, and it was ridiculous that it couldn't be taken.

I now was on my way back to Israel for more appearances. A fatal mistake was about to be made that would seriously damage my reputation and my career, and would almost destroy the trust of the people I respected who believed in me.

The publicity man stayed in Rome for two days after I left. I had no idea what he was doing. It wasn't long before I found out. He had taken one of my pictures and one of Sophia Loren and had arranged with an Italian photographer for a composite of the two. The composite made it appear that Miss

Loren and I were photographed together. The publicity agent released it to the Israeli press. It appeared in papers all over the country with captions saying that I had visited Miss Loren in Italy. That was true, but the picture was not.

It didn't take long for the photographic deception to be discovered. Huge headlines all over Israel declared that Uri Geller's picture with Sophia Loren was a fake. I was really depressed now. This was going to finish me for sure. I went to my manager and told him that, if he didn't tear up our contract, I would take him to court immediately. He had no choice. The fake picture had been done without my knowledge. Combined with the other material my lawyer was gathering against him, this fact would have compelled any court to decide in my favour.

Although the faked picture hurt me terribly, it actually increased the attendance at my appearances. A girl had been assisting me on the business side. She was very bright, even though she wasn't a professional manager. She continued handling all the details for the appearances and did a good job of it.

The whole series of what you might call professional public appearances in Israel had begun in the early spring of 1970. In June of that year I did a demonstration before a group of students and faculty at the Technion Institute at Haifa, the MIT of Israel, which trains the top scientists and engineers of the country. Later, not long after the experience in Italy, a well-known retired colonel of the Israeli Army came to my office. He said that his son had been greatly impressed by what he had seen at the Technion demonstration and that he—the colonel—had been in touch with some American scientists who were interested in what I was doing.

The colonel informed me that Itzhaak Bentov, an Israeli researcher working in Boston, was interested in the reports he had heard and would like to investigate if I were willing to be tested scientifically. Since Amnon Rubinstein had first made that suggestion, I had been thinking more and more about working with scientists. I did have mixed feelings about it, not because I felt there was anything to hide, but because the idea of being tested seemed so cold and unfriendly. Scientists interviewed by the Israeli papers had been saying my powers were trickery and nothing else, and they were sure I was a fake. That kind of thing turned me off. And there was my ever-present fear of failure as well. I was worried that with scientists watching nothing would happen.

The colonel was relaxed and open-minded, although I was sure he didn't know whether to believe me or not. He said to me: 'Look, I don't want to press you or anything, but if you bent a sample of metal for me I could send it to my scientific friend in America, and he could analyse it in his laboratory, just for a start.'

I didn't want to bend anything of my own, because that could be suspect, and the only metal he had with him was an ordinary pin. I reminded him that a pin is very thin and simple to bend, but he said it would satisfy him as a preliminary test. I had the colonel held it in his hand and close his fist gently. I held my hand over his without touching it. Then I concentrated on the pin, as I usually do, saying bend, bend, to myself. When he opened his hand, the pin had broken cleanly in half. I had never touched it.

He was impressed. He immediately put the two broken pieces in an envelope and told me he was going to send them to America. I didn't realize at the time how completely this was going to change my life or that it might possibly change the whole face of science.

I went about my normal routine of giving demonstrations at schools, universities, theatres, and discotheques. In spite of the bad publicity coming from the Sophia Loren incident, most of the appearances were successful and I was able to take care of my mother and make a good living.

I spent a lot of time with Iris and saw less and less of Yaffa—only a few stolen moments. No matter how impossible the situation was, I still loved her. I told Yaffa everything about Iris. As open and frank as I was with Iris, I had never told her about Yaffa. That bothered me. There was a conflict in me; something always held me back. Maybe I knew that my love for Yaffa would always be there, no matter how old I would get, and maybe I did not want to hurt Iris.

I was still debating with myself about scientific tests, trying to get over my fear of them. If a chance to go to America were offered should I take it—or should I just quietly phase out the whole operation and go back to ordinary work?

Word came that several scientists had examined the broken pin the colonel had sent to America. They were definitely interested in testing me, in Israel first, and perhaps later in America. This was a way for me to leave Israel for a bigger country. I thought I probably should be somewhere working with scientists. I was free of my manager, and there was nobody else who could tell me what to do.

A new career was about to start for me. It changed my life into something extraordinary, something almost beyond human thinking. I had never dreamt I would become involved in anything like it.

CHAPTER TWO

AUGUST 17, 1971, was an important day in my life. Dr Andrija Puharich arrived from the United States. He had written some time before to say that he learned of me through the colonel's friend, Mr Bentov. Bentov and Andrija Puharich were friends, I learned. They had decided to come to Israel to check me out and determine if the powers were genuine or not. I had known that Andrija was going to arrive that night, but I hadn't known that they were going to come to the night-club where I was performing.

I had learned that Andrija was an American physician who had spent a lot of time checking out psychic phenomena. He had lectured some time before at the medical school at Tel Aviv University on his specialty, diseases of the ear. The colonel was with him when he came into the club.

The moment I saw Andrija, I knew by instinct that I could work with him. He didn't look like my picture of a scientist, but more like a hippie Einstein. He turned out to be very pleasant and easy to get along with. I felt confident that the forces would work under controlled conditions with him.

I sat down at their table. The first words I said to Andrija were: 'I think we can work together. Don't be put off or disappointed about my stage appearance.' I knew that my being a stage performer might not sit well with a scientist looking seriously into these matters. This, of course, has been a constant problem.

I told Andrija that I appeared on stage because I enjoyed it and needed to make a living. That night I started in my usual way: 'With the co-operation of the audience, I am going to try to demonstrate simple telepathy and psychokinesis. I hope I will succeed.'

The demonstrations that night did succeed about 80 per cent of the time. I didn't feel any hostility from Andrija or the colonel.

Months later, I asked Andrija: 'Did you really believe it the first time?' He told me: 'No, I thought you were doing tricks like any clever magician. Because any magician can do most of those things on the stage.'

In November 1971 Andrija found an apartment in Herzliyyah Heights for himself and his several cases of scientific equipment —magnetometers, cameras, tape recorders, compasses, many kinds of minerals, and pieces of aluminium, tin, steel, and iron. He had electronic gadgets that I wasn't familiar with and mirrors so that he and Mr Bentov could observe from every angle. As we got ready to start the tests, I found that I liked him very much and felt at home with him. So did Hannah, and so did Shipi. He was a jolly man, very open, young-spirited, and extremely intelligent. Andrija wasn't a conventional scientist: he told me he had been exploring parapsychological phenomena for a good many years. This apparently puts a scientist in the doghouse automatically, just because he's willing to explore in this area.

His scientific background was impressive. He had a medical degree from Northwestern and a tremendous technical background in medical electronics with leading American institutions. He was very precise in every experiment he did with me, keeping the most meticulous records and watching out for every kind of trick I could play, even though I couldn't do tricks if I wanted to.

He would be sticking his neck far out in reporting what was happening, and I could see a big conflict in store for him. Should he ignore or hide the incredible things, so that his credibility would not be damaged? Or should he report everything and risk a lot of ridicule? It is hard to function normally when science fiction is turning real in front of your eyes.

I'm sure this worry is one of the big reasons why he later pushed hard to set up scientific tests in America. Without such verification of what was happening, the chances for any of his observations to be believed were slight. What was about to follow was new to me. My impulse was just to go ahead, let things happen, make a decent living, and enjoy life while I was doing it. I realized that the scientific tests were important but had no idea at that time *how* important they would turn out to be. I just had a feeling I was going to learn a lot. The biggest thing was going to come very, very soon.

* * *

When we began the tests, I didn't feel nervous and tense, as I had expected. Both Andrija and Mr Bentov were very sympathetic and didn't try to push me hard. We first tried some telepathy. I concentrated on planting three-digit numbers in Andrija's mind. This, as I have said, is the reverse of what magicians do. Then I moved his watch ahead without touching it. He was particularly impressed when the hands of a laboratory stopwatch advanced more than thirty minutes, which is impossible if the watch hasn't run that length of time. Moving the hands had taken only a few seconds. He filmed the whole process for the record.

I succeeded in doing nearly everything Andrija asked me to do: telepathy, the watches, the bending of metals under laboratory bell jars, moving a compass needle by concentration, and many other things. He became more excited as the tests went on. Then he sat down and explained to me what this could mean to science. He said it is impossible to bend or move metals in ways that defy the laws of physics. He explained the importance of controlled conditions, which could prove to science that such events are real. He explained why he wanted me to repeat the same things so many times. The bigger a phenomenon was, the more proof it would need. If all the tests did check out, he said, there would have to be a complete revision of both philosophy and science. I began to understand more fully how important it was for me to work with science.

Andrija told me he planned to take the results of these preliminary tests back to America, and also to England, to see what support and interest he could find for deeper research. He had already written about the tests to a former Astronaut, Captain Edgar Mitchell, who must have thought at first that Andrija was smoking some new kind of pot.

However, Captain Mitchell later wrote a nice letter to me in care of Andrija. In it he said that he would very much like to work with me on experiments when I came to America, and he was sure that some top scientific laboratories there would be willing to make serious studies of the energy forces. I was impressed to hear directly from him—and flattered. When he had done some ESP experiments on his Apollo 14 mission to the moon, an Israeli newspaper had referred to him as 'the Uri Geller of the Astronauts.'

The first series of tests with Andrija in August 1971 lasted more than a week. Andrija kept a careful log of everything. He left Israel to work on his plans for the future research and was gone for many weeks. He didn't return until the middle of November 1971, this time with more equipment to set up a small laboratory in another apartment he had rented. He said he would need several hours each day for several weeks for the new tests, which I would fit in between my regular appearances in Israel during that time.

The second round of tests was more of the same. They worked well, over and over again. They were also getting very tiresome. I missed my usual contact with people. Andrija again kept very careful records and wrote about them in his book about me: *Uri: A Journal of the Mystery of Uri Geller*, published in America by Anchor Press/Doubleday. What he wrote in the book was more detailed than what I have in my own memory.

With the tests going so well, the researchers were interested in learning more about my background. I told them in detail. Andrija suggested that if he hypnotized me I might recall things that I could no longer remember consciously. I had known some hypnotists in the past and had let them try it with me, but it never worked. Andrija had experience in hypnosis and said he would be glad to try if I would let him.

At first I was afraid of the idea. But after I had thought it over something told me to go ahead with it. Maybe I could learn from it myself. We decided to do it the night of December 1, 1971. I had just finished a public appearance, and Iris was with me. With Andrija at his apartment were Bentov and two other Israelis, friends of Andrija's, who were interested in the experiments. Andrija began the process of hypnosis.

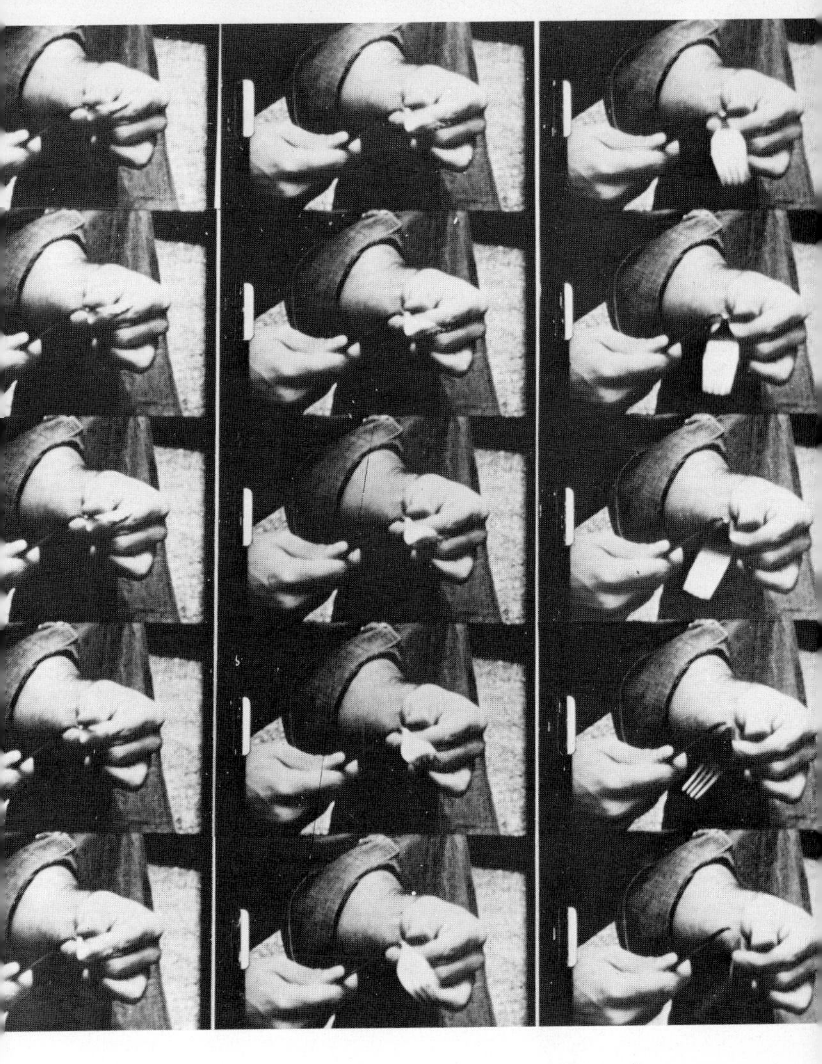

A sequence of frames from a Super 8 movie film taken by James Bolen, editor and publisher of *Psychic* magazine. The fork, which Bolen personally verified as being intact before the demonstration, gradually became pliable at its mid-section as I rolled my thumb and index finger over it. It finally broke apart.

Byron Janis, the world-famous pianist who composed the music for my album, with his wife, Maria (Gary Cooper's daughter), and me.

on the Merv Griffin Show, 19 July 1973.

Muhammad Ali and I.

When I woke up, they told me I had been under for more than an hour. They had taped what I had said. When they played it back I was startled to hear my voice speaking in a distant and mechanical way. Under hypnosis, I apparently had put myself back in Cyprus: on the tape I was with my dog Joker. My voice said, as Andrija reports in his book: 'I come here for learning. I just sit here in the dark with Joker. I learn and learn, but I don't know who is doing the teaching.'

Andrija's voice came on the tape to say: 'What are you learning?'

'It is about people who come from space. But I am not to talk about these things yet.'

'Is it secret?' Andrija's voice said on the tape.

'Yes,' my voice answered. 'But some day you too will know.'

I know that hypnosis can produce strange results, that among other things it can exaggerate fantasies. Still, people usually say what they fully believe to be the truth. I didn't know what to make of what I heard, because my mind was still very fuzzy, and this was very confusing stuff. On the tape I was getting farther and farther back in my childhood. I heard myself speaking Hebrew, and Mr Bentov's voice took up the questions in that language. I was now apparently back to the age of three, to that incident in the Arabic garden when the brilliant light struck me and made me lose consciousness. A shudder went through me at this point.

Then, very suddenly, the tone of my voice on the tape changed to a weird, eerie sound. The moment I heard the change of voice I was seized with fear, even terror. I can't remember clearly what happened after that. They told me I grabbed the tape recorder, stopped it, and ejected the tape. They told me the tape disappeared as if it had dematerialized. I apparently left the apartment quickly, and they later found me in an elevator. I have no idea why. Iris took me home. We never found the tape.

* * *

Later, the others in the room reconstructed what this voice, this flat, mechanical, almost computer-like voice coming through me in the trance, had said. It said that this was the power that had found me in the Arabic garden, and that I had been sent to help man. It said that I had been programmed by these forces—whatever they were—to forget exactly what happened in that garden.

Then it went on to talk about the Israeli-Egyptian crisis. The next few weeks, it said, were going to be very critical. The voice said that these energies were revealing themselves because mankind might be on the verge of a new world war.

Iris confirmed to me that this strange scene had taken place, but there was no tape to prove it. Who knows what someone will say under hypnosis anyway, even though an entirely different kind of voice takes over? What can it prove? However, that was not going to be the only time that the electronic, computerized-sounding voice suddenly spoke on a tape, and it was not going to be the only time that things materialized or dematerialized in front of our eyes. Who in the world would believe it? It was not controlled experimentation. It wasn't even like the telepathy or the metal-bending or the watches. Incredible as those things were—and they still remain incredible to me—they could be done time after time, carefully controlled, and within time and space limits that could be set up in advance. Even so, people have a hard time believing they could happen, especially if they only read about it.

Now a whole series of mind-blowing events started happening, one after the other, like a huge waterfall going far beyond anything in the past. For some reason, Andrija's testing seemed to set them off. When the routine tests seemed to work better after that incident, I was gaining confidence. A compass needle would move 30 degrees when I just put my hand near it, without even concentrating on it. One time Andrija was putting a coded metal ring inside a wooden microscope box to see if I could bend it inside the box without touching it. For some reason, I said: 'Look, I have a feeling I can make the thing disappear.' I had him take a film of himself putting the ring in, and then I concentrated. After a few seconds, feeling sure that the metal ring was no longer in the box, I told Bentov and Andrija to check it. They opened the box. It was gone.

I volunteered to let Andrija hypnotize me again, and he and Bentov recorded the session. I guess I was under about an hour. I had to rush to an appearance before the troops that night, so I didn't listen to the tape. Andrija drove me, and for some reason I told him he should try to remember what I'd said under hypnosis, because I was convinced that the cassette had vanished from the tape recorder.

Andrija stopped the car and checked the recorder. The cassette was still in it. He pushed some buttons to check the tape, but the play button wouldn't work. He opened the recorder to check inside again. The tape was gone from the cassette. I have no idea what prompted me to say I thought the tape would be gone. Can you imagine how you feel when something like this happens? You doubt your own senses completely. In fact you don't want to talk about it except to someone who was there, who shared the experience with you. You know that people flatly will not believe you. But a point comes where you can't go on worrying about not being believed. You have to have confidence in your own observations. However, I knew that the increased strangeness of these events made it all the more important to have the energies verified by science.

As I was getting ready to go out to the Sinai desert to give more demonstrations to Israeli troops, Andrija and Bentov tried to reconstruct what had come out on that second tape. I had said under hypnosis that I was 'flying out of my body' to a wide, flat place with mountains in the background. Then my voice apparently changed to the flat, mechanical voice and warned about new conflicts between Israel and the Arab countries. The voice said I had to use the energies to help the world in this crisis. Andrija and Bentov told me that the voice on the tape seemed not to be coming from me; it seemed to come directly on to the tape.

Now this is, of course, absurd: a disembodied voice speaking on a Sony cassette tape recorder, making all kinds of ponderous statements. Later, when I myself heard this voice again on some tapes, it sounded fantastic, like a computer talking. I said to myself, what is going on? Then I remembered a thought I had had in other times: Maybe there's a cosmic clown up there making a big, cosmic joke. Even though I was hearing this strange voice on the tapes, I didn't know whether to believe or disbelieve.

But things were continuing to happen. An ashtray might disappear from a table in front of our eyes and suddenly reappear in a far corner of the room, rolling over and over. I did nothing to cause this kind of occurrence. I wouldn't be concentrating to try to make it happen. It would just happen.

Looking back, I know I flatly did not believe it the first time I heard that voice on the tape. I thought Andrija and Bentov were tricking me. The second time, when the tape was not played, my suspicion was so strong I opened the tape recorder up with a screwdriver and looked inside for some kind of trick effects, for a second cassette or something like that. I couldn't find anything out of the ordinary.

The third time I just shook my head. Now the voice was saying that the energies were coming from a spacecraft, which it even gave a name: 'Spectra.' The voice said it was from a planet thousands of light years away and that it would help us work for world peace. This to me really was a joke. Why would it have such a common Hollywood-type name? Just what was going on? Sure, I knew I could bend metal, I knew I could read minds, I knew I could do telepathy, I knew I could fix watches and stop them. But never before did things fly around, never before did objects materialize and dematerialize. Previously, in fact, metal objects did not break as they were doing now. And previously, I had heard no disembodied voices speaking on tape.

I began to have strong urges I couldn't explain at all. Out on the Sinai, the night after the tape disappeared, when I'd been entertaining the troops, I asked the commander to let Andrija and me go out on the desert in a jeep. I had never thought much about UFOs, but my interest in them was rising after hearing the tapes. For no reason at all, I felt we might be able to see something of this strange spacecraft. Andrija and I did see a red, disc-shaped light that we thought was following us; oddly, the soldiers with us didn't see it. I was confident that it was a spacecraft and felt sure we could get a picture of one if we kept trying. But cameras were not allowed in that military area, so we would have to wait until another day to try.

The strange incidents with the tape recorder continued. We would put a new cassette, just unwrapped from the cellophane, into the machine for an interview or for recording an experiment. Sometimes, before anyone had a chance to push the playback button, it would seem as if an invisible hand had pushed it, and we would hear the voice from the Spectra spacecraft. Sometimes we would push the button just to test the clean tape, and the same thing would happen. All I can say is that I witnessed this phenomenon, I could not explain it, and I was wishing it wouldn't happen. Maybe my psychic power could work the button, but what about that voice? Where did it come from?

It was one thing to believe in bending objects, telepathy and the starting up of broken watches—but contact from outer space was another thing altogether. There's a limit to what we can accept. Just for me to recount this here is enough to make anyone think that I'm lying or have flipped my lid. I certainly can understand that. But after all the things that have happened and continue to happen, I think it would be wrong *not* to report it.

Andrija wrote about these events in great detail in his book. As a scientist, he was sticking his neck out much more than I was, since I don't have a scientific reputation to maintain. His book was a little too technical and complicated for me, but he did report what happened without exaggerating it, as many people think he must have.

Many incidents he reports sound like science fiction. But Iris and I experienced them right along with him; we know they happened. During this period the testers wanted to see if the apparent materialization and dematerialization could happen under controlled conditions. Andrija wrote down the identifying numbers of a ballpoint pen and a brass refill cartridge inside it. He put the pen in a wooden box and closed the lid. I held my hand above the box for several minutes. I did not touch it.

Finally, when I felt that something had happened, I told Bentov and Andrija to open the box to see if the pen had dematerialized. The pen was still there. They picked it up to examine it and discovered that the brass cartridge had disappeared from inside the pen. There was no rational explanation, of course. It was somehow stranger that only the cartridge had disappeared rather than the whole pen.

A few days earlier, I had picked up the phone to hear the computer-like voice from the tapes instruct me to take a camera to a specific location in Tel Aviv. There, it said, I would be able to photograph this alleged spacecraft Spectra. I rushed with Shipi to the spot, which was on Petah Tikvah Road, and there, after we had waited a while, an oval object appeared in the sky over the Israeli Army headquarters. There, in the presence of several witnesses, I took a picture that shows an object resembling what Shipi and I saw.

Right on the heels of the disappearance of the ballpoint pen cartridge, another mysterious thing happened. By then I was getting what seemed to be impulses or signals one after the other. I suppose you could call them hunches, but they were more than that. Often my watch would jump ahead to a certain time, and I'd have an urge to go to a certain place at the time indicated. This happened on December 7, 1971. I told Andrija that I felt we had to drive to a suburb east of Tel Aviv, where there might be another encounter with the spacecraft, or whatever it was. Andrija, Iris, and I drove that night to an ordinary suburban area with lots of houses; it was not countryside by any means. Near an open area that looked like some kind of excavation, we saw a bluish-white pulsating light, something like a strobe light. Some kind of inner presence was urging me to approach it. The three of us got out of the car, and we all heard an electronic sound, almost like the sound of crickets. I was immediately drawn to the light. I think I told the others to stay back. There seemed to be some massive object under the light, which was still pulsating.

As I got nearer, I felt myself go into a trance-like state. Everything was vague, hazy. I felt I was inside something. It was hard to tell why, but the atmosphere felt different. I think I saw some panels, but I was too dazed to remember. Then a shape that was dark and impossible to distinguish put something into my hands. Suddenly I found myself outside again. I got scared. I started running back to Andrija and Iris. It wasn't until I reached them that I was aware of what was in my hands. It was the ballpoint refill cartridge that had disappeared from the wooden box.

Andrija checked the serial number. It was the one he had written down on the day of the experiment: No. 347299. He had not let me see the number before, as part of the control for the test.

I was in a state of shock for several days after that. It was another impossible thing on top of several earlier ones that I still couldn't take in, and yet it had happened. And it made me realize for the first time that, whatever the energy powers were, they were not from me. They came from some kind of intelligence that to me reconfirmed the reality of God.

It is very difficult for me to unravel my basic feelings about the UFO incidents, the metallic voices on tape, the materializations and dematerializations. It is hard for me to believe that the energies behind the powers are really beings, or that they are really extraterrestrial. I think they are intelligent energies. I don't want to put a form to them. I've never gone to synagogues or to church. But since I believe in God and in higher civilizations outside this planetary system and this galaxy, I can accept what has been happening.

I am convinced that there is no such thing as science fiction, that what is imagined in the mind of a science fiction writer will eventually take place, or it would never have appeared in his mind. Maybe it was real in the past. More likely, it will be real in the future. I believe there is no such thing as time. I don't think we can ever really reach the core of full understanding, because we are human beings and our minds are limited. My mind is not big enough to reach higher levels, but I do believe that anything is possible. It is very complex and difficult for me to explain. Maybe God is the fuel of our souls, the fuel for our going on to higher levels and keeping us going.

While all these unbelievable events were going on I was, of course, seeing Iris, but the memory of Yaffa was still with me. I saw Yaffa only at rare times, but my deepest love was still for her. The sad day finally came when she said that she could not go on, it was too much of a strain on her marriage, and it would be better if we stopped seeing each other. It really broke my heart to know I would never see her again. I hardly wanted to go on living. For weeks I saw her in my mind before going to sleep. I saw her in my dreams, and I saw her when I woke up in the morning. I could think of nothing else but that she was gone, that I had to take it and rebuild myself through a full love with Iris. I did love Iris, but my love for Yaffa was special. No two loves are the same.

*   *   *

After the long series of tests and experiences with Andrija, we decided that I should go to America to be tested in some of the big institutions and universities there. I was still afraid that I wouldn't be able to repeat the things I could do in Israel. The idea of a big laboratory still scared me. I thought it might be better to go somewhere in Europe first to see if I could perform outside of Israel, and maybe to meet some scientists in Europe before I went to America.

A friend of mine, the Israeli singer Zmira Henn, called me to say that a friend of hers in Germany, who had heard all about me, would like to manage my appearances in that country. She told me that her friend, whose name was Yasha Katz, would give me a very good contract and that I would like him and could trust him.

I finally decided to go to Germany in the spring of 1972, and to America later. Meanwhile, Andrija returned to the United States to join with Edgar Mitchell and other scientists in lining up the formal research that he hoped would scientifically confirm what had been going on. He was forming what he called a Theory Group, which was to be headed by Ted Bastin of Cambridge. Andrija was positive that nothing I was doing would be taken seriously until I had gone through a long series of rigorous tests by established scientists in the best possible institutions.

Shipi went with me to Germany. We had grown more like brothers all the time. His parents agreed that it would be a good learning experience while he was waiting for induction into the Israeli Army. He could help out with the tour that Yasha Katz was lining up. I wanted badly to take Iris, too, but it was not possible. She cried in my arms the night before we left, but we knew we would see each other again after I got more experience in the world outside of Israel. Shipi and I took an El Al plane to Germany, and everybody came to see us off —my parents, Shipi's parents, Hannah, Iris. We said a sad good-bye just before we boarded the plane and took off.

Yasha met us at the airport. He was a warm and friendly man, with a crinkly face, sensitive eyes, and a lot of enthusiasm about our prospects in Germany. I liked him right away. He was planning to demonstrate to reporters how these energy forces worked. After it became clear that the powers were a real and valid phenomenon, he would arrange for lecture-demonstrations of the kind we had been doing in Israel. The controversy over whether or not I might be a magician started right away in the German press. But we got a lot of coverage, especially when the Munich newspaper *Bild-Zeitung* decided to do a six-part series on me. It was a pure publicity build-up, but Yasha said that it was important in laying the groundwork for the lecture appearances.

Yasha urged me to try new experiments to get the attention of the press. I told him I'd be glad to try but could never be positive that things would work 100 per cent of the time. I informed Yasha that I often failed altogether.

One reporter on the series asked me: 'Uri, what can you do that will be very big, astounding, and that sort of thing? For instance, could you do something like stop a cable car in mid-air?' There was a large funicular line not far from Munich that was advertised as one of the strongest in the world. He had that one in mind. I laughed when he suggested it. Then I said to myself: 'Now, wait a minute. Maybe I can do it. If I can bend metal, maybe something in the mechanism would bend enough to stop the cable cars harmlessly.'

I was aware that such a thing would be good publicity and a real challenge. Before we decided to try it, we checked with a lawyer, because even if it wasn't dangerous there might be a lot of complaints. The lawyer found no objection. Yasha, Shipi, and I got into one of the cars, along with the reporters.

It was a crazy idea. As we went up and down several times, I kept concentrating on the cars to stop them. It didn't work. I gave up and announced that we might as well quit.

The reporters were really disappointed. On the way down I was talking to a reporter about the scenery, when suddenly the cable car stopped right in mid-air. There was terrific confusion: the control people didn't know what had happened. A mechanic with us in our car gave me a funny look and jumped to the telephone to call the control centre. They knew I was trying to stop the cars, but they were completely bewildered about what made them stop and how. Finally the control centre announced that the main switch had flipped off for no explainable reason. Someone flipped it on, and the thing started up again. Nothing else seemed to be out of the ordinary. The cars had just stopped when the switch flipped.

By the time we got down to the base a lot of excited people were milling around. The operators invited us to dinner afterwards, and people couldn't stop talking about it.

The reporters were hungry for more. They asked me if I would try to stop an escalator in a big department store in Munich. I couldn't resist this challenge either, ridiculous as the idea seemed. I wanted to see if the cable car was just a fluke. The story of the cable car was making headlines all over Germany, especially Munich, and Yasha was confident that an encore would help the appearances to follow.

We went to a huge department store in Munich and went up and down so many times between the first and second floors that people must have thought we were crazy. Still surprised about the cable car, I didn't have any idea whether this stunt was going to work. After something like twenty round trips the escalator suddenly stopped, to my surprise as much as everybody else's. And again the headlines trumpeted the story across Germany.

There was a serious side to the trip to Germany, too. Quite naturally, the German press wanted to know if there was a scientific basis for these events. It was arranged for me to meet in an informal session with Dr Friedbert Karger of the Max Planck Institute of Plasma Physics.

In the presence of the reporter who was following me for four days and a *Bild* staff photographer, Dr Karger volunteered a ring of his, which he held in his hand the entire time. He was so cautious that he never took his eyes off the ring and never let me handle it. I touched it gently and concentrated on it. The ring not only bent out of shape but cracked in two places.

The interview that appeared in the paper tells a little more about what happened:

> *Bild:* 'What happened in the cable car—which was allegedly braked by Geller's unknown power and brought to a standstill?'
>
> Dr Karger: 'Obviously it was not an electrical effect, but a mechanical change, which for the time being is inexplicable. In Uri's presence, without being touched by anyone—the switch dropped. How? We don't know.'
>
> *Bild:* 'Does science seriously regard as credible these and other similar incidents?'
>
> Dr Karger: 'In universities all over the world, you will find an ever growing number of departments of research in this type of phenomena.'
>
> In Munich Uri Geller had altered a decorative ring that belonged to Dr Karger. The ring was not only bent, but it was also cracked in two places. Immediately after the demonstration, *Bild* asked Dr Karger, 'Couldn't the ring be split just by applying a strong pressure?'
>
> Dr Karger: 'No.'
>
> *Bild:* 'A laser beam?'
>
> Dr Karger: 'Nonsense.'
>
> *Bild:* 'Did Geller have any chance at all to play a "trick" on you?'
>
> Dr Karger: 'Actually he could only have tried to hypnotize me. This I consider not very likely. A disassociation through hypnosis would have been the "trick" possibility.'

In the Max Planck Institute, Dr Karger's colleague, the physics engineer Manfred Lipa, 27, closely examined the cracked ring.

Lipa: 'If Dr Karger had not told me anything, I would state: The ring has been mechanically altered by a tool, with a pair of pliers, for example, or with a small chisel or a hammer. Then near the crack site, one can ascertain clear signs of reworking.'

But Dr Karger assured us, 'During the demonstration I never took my eyes off the ring or let it out of my hand. Geller only touched it lightly with his fingers.' Also the *Bild* photographer, Joachim Voigt, who was present during the demonstration confirmed: 'If Uri had been able to conjure up a pair of pliers, or any other tool, I would have noticed it—I was fully aware.' Uri Geller—a phenomenon? A charlatan? Or a great artist, who with elegant tricks keeps everybody including science holding its breath? Heretofore it has not been possible to unlock the secret of this uncanny man.

Dr Karger summed up the incident for reporters: 'The powers of this man are a phenomenon that in theoretical physics cannot be explained. Science already knows of similar cases. It is like atomic science. At the turn of the century, it was already known as a reality. It was just that at that time one could not yet explain it in terms of physics.'

Dr Karger wanted to start a research programme of his own as soon as possible. He put in an overseas call to Andrija in New York. Because the plans with Captain Mitchell and other American scientists were moving along at the time, Dr Karger agreed instead to join Andrija's Theory Group and postpone his own investigations until later.

I could see how hard it would be to control all that was happening for a concentrated research programme. I faced the scientific studies in America with mixed feelings. The material I was using in my lecture demonstrations was pretty much under control and could probably serve well for a start in the experiments. But how would it be possible to tame the amazing and startling uncontrolled events that lately had seemed to be taking me over? Only time could tell. I would just have to go along and play it by ear.

CHAPTER THREE

GERMANY IN 1972 opened my eyes to a different world. My first appearances, at the Hilton Hotel in Munich, drew a lot of attention. Shipi and I were invited to a full round of receptions and cocktail parties and made many new friends. Among them were Lo and Ernest Sachs, who have a magnificent home outside of Munich in Grunwald, with large gardens, a swimming pool, and rare antiques. They made us feel completely at home there. It was the first time I had been exposed to such a style of living. Ernest's brother, Gunther, is the internationally known millionaire who was married to Brigitte Bardot. Having been starstruck from my earliest days, I was hugely impressed, though the connection was remote.

The friends I met in Germany were warm and cordial, and displayed none of the historical prejudice against Jews. Lo Sachs was a gracious hostess, and we visited there often. I did notice that some of the very rich people we met were bored much of the time. That woke me up to the fact that money alone isn't enough. I had been thinking all along that money meant total freedom from cares or worries, and Germany taught me that there can be so much emptiness and sadness even with money.

In spite of all the press coverage, the appearances didn't take off the way Yasha had hoped. Sometimes we ran into difficult situations. Once I was scheduled to fill in as a last-minute substitute for a ten-day engagement at the Europa Theatre in Hamburg. We flew from Munich, arrived late, and were rushed from the airport to the theatre. Backstage, we discovered that the entire programme consisted of magicians and their acts, complete with top hats and capes. We had not been told about the programme when we signed the contract.

Now this to me was a very serious mistake. It's not that I'm against show business, but the acts of magicians are sensational and full of showmen's tricks. My demonstrations are simple and direct, but they are real. If I appeared at the same time as a group of magicians, I would automatically be classified as one of them. That would be very bad not only for the scientific tests being lined up for me in America but also for my credibility. Yasha and I protested loudly, but there was no choice. We were obliged to go on under the contract. The theatre announced that my appearance was a lecture and demonstration, not an act, but it was not a very effective disclaimer. Telepathy and the bending of keys can't possibly compete with acts where women are sawn in half or rabbits are pulled from hats.

The magicians on the programme, oddly enough, understood that I had nothing hidden up my sleeves and, by the time I had done several performances, were really interested in how the powers worked. But the very fact that I had appeared on the same bill with magicians was eventually going to backfire on me, and I sensed it at the time.

I met a man named Werner Schmid at this time. He is a big impresario in Germany and had produced the German versions of *Fiddler on the Roof* and *Hair* and other big musical shows. After introducing himself to me following one of the performances at the theatre, he said: 'I don't know how to say this, but watching what happened tonight has changed my whole life. I've been dreaming about something like this all my life.'

I didn't know exactly what he meant at first. At lunch the next day he told us that he was writing a musical about meditation and mystical powers. When he watched me on the stage, he saw his musical happening right in front of his eyes. He couldn't believe it. He said he wanted me to be in the musical as both an actor and a demonstrator of the unknown forces in the universe. I have to admit I was intrigued by the idea, even though I wasn't sure how he was going to do it. I had never sung in public, but I was willing to take lessons and give it a try.

When I talked on the phone to Andrija in New York about the idea, he didn't like it at all. Of course, all he had in mind was to get the scientific tests started. He told me that he had succeeded in getting the Stanford Research Institute interested in setting up a programme to test the powers under strict laboratory conditions.

Andrija was on his way back to Europe to meet me and to set up the test plans in detail. It was now October of 1972, and he was aiming at beginning the tests at SRI in November. He wanted me first to come to America and meet several scientists in the United States who, he thought, would be able to lend support to the serious work at the laboratories. They would be more likely to do so if they could observe the energy forces in person.

When Andrija arrived in Germany, he found Werner to be kind, warm, very sensitive, and sympathetic to the whole programme. In addition, when Werner was around, all kinds of unexpected things would happen. For instance, a lamp would suddenly levitate and fall; knives and forks would bend across the table from me in restaurants without my having touched them; and some would dematerialize in front of us and much later drop down on the table apparently from nowhere. Yasha kept track of most of these occurrences, writing down the dates and times, and from his notes one could almost see a pattern of signals regarding yes or no decisions on the best course to take at the time. It may be that these events don't sound real or even interesting as you read about them. But their impact when they happen—most often when my mind is on something else—is shocking to me and the others around me.

With the schedule in Germany not living up to its promise, our plans gradually re-formed. It was agreed that I would go with Andrija and Shipi to the United States in late October. Yasha and Werner would come later. Yasha would work on a series of college and university appearances, and Werner would explore the further possibilities of his idea for a musical there rather than in Germany. It was a far-out idea, I knew, but still worth exploring as long as it didn't interfere with the serious scientific work to be done. Also, a lecture tour would give me an income to live on while the experiments were going on. The musical idea was speculation; no one knew if that would work out.

As Andrija prepared to go back to the States ahead of the rest of us, he asked me to travel to England to meet some scientists and certain other people who were considering giving financial support to the scientific work. Shipi flew with me to London, where we met and talked to some of these people.

During our flight back to Germany, an incredible thing happened.

I was sitting on the left side of a Lufthansa jet. Shipi was beside me. My Nikon camera was under his seat. All of a sudden, it rose up and simply stopped in the air in front of me. Shipi and I were both shocked. I took it in my hands and figured that I might be receiving some kind of signal to do something.

I looked out the window but saw nothing but blue sky and white clouds. I decided to point the camera out the window anyway and take some shots. I don't know why I had this urge, because it was rather pointless, really, except on the off-chance that the levitation of the camera meant something.

I took several shots but left some film unexposed on the roll. I put the camera away and charged the experience off as another in the long series of puzzlements. I just about forgot the incident in the pressure of finishing my schedule in Germany. The episode was to have its own conclusion later.

Andrija met our plane at Kennedy Airport in New York and drove us out to his home in Ossining, an hour or so away. His driveway led through stone pillars to a large, beautiful house with lovely surroundings, lots of grass and trees. My feelings were still mixed about the laboratory studies, and I guess the fear of failure was the worst part of it. Looking back on it now, I know I still didn't have enough confidence in myself or in the persistence of the powers. I still wasn't certain I could repeat them time after time in the right surroundings or when there was outright hostility in the air. I was beginning to find that things would go perfectly well in the presence of sceptics but not well at all when there was total hostility.

The incidents in the previous few months numbered in the dozens. I was growing more convinced that they were under the control of impersonal, computerized intelligences. There seemed to be no other possibility.

I was still bothered by the capricious way the powers acted. Questions continued to bug me: Why should they make things materialize and dematerialize without giving clear signs of what was meant? Why did they seem to be playing games with us? Were the incidents symbols of something we were missing altogether? Why were they performing on our stupid level? Why did a whole flood of activity happen when certain people were around, and not with others? Why did the powers continue to be so clownish?

Amid the excitement of being in America, these things

weighed heavily on my mind. I felt I was being manipulated by forces not under my control.

The programme that was shaping up consisted of two parts. One, of course, was the testing at Stanford Research Institute; the other was a publicity process much like the one we had done in Germany to lay the ground-work for lecture-demonstrations in the United States.

My first visit to America in August 1972 was brief. I met Captain Edgar Mitchell, a rugged, handsome, and confident man. I liked him. I also met Professor Gerald Feinberg, of the Columbia University Physics Department, and Dr Wilbur Franklin, of Kent State University. I did several informal tests for them, moving a watch ahead, breaking a ring, and concentrating on a steel sewing needle, which broke with a loud crack. They both agreed that very serious scientific studies should be carried out.

Later, Captain Mitchell was eager to introduce me to Dr Wernher von Braun, the famous scientist and rocket expert. He was very cordial—and naturally very sceptical. We met in the offices of Fairchild Industries, where he is vice-president. I could tell he wanted to challenge the existence of the forces, but in a very friendly way. I especially wanted to demonstrate them to him because of his intelligence. Besides, I didn't want to disappoint Captain Mitchell.

I asked Dr von Braun to take off his heavy gold wedding ring and hold it in the open palm of his hand. I began concentrating on it. I put my hand near his, careful not to touch either his hand or his ring. Suddenly, the ring bent into an oval shape. Dr von Braun admitted that he had been sceptical and was completely astonished when it happened. He couldn't think of any explanation at all. Later he told a reporter: 'Geller bent my gold wedding ring without touching it, while it was in the palm of my own hand. How he did it, beats me. I can offer no scientific explanation. All I know is that the ring was perfectly round before. Now, it's oval.'

What happened next was still more interesting. He had an electronic pocket calculator that wasn't working. He thought the batteries hadn't been recharged, but his secretary assured him that they had been. He consented to let me try to start it. I held the instrument between my hands and concentrated on it. In less than a minute, the panel lit up—but the numbers weren't coming out right. I took it back and again held it less than a minute, and the instrument started working properly. The experiment for Dr von Braun was a success.

All of the demonstrations for Dr Feinberg, Dr von Braun, and many others at the time were important in helping convince the Stanford Research Institute that the research programme planned for me was worth while. Meanwhile, the mysterious slow-motion voice messages continued to come in on the tape recorder. To see the tape recorder button suddenly pressed in, as if by an invisible hand, was a shock. As if that weren't enough, some crazy thing would always happen beforehand that seemed to indicate that the recorder—with a blank tape in it—would go on. Maybe an ashtray would jump off the table to the floor. Not slide off, but jump. Or maybe a small vase from another room would drop in front of us on to the table. These things would drop gently. They wouldn't break. Usually, they seemed to appear just a few inches above the table or floor where they were about to drop. Even on soft surfaces they would often make a kind of metallic ping, as if to draw our attention to them.

I don't know how to ask a reader to believe things like this. But they happened, they are still happening, they repeat themselves. That's the best way I can put it. Otherwise, all of us who have seen these things happen are wildly insane or hopelessly stupid observers. Since the witnesses include many of the world's respected scientists, I think that explanation is unlikely.

The dreamlike voices on the tapes were the most frustrating

thing of all, because the tapes would either literally vanish inside the recorder as we watched or would be erased when we tried to play them again. That meant the best evidence was destroyed, leaving us with the fantastic testimony of witnesses.

The voices would often give specific instructions. They showed ambivalence about my going through formal scientific tests, however; they seemed to indicate that discussions and informal demonstrations with the scientists would be acceptable but research in depth would not be. I had mixed feelings about the instructions. I wanted to do informal and formal tests, if I could once get over my fear of scientific laboratories. It was hard to be rational when everything that was happening was not.

Shipi and I went back to Germany after the August 1972 visit. We would return to America in November if all went well with the Stanford Research Institute arrangements. I had met one of Andrija's assistants who had been living in Rome and would now be joining the group to help arrange the details for the scientific experimentation and the American lecture tour schedule. Melanie Toyofuku is a lovely Japanese-American girl with a brilliant mind and a tremendous ability for organization. She had been working in film production in Italy but was extremely interested in psychic research too. Later, Solveig Clark, an executive with a large American corporation, joined our group on a part-time basis. Like Melanie, she was charming and attractive and had a talent for getting things organized and done quickly. Both women were strongly in favour of learning more about the forces and were present when many incredible things took place.

Shipi, Melanie, and I arrived back in New York in the first part of November 1972. Much planning was needed to co-ordinate the scientific research with the lecture tour, and possibly the musical, which Werner was still interested in doing. Again I met a lot of interesting people, including Bob and Judy Skutch, who were deep into parapsychology research and psychic healing, and Maria and Byron Janis, who were to become two of my closest friends, almost family. When I meet some people, I know immediately there will be a deep and lasting friendship. I knew that immediately with Maria and Byron. With Melanie and Solveig it was the same way, as it was with others I met later.

So many strange things happened after we arrived in New York, it's impossible to tell them all.

The day after we arrived in Ossining, I noticed Andrija's black retriever, Wellington, lying in the kitchen doorway and trembling noticeably. The telephone rang, and Andrija went to answer it in the kitchen. It was in my mind that he would have to step over the dog, but suddenly Wellington just wasn't there. I don't mean he got up and ran away. He was there one second and not there the next, just like some of the inanimate things that had been appearing and disappearing.

Within seconds, I saw the dog far down the driveway and coming towards the house. We called to him, and he came, still trembling and upset. We were all shocked. No one could make any sense of it. As Andrija said, how could a living thing be translocated like this in a matter of seconds? It would have to be taken apart atom by atom, then reassembled. Or the atoms had to be accelerated in some unknown way. But of course, the same would have to be true of all the inanimate things that had disappeared and appeared. I wasn't to know until much later what kind of event this incident with Wellington foreshadowed.

Just before we were to leave for San Francisco to begin the Stanford Research Institute test, a disturbing thing happened. Andrija and I were in his living room, when an ashtray and a key suddenly appeared in front of us on the table.

Andrija took this as a signal that a message was coming in from the computer voices. He took out the tape recorder, and we waited. He was right. The 'play' button of the machine activated itself. A voice came out of the speaker.

The voice said very firmly that I was to meet with scientists only socially, which would throw the whole carefully planned programme at SRI out of kilter. By now, I was becoming convinced that I should listen to the voices: all the signs seemed to indicate that they were programming the energy forces that showed themselves through me.

I was disturbed by this message, and Andrija was in a spot. We were due to arrive in San Francisco in a couple of days. He was certain my credibility would be shot if the phenomenon was not validated by science. I had my own fears about science, and now this taped message backed them up.

Andrija felt that we *had* to go through with the tests regardless of the message. Whether responding to my own feelings or somehow taken over by these strange intelligences, I felt I could not go against the instructions. I acted very strangely as an argument flared up. Andrija and I both got furious, and suddenly I found myself throwing a sugar bowl at him. At the same time, the house seemed to rock and a grandfather clock in the front hall went across the floor and was smashed. Melanie and Shipi saw it all happen, and it scared everybody there. I finally agreed to go out to San Francisco and explain to the scientists that I could not go on with the research programme. Later, in the middle of the night, when Shipi and I were asleep in an upstairs bedroom, we distinctly heard a loud voice that woke us up. It seemed to come out of nowhere. It was the same voice that had come on to the tape recorder earlier. All it said was one short sentence; 'Andrija must write a book.'

We were all happier about this. It apparently meant we were free to discuss the tape recorder incidents with others, and it might also have meant that the restrictions would be eased. I didn't know for sure. I did know that my fears about meeting the scientists at Stanford Research Institute had come back stronger and that I didn't want to bring the wrath of the gods down on my head. We took off for San Francisco with much on our minds.

As we approached San Francisco, I was still afraid of meeting the scientific group. I thought to myself: 'Oh, my God, it's going to be like lying on an operating table with a huge lamp over me. They'll be bending down looking at me, wearing face masks and watching everything I do, with everything all sterilized.' It was the typical Hollywood concept of a laboratory. I felt this fear even though I was going to tell them that I couldn't work with them in deep research.

Andrija, Shipi, and I arrived at the San Francisco Airport. We got on the moving sidewalk, and there in the distance were Captain Mitchell and the scientists. As I came closer to them, I was nervous. The damn sidewalk was moving too fast. There was no way out. I couldn't run back. It was like parachuting again. I was already planning the meeting, how to shake hands, how to tell them I was afraid to do these experiments. And then—bang—I was there, with Edgar Mitchell shaking my hand. They were human beings, and they were beautiful.

There were three other scientists with Captain Mitchell: Dr Hal Puthoff and Russell Targ of SRI, and Dr Wilbur Franklin of Kent State. Captain Mitchell is a fascinating guy with a head on his shoulders. He's very cool and knows what he wants. He's kind, he will talk to you, he will explain things to you, he will give you a chance to talk, and he will listen. Dr Franklin is a merry fellow, blond, short, with glasses, very intent on making experiments. Hal Puthoff and Russell Targ were relaxed and pleasant, soft-spoken and not at all formidable, as I had imagined. I began to feel more relaxed the minute I met them all.

As we drove from the airport to Palo Alto, near SRI,

we had a long talk about my fears of the laboratory. I told them about many of the strange things that had been happening, and they were willing to listen. I even blurted out some things about the tapes, which shocked Andrija, who felt they shouldn't be discussed with anyone. They all listened carefully and didn't ridicule anything I was saying. I told them about some of the uncontrolled phenomena—spoons breaking or keys suddenly materializing—that seemed to act as signals indicating which way to go on certain decisions. As I began to warm up a little, I told them we'd soon see if we had interpreted any of these signals rightly. Meanwhile, I'd show them some examples of the things I did for the lecture-demonstrations.

In the apartment rented for us in Palo Alto, I had them make five drawings out of my view and got four of them right. Then I bent a machined copper ring Dr Puthoff had brought by concentrating on it without touching it. I tried to move the hands of Russell Targ's watch but failed. But the copper ring continued to twist itself into the shape of a dumb bell as we talked. Meanwhile, Hal Puthoff offered a heavy chain bracelet which he held in his hand. It broke without being touched. The copper ring continued to bend into a figure-eight shape.

These seemed like fairly encouraging signals, but I still felt that proceeding with the formal lab tests would be a violation of the instructions. I had time to think it over, since the next day, November 12, 1972, was a Sunday. We went to the beach with Russ and Hal, which was pleasant and relaxing. I was like a mouse getting used to a new environment. We had dinner at Hal's house, where I met their families and began to feel more at home.

We went to visit the SRI labs the next day, and the atmosphere wasn't anything like what I had feared. There were no operating tables and no masked scientists in white coats. It was very informal.

When they asked me to concentrate on a magnetometer,

which tells how strong a magnetic field is, I was as surprised as anyone when the needle moved sharply without my having touched the instrument at all. I concentrated very hard, though, to do it. They told me this was scientifically impossible, but I was able to do it every time they asked. They said my concentration was apparently able to produce a magnetic field that would register on the instrument.

Already I was more confident. They tested a metal ring under water, with an ultrasonic gadget that used a TV screen to monitor what happened. The device was able to show the ring becoming flatter, and at the same time a distortion appeared on the TV screen every time I concentrated. It was during this experiment that the computers of an Air Force project on the floor below were rumoured to have gone out of whack.

As more instruments began to show that the energy forces were working, I began to warm up. The powers were acting like a little child with a bunch of new toys. Everything brightened up, and I said to myself: 'Hey, maybe I can work under these lab conditions.' I was so happy that things were working out, it felt just like my first parachute jump. I had jumped then, I had parachuted. I reacted to the scientists as they looked at a meter or a needle moving and told me: 'Hey, something is really happening here.' They would move the control knobs, check the charts, check me and my hands. And I'd say: 'Am I really doing something to the machine?' They'd answer: 'Well, the instrument never acted this way before.'

As long as things were moving along so well, I decided to go ahead with the lab tests until the powers stopped or faded off. Andrija had to go back to New York, but I stayed there and continued working without him. After a lot of informal tests I agreed to try the telepathic tests they had lined up for me. For one of them they put me inside a shielded room that looked like a refrigerator. The walls were of thick, massive steel. There were two huge metal doors, and when they closed them, wham, one door would lock, then the other. And then there would be dead silence. It was so silent it reminded me of underwater diving, and of the caves in Cyprus. I don't get claustrophobia. I enjoyed the silence, perhaps because I could really concentrate.

There was a lamp inside, of course, and a pad and a pencil. Over a two-way intercom, they would give me instructions. Someone would make a drawing, which of course I could not possibly see. They would say, 'All right, the drawing is ready.' And I would close my eyes, concentrate on that screen in my forehead, and capture the drawings they were sending me.

For other telepathy tests I was placed in a Faraday cage, the double-screened copper box that screens out all radio waves. This in turn was inside a sealed room. There was no way whatever for me to cheat during any of these tests, even if I had wanted to. The results were more than they had hoped for.

The results of some of these tests are reproduced in the illustrations to this book. They were reached against what the SRI figured as 1,000,000 to 1 odds.

So much had been going on that I had neglected the film I had shot through the window of the Lufthansa plane over Germany. I told Hal Puthoff about it, and he had it developed in a lab he trusted. Several of the shots showed clear, unmistakable UFOs.

I didn't need proof that it was genuine, but we took the transparency to a professional photographer at SRI. He measured the window frame and made a lot of calculations. He concluded there was no way the picture could have been faked.

As word got around that SRI was getting confirmable results from the experiments the controversy began to grow. There were more rumours about the Air Force computer programme. Whether or not there was any truth to the rumours, I don't know, but the Stanford Research scientists had me concentrate on a videotape reel, and the image on this wide magnetic tape was either distorted or wiped out by concentration. Since computers store their information on magnetic tape, there could have been a connection.

Not long after the rumours started, the Advanced Research Projects Agency, which was running the Air Force tests, began insisting that I was a highly skilled magician and a fraud who was deceiving the scientists at SRI. They sent Dr Ray Hyman, a professor of psychology at the University of Oregon, to check. He issued a report saying that I was doing what any magician could do and was smart enough to put one over on the dozens of scientists I had demonstrated for. I had confidence by then. I said to myself, If they don't believe, they don't believe, and that's it.

The first series of tests ended in the middle of December 1972. Shipi and I rejoined Andrija in Ossining. We learned that the Advanced Research Projects Agency was intensifying its campaign to discredit both SRI and my own capacity for demonstrating the unknown powers. John Wilhelm, *Time*'s Los Angeles reporter, came east to talk with us on January 18, 1973, and told us that George Lawrence of the project was trying to discredit Mitchell, Puthoff, and Targ. He also told us that Leon Jaroff, the science editor of *Time*, had already made up his mind to write a story that I was a fake, and nothing would change his mind. I later learned that Wilhelm, too, turned negative.

Andrija, in the meantime, was preparing a summary of the things that had happened at Stanford and elsewhere in recent months. The summary clarifies the types of things that were happening:

They included *telepathy*, such as reproducing the pictures that were 'sent' to me in the metal vault and Faraday Cage at Stanford Research Institute.

There was *clairvoyance*, which was checked out under controlled conditions at SRI, where, time after time without fail, I was able to tell what number was on the face of a die placed inside a steel box. There were many other tests like this.

There was *moving the hands of a watch*, as I had done with Captain Mitchell's watch.

There was *repairing a broken watch*, which I had done constantly during various lectures and demonstrations.

There was the *repair of electronic circuits*, as had happened with Wernher von Braun's calculator.

There was *taking a picture through a lens sealed with a solid black lens cap*, which I had done with several photographers and later was to do for Lawrence Fried for the magazine *Human Behavior*. He sent me a long affidavit describing how he made sure there was no possibility of my being able to remove any part of the taped lens cap.

There was, of course, the *bending of metals*, which included everything from stainless steel to brass, silver, and copper.

There was *erasing videotape images*, as I had done at Stanford Research Institute.

There was the causing of objects to *disappear from one place and reappear in another*. This was of course the most unusual thing of all, especially since it happened only at the will of the energies, and my concentration had nothing to do with it.

A videotape camera at SRI caught one incident involving an SRI watch locked in a briefcase. Targ, Puthoff, Mitchell, and I were nowhere near it when the watch dropped lightly on the table in front of us. On the video film replay, the watch appeared at the top of the screen, falling downwards. The watch then disappeared and reappeared twice as it fell, coming back on the screen just before it hit the lucite table. The tape was replayed many times on a stop-motion basis. You could clearly see the watch vanishing and coming back on the screen, as if it had materialized and dematerialized during the fall. There was no reasonable explanation at all.

One day I was having lunch with Captain Mitchell and Russell Targ in the SRI cafeteria. We got to talking about Mitchell's walk on the moon and all the experiences he'd had. (He told me that he left a very good camera on the moon. From that moment on, incidentally, I've wanted to see if I could bring it back to earth by means of the materialization-dematerialization process.)

We were finishing our lunch when the most incredible thing happened. I was hungry that day and ordered two desserts. The second was vanilla ice cream. I took the first spoonful and I felt something metallic in my mouth. So I spat it out. I found myself holding a miniature arrowhead in my hand. I was furious that the cafeteria was so careless with its food; after all, I could have broken a tooth or a filling by biting on it. Russell Targ looked at the arrowhead and passed it along to Edgar Mitchell. Mitchell said: 'My God, this looks familiar!' He didn't know exactly why.

I told the waitress to find out where the ice cream came from and warn the supplier about this kind of thing, because people could get hurt. She looked at the object and asked me to give it to her, but I said no, just in case something happened to my teeth later.

We went back to the laboratory. We were sitting around talking when all of us saw something fall on the carpet. We picked it up, and it was the rest of the arrow. Together, the two pieces made a tie pin.

Edgar Mitchell looked really shocked. With the parts together, he recognized a tie pin he had lost several years before, which now had suddenly come back in two parts. But where did it come from? I certainly didn't know. But it gave me one thought: Maybe that camera is going to come back from the moon one day, and it would be one of the most wonderful surprises if it does. Is this a fantasy? With everything that has been happening, one thing on top of another, I can hardly tell what is fantasy and what is reality.

Two other incidents, almost as strange, especially stand out in my memory. One happened a little earlier, in August 1972, when I was in the United States for my first visit. Andrija had invited Captain Mitchell and some other scientists to an informal reception so we could make plans for the experiments that were to follow. Somebody asked me if I could do anything with a bean sprout. I was reluctant to try, because I don't like to tamper with living material. I kept saying I couldn't do anything with the sprout but everybody kept encouraging me. So I took the bean in my hand and concentrated on it. When I opened my hand the bean had sprouted and was almost an inch longer than it had been.

Everybody was excited. They asked me if I could make it go back to its original form. I shut my eyes and concentrated very hard, and when I opened my hand again it was its original size and form. This excited the scientists still more. But it scared me. I don't do it any more because it has to do with a living thing.

Word was getting around that the SRI tests were going to validate many of the experiments I had done there. Andrija told me that would be a major breakthrough in science. Further, Hal Puthoff and Russell Targ were going to prepare a scientific paper they felt was important enough for *Nature*, which Andrija said was a giant step. Meanwhile, *Time* was trying to get the results of the tests, which SRI naturally didn't want to give out in advance of a scientific announcement. The magazine pressed Andrija and me to give them the results, but we couldn't do so under the circumstances.

Denied information from both us and the Stanford Research Institute, the *Time* editors seemed to grow angry. Leon Jaroff told Stanford Research Institute that, if they didn't get the full report on the findings, they would print a story knocking both SRI and me.

It looked to me like a war between the executives of *Time* magazine and the heads of the Stanford Research Institute.

Charles Anderson, the president of SRI, defended his people in a way that was enormously impressive to me; he was the strongest man I've ever seen in the face of pressure. He stood behind the scientists on his staff when rumours said that even his scientists were in collaboration with me. I think Anderson had real guts in this situation. It looked as if *Time* was out to clobber everybody concerned with this, and we could only sit back and wait for the blow to come.

CHAPTER FOUR

THE STANFORD RESEARCH INSTITUTE tests led to some important conclusions, which were to be announced to the public at a colloquium sponsored by the Columbia University Department of Physics in March 1973. SRI was preparing a report to the colloquium. Among the data to be presented was evidence of my success in hidden object experiments, against odds of a trillion to one; and of my ability to influence a gramme weight to weigh more, then weigh less, when measured with precision lab instruments.

SRI's most important findings for the Columbia meeting were: 'As a result of Geller's success in this experimental period, we consider that he has demonstrated his paranormal perceptual ability in a convincing and unambiguous manner.' And this: 'We have observed certain phenomena . . . for which we have no scientific explanation. All we can say at this point is that further investigation is clearly warranted. Our work is only in the preliminary stages.'

For conservative scientists these were startling statements. I myself soft-pedalled the results, because I started sensing that *Nature* would be cautious about publishing the results in spite of the presentation at Columbia. Even if nothing was published,

I had SRI's reaction, and knew I had to keep going. But I was also happy deep down that I could succeed with scientists under controlled conditions.

I had succeeded. It was real. Scientists could see that it was real. No chemicals, no laser beam, no sleight of hand. And there was more to it than just bending keys, telepathy, and starting up watches. I was now convinced that the phenomena were symbols, clues from enormous intelligences that seemed to be revealing themselves through the tapes, through the materializing and dematerializing objects and through living things. There was also evidence coming through about UFOs and spacecraft.

Neither Russ Targ nor Hal Puthoff knew what to think about the UFO picture I had taken on the Lufthansa plane or about the voices on the tapes. They had their hands full testing the material that could be repeated over and over again in the lab. They didn't want to get into speculation. Even if they had wanted to explore the voices, they couldn't have got very far, because the tapes had dematerialized or had erased themselves.

It was still hard for me to accept those voices. But Shipi, Melanie, Solveig, Byron, and Maria, as well as Andrija and I, all heard them at one time or another. I can guarantee that none of them is a psychotic or fantastic liar. We were not deluded or imagining or kidding ourselves. Most of us saw the tapes dematerialize right in front of us after hearing them, or found them automatically erased after hearing a message. What scientist or layman would believe that? I wouldn't, if somebody just told me about it. I would have to have the evidence in front of me. And a name like 'Spectra' makes the whole thing sound like bad fiction. But it was heard clearly on the tapes.

And yet the tapes bring with them a tremendous message to the world, even though they do sound like science fiction.

For instance, a portion of one of the tapes made approximately this statement to Andrija in 1973:

> You see, the procedure is this. We accept the thesis that we are here and that we want these things done, we can do them through you. You also have to struggle—we have also to struggle. Supposing all healthy biologic events surround the birth of a child. It will take nine months and it will take mating. The greatest of men are not born in an instant. All the birth pangs that any other mother would undergo, their mothers had to undergo, too. But the point is this: Supposing tonight I sit down here—which is perfectly possible—I can sit here for an hour and tell you what is going to happen to the minutest detail—how often you are going to sneeze, how often you will sit—that can be done, but that is not the way to do it. What you are doing is just the right thing. Struggling a little, getting creative imagination into exertion, awaiting a certain little point for guidance. . . .
>
> We have to look upon this as a long-term contract between you and us. Your co-operation is so urgently needed. If we develop these techniques, we shall have taken long strides: indicate the formula and the method. But we understand how much labour, application, patience it involves to get into operative forces. So our plans are definite. We feel that you must put in some real effort. We shall co-operate, but your will has to exert itself.

Or sometimes the voice would talk more about theoretical matters, like this one in 1973:

> The ultimate powers, whether on the particle level or the cosmic level, are in rotation and drawing off the gravitation power from the centre of the system. There are special rays . . . where the skin of the envelope of the cosmic rays is utilized for power. The computerized beings in space

vehicles draw on this energy. This rotation energy can be used from outside the galaxy. It does not exist in a usable form at the particle level. The computerized beings are under the direction of the 'controller', or what earth man calls God, or gods. In the future, this general idea would be formulated in rigorous mathematical language.

Is it hard for a reader to believe that all this and much more actually came through on a cassette tape recorder that automatically activated itself? Of course it is. But it is part of the story and can't be ignored. The voices are also a clue to the source of the energies that flow through me, energies that are directly confirmed in the physics labs.

Andrija has recorded much more than these brief portions in his book *Uri*. Many of the other tapes affirm for me the existence of God, although I believe that anyway, tapes or no tapes. Some of them describe the vastness of a universe that never ends. Some emphasize the importance of the free will of the human individual. Some talk about previous explorations of the earth by spacecraft and predict another large spacecraft probe of the earth in the near future. Not an invasion, just a contact. Some indicate that the owners of the voices have been observing the earth because all the universe is interrelated, and every small event affects everything else. On this subject, the tapes stated that they were out to stop the earth from destroying itself.

I don't know whether these voices are beings or cosmic computers. I do think they are intelligences of some kind. They were so persistent that I have come to accept what they said, because—at the same time—actual, down-to-earth, material things were taking place while the scientists were studying the energy forces.

All this, as well as my own instincts, was pushing me to go beyond the scientific tests and continue to make the energy forces known to the masses of people, if only to show them the small but unbelievable symbols found in the bending of a key or other phenomena. I think the symbols might suggest that we're on the edge of big discoveries of new energies, new intelligences, and new contact with other forces or superior beings in the universe, which will help us join together instead of tearing ourselves apart. It isn't all that illogical. I think every astronomer today accepts the theory that there are millions of other planets with the probability of intelligent life on them.

Time magazine was still pushing for more information as the time for the Columbia University meeting got nearer. Andrija and I agreed to go to their offices for an interview. Neither of us liked the idea, because it looked to us, from what we had heard, that Jaroff, the senior editor on the project, was sceptical almost to the point of hysteria.

Our hunch was right. At *Time*, the atmosphere was hostile and negative. There was no sign at all of honest scepticism. There were a couple of magicians there, and one of them brought up the fact that I had appeared in Germany on the same stage with magicians. The atmosphere was not at all good for any kind of demonstration, but I did some and they worked, including the bending of a key and fork supplied by the editors. Andrija remarked after we left that the entire meeting had the atmosphere of a lynch party.

I was very down when we left the *Time* offices. It was easy to sense what they were going to write, and the atmosphere at the meeting confirmed that the rumours we heard were true. The article appeared under the heading 'The Magician and the Think Tank' in the March 12, 1973, issue, just about the same time that the SRI results were presented at the Columbia University colloquium.

It was a strange conjunction of events. The *Time* article was vicious, filled with outright falsehoods and innuendoes. Without even knowing what the SRI conclusions were, the writers tried to make it appear that I had pulled the wool over the scientists' eyes with a series of tricks. They always seemed to want to do this—to make it appear that I was more clever than a whole group of top scientists. If I were, I would have to be a lot more brilliant than I am.

But at the same time that the *Time* story appeared, the results presented at Columbia confirmed the authenticity of the tests under controlled laboratory conditions. *Newsweek* covered the colloquium with a cautious but fair article that said the evidence showed the need for serious follow-up study. My confidence that *Nature* would eventually accept the paper that Targ and Puthoff were preparing began to grow.

So it was a mixed reaction. Actually the *Time* story started my name circulating around, and I got invitations to appear on some of the top TV talk shows in the United States.

Jack Paar was the first. It was my first big television appearance in America, and I was really excited about it. It went fantastically well, the demonstrations worked, and the appearance helped set up some of the lecture-demonstrations at colleges that Yasha and Werner were working on.

I was pleased when I was invited on the Johnny Carson show, because I knew he commands a huge audience. I wanted very much for things to go well, and because of that I was unusually tense and nervous. Nothing seemed to work at first, although a spoon did bend as Ricardo Montalban held it, and I was uncomfortable because they were hurrying me along. Very little happened on that show, and I felt terrible. I'll never forget it. Millions of people were watching, and I had to pretend that I was happy and smiling. Inside I felt this awful depression.

It was terribly embarrassing. The funny thing was that after the show, backstage, things really started happening. A medal disappeared and reappeared, objects flew around the room, everyone was astounded.

On the other hand, I was on the Merv Griffin show twice, and each time it went beautifully. Rings broke in half, the telepathy worked. With Mike Wallace on 'Sixty Minutes' the results were good in spite of his scepticism. The Carson show was the only failure, perhaps because I wanted so much to succeed.

Meanwhile, I was getting restless living at Andrija's place out in Ossining, even though it was beautiful. I have always liked to be active, and I felt the strain of being hemmed in. I wanted to meet more people. I liked the excitement of New York and wanted to live in the city. Yasha and Werner had set up an office in their apartment there, and it had enough room for Shipi and me.

Andrija was beginning at that time to write his book on our experiences. We had our fights and our differences, sometimes quite intense. But I loved Andrija, and I still do. He is like a father to me. But there comes a time when the son grows away from the father, and this happened with us. We agreed that, even under these strange conditions, he could not possess me and I couldn't possess him. I wanted to work for myself, to think for myself, to grow up, and to advance alone.

I told Andrija this, and he agreed. I said I wanted to test myself, at least for a while. When I moved into New York to stay with Yasha and Werner, I felt a new independence and a new sense of security. I began to understand that, no matter what happened, some people would always be against the idea of the powers, and nothing I said or did would change their minds. This situation would continue until the scientists confirmed that the forces were real. But I was learning. I began to see that even critical articles served a useful purpose, because the detractors were offering publicity to me and keeping the events much in the public eye.

Meanwhile, I was doing follow-up experiments at SRI and making the rounds on a lecture tour of colleges and universities.

I visited Yale, Stanford, Berkeley, Kent State, Bowling Green, North Carolina, and many other schools. The student audiences were alive, enthusiastic, and open-minded. They wanted things to happen.

While I was in Hollywood for the Carson show, Maria Janis asked her old friends Jimmy and Gloria Stewart if they wanted to meet me. I went to the Stewarts' house with Byron and Maria for drinks early one evening. Jimmy asked me to bend a key for him, which I did. Then he took us down the lawn to his garden, quite a way from the house. Suddenly we all heard a loud thud, like something heavy falling on the grass. Maria ran in the direction of the sound, about twenty feet away, and came back carrying a stone carving of a hippopotamus, about five inches long. Both the Stewarts recognized it as an artifact from a shelf in their library. Their two golden retriever dogs kept jumping up and sniffing at the statuette and continued to behave excitedly after it was put into a tool shed at one end of the garden. They stood there, pointing at it, until we went back to the house. Many other startling events took place with other famous people.

It seemed that phenomena would often happen when I was with Maria and Byron. They were always sympathetic to the whole possibility of life in other worlds. Maria's beautiful abstract paintings, which are shown in galleries in many countries, reflect the endlessness of the galaxies and stars. I have always felt since meeting her that a big part of her soul and body and mind belong on higher levels. Byron's music affected me the same way. When he plays the piano, whether it's Chopin or Rachmaninov, he seems to carry the music far beyond the keyboard or even the composer.

The same strange things would constantly happen with the staff who worked with me in lining up the details of the tours and lectures, the motion picture that was brewing, and the album being planned. Shipi, Melanie, Solveig, Yasha, Werner, my lawyer Larry Lighter, and Trina Vatter, who joined us later—not one of them was interested in only the business side. Each was intrigued by the mystery of these forces, and nearly every day at least one of these friends was part of the strange events that seemed to be increasing instead of decreasing as time went on.

Each of them feels that experiencing the phenomena has changed his life—especially Shipi, who has always been all over the place, handling details, following them up, keeping things running smoothly. I have never forgotten that, if it weren't for Shipi, I would probably still be a clerk with an export company. He was the one who kicked me in the tail and told me to get out and show people what was going on.

The rest of the group worked as hard as Shipi, because, I guess, they all believed that the new energies, the new forces, were more important than what could be shown on the television screen or on the lecture platform, what could be discovered in the science labs. What happened in those places would happen every day in our office.

Can you imagine your shock if during the week a glass suddenly jumped off a desk at your office and landed on the floor without breaking? If a light switch clicked off by itself and then clicked on again, with no one near it? If the head of a spoon just broke off when you were sitting at your desk and stirring a cup of coffee? If your office clock jumped ahead a few hours? If a paperweight lifted off your desk, disappeared, and then instantly rolled over in the far corner of the room? If a priceless Chopin manuscript vanished in front of your eyes, as happened to Byron, and showed up inside a newspaper soon after? If a cigarette lighter disappeared from one office and reappeared in another, with all the doors in between closed?

This happens all the time, day after day, among us. There is no accounting for these appearances, and we simply had to grow used to them. I tried to analyse why I was being pushed from inside my mind to communicate with as many people as

I could, whether on TV or in a lecture hall, or through an album, a motion picture, or a book. I guess my inner feeling, my inner voice, will tell me when to stop. In the meantime, I am compelled to let people know more, to educate them somehow.

There are others I'm very close to, so much so that we all feel part of each other. We are all of different religions and backgrounds, but we all believe in one God. Bob Williamson, who managed the Hyatt Hotel near SRI, became a close friend, and we are in touch with each other constantly. Dr Louis Shenkman, on the Bellevue Hospital staff, and his wife, Edna, have made me feel I'm part of their family. I don't have to demonstrate to friends and associates to convince them that the powers exist, yet whenever I'm with them the most extraordinary things take place. For instance, I was in the Shenkman apartment overlooking the Hudson River when I decided to try out a Polaroid camera I had just bought.

There was nothing at all visible in the sky above their balcony except a nice view of the New York skyline. I pointed the camera nowhere in particular and clicked the shutter. The Polaroid print I developed a minute later showed a well-defined UFO in the sky.

How can things like this be explained? As isolated events, they could be considered freaks or accidents of nature. But when they become part of a pattern that goes on and on, practically every day in the year, there is no way they can be dismissed, especially when the effects are being confirmed by several scientists in different parts of the world.

As 1973 went on, the list of confirmed tests, often with scientists present, was growing, albeit in less formal situations than at Stanford. In a demonstration, I had cracked a gold ring for Andrija, who sent it to Professor William Tiller of Stanford University. He had it analysed by the Stanford Department of Metallurgy. They used a scanning electron microscope. The break was not at all similar to the normal kind of fracture. They tried but couldn't duplicate it. What they saw under the microscope, they said, 'sheds little light on why the ring failed.' I had touched the ring only lightly.

Eldon Byrd, a physicist from the U.S. Naval Ordnance Laboratory, performed one of the most interesting tests. The lab was working with a new metal called Nitinol, which has a strange property. If Nitinol is bent by hand and then put in hot water, it springs back to its original shape so quickly that it almost jumps out of the water. I bent a piece by stroking it lightly.

It continued bending, after I had stopped, to a right angle. Byrd was surprised, because the metal usually bends in an arc. But the biggest shock was to follow. He placed the bent Nitinol in hot water, and it immediately curled up in a manner exactly opposite to the property the metal had always shown. The test was run over and over again, with the same results. They are still studying what happened to search for the reason.

Experiments with 'psychic photos' continued. I did them with several leading photographers. In each case, I took a picture of myself through a solid lens cap tightly taped on the camera. In nearly every case there would be at least one image on a roll of their own film.

Movie films recorded the end of a fork breaking off with light pressure. *The Modern Churchman* published a series of tests on metal-bending conducted by Dr Ted Bastin of Cambridge University. The Kent State University Department of Physics issued a scientific paper by Wilbur Franklin and Edgar Mitchell on metal I had fractured; again, a scanning electron microscope had been used to examine the peculiar way the metal broke. The report concluded that the 'Geller Effect' was new and unexplainable and that there was definitely a connection between physics and ESP.

Momentum continued to build fast in 1973. Newspapers and magazines joined the broadcast media in reporting on what

I was doing: not just *Time* and *Newsweek*, but *Business Week*, *Science* (published by the American Association for the Advancement of Science), *Paris Match*, *Stern*, *Spiegel*, *Physics Today*, *Today's Health* (an AMA publication); *Human Behavior*, *Psychology Today*, *New York Times Magazine*, *Technology Today* (MIT's publication), and scores of others everywhere, to say nothing of the leading newspapers and the scientific journals all over the world. Many of the magazine articles were cover stories.

The most important part to me was that the coverage in the media helped prod scientists into giving the forces serious consideration. Science had to react, and I was glad that it did, now that I was rid of my fear of it.

By the fall of 1973, I knew that the energies would eventually be validated by science, even though it would take some time for science as a whole to accept them. The scientists had to be cautious and could take only one small portion of the 'Geller Effect' at a time. For instance, the first SRI paper concentrated only on the telepathy part of the phenomena, even though all kinds of effects with metals and instruments had shown themselves. And it took months before the paper was finally published in *Nature*. The University of London tests at both Birkbeck and King's Colleges concentrated on the metals and instrument experiments, and it would be a long time-lag before their papers would appear in scientific publications.

Important as all the scientific confirmation was, it wasn't the whole story. The whole weird experience with mechanical voices on tapes, the links with the UFO appearances, the photographs of them, the unexpected materialization and dematerialization of objects—these could not be controlled and brought into the laboratory. Scientific verication of the controlled tests could do no more than suggest that the other fantastic, incredible, unearthly phenomena were not as insane as they sounded. In addition, documented facts resulting from TV demonstrations all through Europe and from the playing of my album on the air would soon show that these powers could be triggered in other people all over the world.

This was, of course, the most mind-blowing thing of all, because it meant that the unknown energies were being transferred to others, who could in turn be examined in the laboratory under repeatable conditions.

So there is no question in my mind that the earth is on the verge of discovering a whole new power, a real and unquestionable power that goes far beyond me or Andrija or Shipi, who helped bring it out, or the scientists who are brave enough to test it at the risk of being ridiculed. That's why it seems important to bring the word to people everywhere, so that it can be accepted and all of us in the world can put it to good use. I am convinced that it is a power only for the good of man and the earth. I do not think—and maybe I'm naïve about this—the intelligences, as awesome as they are, creating these energies will permit them to be used for harm.

But nothing, absolutely nothing, of all the strange things that have happened to me since that day in the Arabic garden was so dramatic and awe-inspiring as what happened to me on the late afternoon of Friday, November 9, 1973.

As I tell it in all its detail, I may have to ask you to suspend your disbelief, as I have had to do.

CHAPTER FIVE

THERE IS NO WAY I can tell this story without having it sound like science fiction. There is nothing I can do about that. Because it is so hard even for me to believe what happened, I have thought a long time about whether or not I should include it in this book. And yet, what happened, happened. The times and places involved are real, clear, unquestioned. The main problem is the physical impossibility of what happened in terms of ordinary time and distance, and the laws of physics as we know them. I finally concluded that, as long as I and the others who were involved know it is the truth, the story should be told. My friends and associates have all gone over it together, reconstructing every detail of the event, and except for minor differences of opinion, this is what happened on Friday, November 9, 1973:

About 4 p.m. I left the apartment I was staying in on the East Side of midtown Manhattan to buy a pair of binoculars for my friend, Dr Louis Shenkman. I found a pair I liked, bought them, and walked to Maria and Byron Janis's apartment building, also on the East Side. Maria has a studio in the basement of her building, and Shipi was helping frame some paintings for an exhibition of her work.

I arrived at her studio just about 4.30 p.m. The three of us chatted for a while, and then Maria and I went upstairs to their apartment to say hello to Byron. Shipi stayed in the basement working. Byron and Maria and I often have long talks, and we were just getting into an interesting discussion when I realized it was getting late. I had a date with a girl from Israel, whom I was going to meet at the Biltmore Hotel at 6.30. Now it was almost 5.30, and I wanted to go to Bloomingdale's to buy a present, then run home to shower and change before meeting my date. I wasn't sure what time Bloomingdale's closed, so I said good-bye to Byron and Maria and headed towards the store at the corner of Fifty-ninth and Lexington Avenue—only a few blocks from my apartment.

Bloomingdale's was very crowded, so I went to Hammacher-Schlemmer's, which is also near the apartment. It was now somewhere between 5.30 and 6 p.m., but I don't know the exact time.

In putting this together, I asked all those who had something to do with it to figure out what happened during this period. Maria said that I left their apartment about 5.30. She and Byron continued talking and, Maria recalls, even mentioned that I seemed to be in a particularly high state of energy. Maria was planning to phone Andrija out in Ossining to ask him some questions about a book she had borrowed from him. Solveig Clark told me later that she left her office in the General Motors Building at exactly 5.30, her usual quitting time. She was rushing to Grand Central Station to catch a train due in Ossining at 7.04 p.m. She was going to help Andrija with the manuscript of his book *Uri*, which he was writing at the time. Andrija was going to meet her at the station. In other words, she was on her way to Grand Central at the same time I was heading for Bloomingdale's.

Shipi left Maria's studio and started back to the apartment, which also was Yasha's and Werner's office. Yasha and Werner were there in the apartment-office, expecting Shipi and me at any minute. Shipi is not sure exactly at what time he left the Janises', but he guesses it was some time after 6.00.

I did some window browsing at Hammacher-Schlemmer's and then looked at my watch. I saw that it was nearly 6.00. I had to get back to the apartment and change, then get to the Biltmore. I often jog when I'm going places in New York, for the exercise, and since I didn't want to be late I started jogging about a block away from the apartment, which was east of Second Avenue and almost to First Avenue. It was now just a few minutes past 6 p.m.

Andrija was out at his home in Ossining, more than thirty miles away and about an hour away from Manhattan from door to door, either by train or by car—sometimes longer during the rush hour. He told me later that he was lying on his bed watching the six o'clock news on TV and waiting to go to the station to pick up Solveig when her train arrived at 7.04.

So, a very few minutes after 6.00, I was starting to jog about a block away from the apartment. Andrija was watching TV in Ossining, more than an hour away. Solveig was en route to Ossining, due to arrive in about an hour. Yasha and Werner were waiting for Shipi and me in the office part of the apartment, Maria and Byron remained in their apartment after Shipi left.

I clearly remember approaching the canopy of the building right next door to ours. I remember almost reaching that canopy. Then I remember having the feeling that I was running backwards for a couple of steps. I don't know whether I really did or not, but that was the feeling. Then I had the feeling that I was being sucked upwards. There was no sensation in my body. I closed my eyes and, I think, opened them almost immediately.

When I did, I found myself being propelled in the air a foot or so away from a porch screen, over the top of a rhododendron bush, about to crash through the screen at a point eight or ten feet off the ground. To prepare for the impact, I turned my left shoulder towards the screen and put my hands out in front of me. I crashed through the screen and landed on a circular glass-top table. It was heavy plate glass. My hands hit it first, and it slid forward, then hit the floor and shattered. My knee struck a wooden part of the table, and the table toppled over. I landed on the floor of the porch. I was conscious all through this, but slightly dazed when I hit the table and floor. My knee hurt, and I was afraid to move in case I had any broken bones. But what shocked me was that I recognized the porch and the table because I knew them so well. This was Andrija's screen porch in Ossining—there was no mistaking it. One moment I had been on the East Side of Manhattan. The next, I was crashing through a screen porch in Ossining. The only sensation I had was crashing through the screen and hitting the table and floor. I called out loud as I could to Andrija, but there was no answer right away. I remember being cold and very thirsty. I still was afraid to move.

Andrija added more for me later. He had watched just about half of the six o'clock news. About 6.15 p.m. he heard a crash, followed by a thud, as if something hit the side of the house. He jumped up from his bed right away (his bedroom is on the second floor, on the same side of the house as the porch) and began investigating all through the house. Since it was a windy evening, he thought maybe the wind had caused a tree to topple against the house. He ran from room to room, on all three floors, but couldn't find anything wrong. Then he went out the front door to the porch. The screened part is several feet away from the door. Although he couldn't see anything in the dark, he heard me calling him. To get to the screened part of the porch, he had to go back into the house and through the dining room and study.

He threw on the light switch and opened the door to the porch. He told me that he saw me lying in a heap beside the broken glass and table, and then looked up and saw a huge gaping hole in the screen, which was pushed in from the top above his head level. He saw that I was holding a package, which contained the binoculars I had just bought in New York.

My mind had cleared enough by now to help him as he quickly checked me for broken bones and half dragged me to the couch in the study. Being a medical doctor, he checked me completely. There didn't seem to be any injuries, and I didn't feel any pain except for my knee. I got up and walked around and felt shaky, but all right.

I couldn't figure anything out at the time. Maria, back in her New York apartment, remembers that she decided to call Andrija somewhere between 6.10 and 6.15. The phone rang in Ossining just as I was walking around and trying to figure out what had happened. Andrija picked up the phone. He sounded stunned. He said something like there's a friend here who wants to talk to you. He handed the phone to me, and I said 'I'm here.' Now Maria was shocked. She had seen me in New York less than an hour before, as I had left her apartment about 5.30. I told her that I had been in New York one moment and in Ossining the next. Andrija got back on the phone and described the scene of the porch when he found me there.

I still felt weak, but I phoned Yasha and Werner. They later told me my voice was shaking. It was now about 6.20. Shipi had not yet arrived from Maria's apartment. I told Yasha I just wanted to let them know what had happened and that I would call them back after I pulled myself together.

Shipi arrived at the apartment right after my call. He found Yasha and Werner in a confused and excited condition. When they told him that I was in Ossining, he said it was impossible, that he had just seen me leave Maria's and Byron's apartment a short time before. Shipi later said: 'In the beginning, when these strange things happen, you get scared. Then you just get accustomed to them.'

Of course, Andrija and I, as soon as we collected ourselves, thought the same thing. This whole event was either total insanity on the part of everyone involved—Yasha, Shipi, Werner, Maria, Byron, Andrija, and myself—or the most dramatic phenomenon yet. The facts were there. No human form of transportation could have delivered me from the East Side of Manhattan to Andrija's house in Ossining in practically an instant, between 6.10 and 6.15.

Andrija felt we might find an answer if we tried the tape recorder again. He fetched it and turned it on. The mechanical voice came on almost immediately and made it clear that the forces had literally transported me almost instantaneously from New York to Ossining. Then the voice went on to make important statements about future planning for both Andrija and me. The tape message was quite short. There was mention of the difficulty Andrija and I were having with each other, and it went on to say that I should be going out more on my own and that free will in man must always be foremost.

During all this, Solveig Clark was on the train to Ossining. She wrote out to the best of her memory what she recalls of the incident:

I had promised Andrija Puharich that I would come up for the weekend to help him with his writings . . . and that I would take the express train from Grand Central, arriving at Ossining at 7.04 p.m., and he would meet me at the railroad station. The train arrived on schedule, but Andrija was not there to pick me up. I waited some ten minutes, thinking he would be along shortly, but when I was the only one left at the station, I went over to the public phone inside the station and dialled Andrija's house.

I was startled to hear Uri's voice at the other end. The reason I was surprised was that I had spoken to him earlier in the day, and he had not mentioned going up to visit Andrija. I immediately sensed something crucial had happened when I heard the tape-recorder going in the background.

Uri tersely said: 'We'll be there to pick you up in fifteen minutes,' and hung up.

I waited in suspense, prepared for anything. They arrived at the station in Andrija's VW—his Mercedes was being repaired.

I climbed into the back seat. Uri, as I had surmised, had had no intention of going to Ossining that Friday. He had a date with a girl, and had to hurry home to change.

When we got to Andrija's house, Andrija flipped on the light switch on the porch, and I saw the scene. It looked like a disaster area. A huge gaping hole in the screen—way up high, above the top level of the rhododendron bushes that surrounded part of the porch. The wooden table was on end, with shattered plate glass everywhere, some in large chunks, some in slivers.

Uri had gotten over his shock and was in a state of wonderment and excitement over what had just happened. If it had happened to anyone else, I'm sure that person would be in such an emotional state of utter shock that he would have been a basket case. I felt pride in Uri's strength of mind and constitution to be able to go through such an experience and still keep his equilibrium and joking sense of humour. It made it all seem perfectly normal like a high adventure in the natural human world that we are accustomed to.

I have put Solveig's words here because she has a very clear mind and is such a good observer. She was also very much needed for a down-to-earth reason when she arrived. Whatever the cause, I had never been so hungry in my life. She got together some scrambled eggs and salad for us, while we tried to figure out more about what happened.

Just to double-check, Andrija got a light and looked to make sure there were no footprints outside the porch. There weren't. We both checked the screen: there was no question that it was punched in *towards the inside* of the porch. The screen was torn at a very high place, so I would have had to have come in at least six or seven feet above the floor. There were no cars around, nothing. I kept saying to myself: Why was it? There hadn't been any sensation in my body at the time. It was as if I was not on the New York sidewalk any more, and then suddenly appeared in the air, outside a screen, ready to hit it. Everything happened fast. Crashing through the screen. Falling on the table, the glass top falling off the table and breaking, hitting my left leg, falling on the floor, finding myself 36 road miles out of Manhattan. What kind of transformation or transportation did my body undergo? Was I really torn up molecule by molecule? Was I pushed through a dimension, teleported by a ray or by a spacecraft? What happened? I don't know. The tapes didn't go into any detail on this. And how could the binoculars stay with me through it all?

The more I think of it, the more I see how small we all are. How much we don't know, how much more there is to know. If you take a radio and put too much power into it, it will blow out, an overload. That's the way our minds are. If we suddenly know too much, we'll go crazy. Maybe I don't want to know more about it. Maybe I should just let things happen. I don't want to take an overload. But I also like to keep going at full capacity.

As we ate the supper Solveig cooked for us, I felt better, and I remember asking Andrija: 'Would you mind driving me back to Manhattan?'

'After what happened, I'll drive you anywhere,' he said.

It was cold, and I wasn't dressed for the weather. I had on an old Eisenhower jacket of Shipi's that didn't even fit me. But Solveig, Andrija, and I piled into the VW and started back for Manhattan. Andrija and I talked a little about what information the tape had offered, and we even had the Sony recorder with us. The cassette was still in the recorder, which was a little unusual, so we let Solveig hear just a couple of sentences of the strange voice. She said it made a tremendous impact on her. Solveig speaks several languages and is very interested in different ways of speaking. She said that the male voice she heard on the tape had nothing really special about it, except that it seemed to speak English very correctly and that it sounded like a human voice that didn't carry any humour, any accent or ups and downs. But, she said, it carried a lot of authority. She didn't feel any kind of eerie chill or anything like that, just a lot of force and command.

The drive back to the New York apartment took a little less than an hour. Only during that drive did I fully comprehend that I had not arrived in Ossining by means of any normal transportation. I suddenly was shocked again. Really shocked. The long, tiresome road back, the traffic, the lights of the city—I hadn't seen any of these on the way out there. And then I thought about the many other things that had happened, about Andrija's dog and about the objects that had dematerialized and materialized one after the other, and were continuing to, in people's homes and in the laboratories of famous scientists. Everything was pointing to a whole new world, where science was on the dangerous edge of joining with miracles, and I was able to play a part in it. The more I thought about it, the more my confidence grew. I was lucky enough to be a channel for tremendous energies and powers that needed only to be brought out and studied impartially.

I could sense all this not just from the symbols on the surface, like the bending of metal, but from the poems flowing through me. Their words and meanings, even if they were obscure, seemed to be joined to the more simple demonstrations. And together they may be a bridge to deeper understanding of the universe, of space, of intelligences far greater than ours, and of a God far greater than the intelligences themselves.

All these thoughts came to me in a cramped Volkswagen on a cold night, driving back to New York on a journey that had taken a fraction of a second only a few hours before, in as wild a science fiction scene as any writer could imagine. And yet it had been real, completely real, on November 9, 1973, shortly after 6 p.m. And if it was real then, it will be real in the future. Whatever this Spectra is, whether it's a UFO or some other spacecraft or a Sony TC-120, I'm convinced now that it's not an illusion, not a delusion, not a figment of the imagination, not a freak of nature, but a reality.

But it's also not a God. It must be some kind of great, intelligent, interspatial energy that is serving us and serving God at the same time. What part of what galaxy it comes from doesn't matter.

It is strange, this sudden mixing of what science has learned with this new, great force, whatever it is. In the words that come through me that I try to grab and write down—and please don't worry whether they are poetry or not—I receive flashes of light that go beyond the narrow limits of our own contained vision:

Yes, but I know the truth
It lies way deep inside you
The truth of mystic knowledge for which all splendour is
only a camouflage

The knowledge to control, accomplish and achieve the
unbelievable
The unbearable duty that has come upon you without any
warning or notice
The knowledge that will give you power, courage, and
greatness
To behold and bloom the biggest, tremendous, positive,
outraging, thunderous act
That will change all known knowledge on earth and even
furthermore.

I *know* the mysteries of the universe are on the verge of breaking through, and that these energies, just now appearing, will be the key to restoring both harmony and order for all of us, not on some distant day, but in the close, near, immediate future.

Epilogue

A GREAT MANY PEOPLE felt that when *Nature* published the results of the Stanford Research Institute tests the controversy would ease off, and more interest would develop among scientists in getting deeper into the subject. I was really excited when I learned that *Nature* was going to publish the SRI paper in its October 1974 issue, even though it had been in the works for a long time. While the reaction in the general press didn't quiet the controversy, it did seem to show that new scientific interest would develop in a field that had been ridiculed or ignored for a long time.

Even the *New York Times*, which doesn't usually give much attention to paranormal matters, came out with an editorial which said: 'The scientific community has been put on notice "that there is something worthy of their attention and scrutiny" in the possibilities of extra-sensory perception. With these words, the respected journal *Nature* called on scientists to join —or refute—millions of non-scientists who believe human consciousness has more capabilities for real perception beyond the five senses. . . . The editors of *Nature* have taken an important step to stimulate scientific discourse, openly posing the issue "whether science has yet developed the competence to confront claims of the paranormal."'

Nature printed its own editorial saying the SRI paper was bound to create a stir in the scientific community, and it did. The *New Scientist*, which had access to the SRI paper before publication, ran a cover story the same month *Nature* published its article. The *New Scientist* was highly critical, as a magazine has every right to be. But its article spent page after page criticizing the SRI paper not in any scientific way, but using interviews with magicians and speculations that had nothing to do with the scientific method the writer thought so much of. In other words, the *New Scientist* writer himself broke every rule he claimed was necessary for a scientific experiment. The most flattering thing he said about me was that Russell Targ and Hal Puthoff 'are no match for Uri Geller'. Since both these men are laser physicists, and have been for many years, I'd be proud if that were true—which it isn't.

The wildest charge that the *New Scientist* made in its article was its suggestion that I have a miniature radio implanted in my teeth, based on a design Andrija Puharich had developed to help deaf people hear. Since the magazine used over a page to create this untrue story, I think it's important to say that John K. Lind, a New York dentist, examined me in his office in December 1974. His report said 'I can attest to the fact that clinical and radiographic examination of his mouth, teeth, and jaws reveal no foreign objects implanted such as transistors, metal objects, etc.' *Time* continued to try to discredit the SRI tests in its November 4, 1974, issue by talking about the *New Scientist* article.

But the most important thing was that the portion of the SRI tests that appeared in *Nature* was only the tip of the iceberg, leaving alone such other phenomena as metal bending. The tests at the University of London had not been completed at the time the first *Nature* article came out, and the important part about these, as I have mentioned earlier, is that they include confirmed tests on other people who were triggered by my television appearances. In other words, I wasn't even in England when those tests were concluded on other people, so there is no chance of connecting those tests to mine. Yet they are showing similar results and point towards the conclusion that these energies and forces seem to be coming into play as something new in the universe.

John Hasted wrote me and said the disappearance of an

object from one place and its reappearance in another—a phenomenon he had observed several times—made him 'suppose that on its journey it did not have normal existence in our space. . . . Did it cease to exist on the journey, or did it continue to exist in some other way?' He mentioned his 'hunch that the disappearance-appearance events are fundamental, and suggest that they might be at the bottom of the metal-softening and also the electrical phenomenon.' And, incredibly, he told me that after I visited with him at his home, he has been able, repeatedly and seemingly at will, to induce a clock in his house to strike.

John learned early in 1975 that *Nature* was to publish the paper he and David Bohm had collaborated on after their experiments with me. It appeared certain that other papers on the 'Geller Effect' would be accepted by leading scientific journals, and the direct physical effects of these forces would be presented formally to the world of science for the first time, fully documented and verified. The new studies would now complete the picture. Further, an international conference of many leading scientists was scheduled in Tarrytown, New York, for February 1975, to analyse the effect of these newly discovered forces and what their impact would be on science. These were signs of new interest in the mysteries of these energies, which are still waiting for a scientific explanation.

Personally, I continued to run into more and more unexplainable happenings in the beginning of the New Year. One of these was described in a letter from Robert Stigwood. He had burned himself before a flight to New York and had an uncomfortable blister on his hand. 'About an hour out of London,' his letter said, 'I opened the *Daily Mail* and started to read a serialization about you.' Robert said he then 'carefully folded the page from the newspaper with the photograph showing in front and placed it in my jacket pocket' and for the rest of the flight 'placed my blistered finger against the photograph.' He fell asleep and forgot the blister until he was walking in the airport in New York. 'I looked at my finger and the blister had disappeared. I was obviously very surprised and could find no logical explanation for this phenomenon.'

Another amazing event took place in the apartment of the mother of a friend of mine in Italy. I visited her during January of 1975, and we had a long talk about the paranormal. While we were talking, a small ashtray levitated from a table and dropped on the floor. But some minutes later, an even stranger thing happened.

We heard a faint crash that seemed to come from a glass cabinet in the room that contained shelves of porcelain dishes she had collected. We went over to the cabinet and saw a small blue statuette lying on the shelf. It was a miniature Egyptian statuette, made of a light blue ceramic material, small enough to lie in the palm of the hand. My hostess was shocked, because the cabinet was locked, and this object had never been in the cabinet before. She had never seen it, anywhere.

She unlocked the cabinet and took it out. As she did, the object suddenly cracked in half. She was so surprised that she dropped it, and I was able to catch the two pieces as they fell. The inside was made of a crumbly, plaster type of material. The statuette was that of a male Egyptian, and it looked very much like an inexpensive souvenir of the kind made in Hong Kong or Taiwan. It had an unusual stale odour about it.

My hostess was a little frightened by the experience. She urged me to take the object with me, which I did. I wrapped it carefully and put it in my suitcase back at the hotel. As I did, I couldn't help remembering the old stories I had read about King Tutankhamun, and the curse that had followed the scientists who had unearthed his tomb. However, I didn't think much more about it until I went to New York, where I showed it to Solveig Clark and told her the story.

She was fascinated by the piece and seemed to think it was of far more interest than a souvenir trinket. When she asked if she could take it to the Metropolitan Museum of Art in New

York to have them examine it, I of course agreed, but I didn't expect anything to come of it.

She went to both the Metropolitan and the Brooklyn Museum, where there are several Egyptian experts. Both museums not only certified it as dating from 1200 B.C. to 700 B.C. and named the possible dynasties it was from, but also said that the figure was in an extremely fresh state of preservation. Again, a mystery remains: How could this rare, ancient object get into a locked glass cabinet of a woman in Italy who had never seen it before? So the puzzles are continuing, with still no clear answer except they are becoming more clearly verified and documented to the point where they can no longer be doubted, even by sceptics.

When everything is added up, I don't really know what the intelligences want. If I know one thing, it is that these intelligences are working and communicating, no matter how hard that is for anyone to believe. My theory is that the energies are coming through me from a higher source. I am not talking about God here. I'm talking about things under God. Still, I really don't understand all the things that are happening with me, or through me.

What I'm trying to achieve is this: I think it's important for the world to know about these intelligences, because they are real and they are going to prove out, even if it takes time. Another approach would be to hide everything, keep it confidential. I don't believe in that. I want to put everything out on the table. I know that these forces will work only for the good of mankind and that nothing sinister is going to arise from the situation. Everything will then be working as a positive force.

I'm working hard now for that reason, and for the security I've never really had in the past. Like everybody else, I want to be free of worries about telephone bills, monthly payments, getting behind in the budget, and that kind of thing. If I can get a reasonable amount of security, I can sit down for a month or more and think about what I really want to do. Shall I work solely with science? Shall I continue roaming around the world? Shall I explore myself? Or what? I'm not sure yet. That's why I'm giving lecture-demonstrations all over the world, recording an album, doing TV shows and a motion picture. I have written this book for people who want to be aware of and share the incredible events that I have experienced and continue to experience.

The big thing is to try to understand why these things happen. Why does a piece of metal lose weight under these forces? Why did the tapes come on with those low, mechanical voices? Why have I been able to take those UFO pictures? I don't even like to use the term 'UFO', because to many people it's never been credible. They think you're crazy. But even though I don't know what they are, I know they exist. It might be that big cosmic clown I've mentioned before, playing with us. He might be dropping a lot of clues, but he seems not to be communicating with us as fully as he could.

I keep thinking there must be a reason. There must be a reason for all the controversy that has boiled up, for critics to strain so hard against this, even in the face of solid evidence There must be a reason for these intricate, complex experiences.

I feel that so much of everything goes back to that Arabic garden in Tel Aviv so many years ago, when I was so young. It is a scene that comes back to me often.

And some things—at the base of everything—come clearly to my mind and my heart.

I believe that God exists. There is no question about that.

I feel that under God are endless intelligences, many of them greater than ours.

I am convinced that there are people here on earth with incredible power, and many of them are not aware of it.

I think that everyone has a message of some kind. What has happened and is happening with me can happen to you.